MW00654088

Grace and its fruits

Selections from John Calvin on the Pastoral Epistles

John Calvin

Grace and its fruits

Selections from John Calvin on the Pastoral Epistles

EVANGELICAL PRESS

EVANGELICAL PRESS
Faverdale North Industrial Estate, Darlington, DL3 0PH, England

Evangelical Press USA
P. O. Box 84, Auburn, MA 01501, USA

e-mail: sales@evangelical-press.org

web: http://www.evangelicalpress.org

First published 2000

British Library Cataloguing in Publication Data available

ISBN 0 85234 445 7

Printed and bound in Great Britain by Creative Print & Design Wales, Ebbw Vale.

Contents

		Page
Foreword by Michael Haykin		7
Preface		9
Introduction: The life and times of John Calvin		13
1.	Our election revealed in Christ Jesus (2 Tim. 1:9-10)	27
2.	The one mediator (1 Tim. 2:5-6)	45
3.	The mystery of godliness (1 Tim. 3:16)	65
4.	God desires all men to be saved (1 Tim. 2:3-5)	83
5.	The purpose and grace of God (2 Tim. 1:8-9)	101
6.	Strength for the battle (2 Tim. 2:1-3)	117
7.	God's firm foundation (2 Tim. 2:19)	139
8.	Clay pots and vessels of gold (2 Tim. 2:20-21)	155
9.	The Scriptures: God's profitable Word (2 Tim. 3:16-17)	173
10.	Rules for ministers and all the faithful (Titus 1:7-9)	193
11.	The good fight of faith (1 Tim. 6:12-14)	213
12.	A crown of righteousness (2 Tim. 4:7-8)	235
13.	A lesson on prayer (1 Tim. 2:8)	257
14.	Abundant grace (Titus 3:4-7)	277
15.	Grace, godliness and glory (Titus 2:11-14)	297

Foreword

Charles Dickens' famous line in *A Tale of Two Cities* — 'It was the best of times, it was the worst of times' — seems well suited to contemporary Western evangelicalism. On the one hand, the last few decades have seen much to praise God for, and much to rejoice about. In his goodness and grace, for instance, he has restored Reformed truth once more to a position of influence. And yet, as an increasing number of evangelical authors have noted, there are still many sectors of evangelicalism that are characterized by great shallowness and a tendency to trivialize the weighty things of God. So much of evangelical worship seems barren. And when it comes to spirituality, there is little evidence of the riches that should be there — only poverty.

As it was at the time of the Reformation, when the watchword was *Ad fontes* —'Back to the sources' — so it is now: the way forward is backward. We need to go back to the classics of evangelicalism to find the pathway forward. We cannot live in the past. To attempt to do so would be antiquarianism. But our evangelical forebears in the faith can teach us much about Christianity, its doctrines, its passions and its fruit.

They can also serve as role models for us. As R. C. Sproul has noted of such giants as Augustine and Martin Luther, John Calvin and Jonathan Edwards, 'These men all were conquered, overwhelmed, and spiritually intoxicated by their vision of the holiness of God. Their minds and imaginations were captured by the majesty of God the Father. Each of them possessed a profound affection for the sweetness and excellence of Christ. There was in each of them a singular and unswerving loyalty to Christ that spoke of a citizenship in heaven that was always more precious to them than the applause of men.'[1]

To be sure, we would not dream of placing these men and their writings alongside the Word of God. As John Jewel (1522-1571), the Anglican apologist, once stated, 'What say we of the fathers, Augustine, Ambrose, Jerome, Cyprian? … They were learned men, and learned fathers; the instruments of the mercy of God, and vessels full of grace. We despise them not, we read them, we reverence them, and give thanks unto God for them. Yet … we may not make them the foundation and warrant of our conscience: we may not put our trust in them. Our trust is in the name of the Lord.'[2]

Seeking then to honour the past and yet not to idolize it, we are issuing these books in this series, *Living classics for today*. It is the hope of the publishers that they will provide riches for those areas where we are poor, and light of day where we are stumbling in the deepening twilight.

Michael Haykin

Notes

1. R. C. Sproul, 'An Invaluable Heritage', *Tabletalk*, 23, No. 10 (October 1999), pp.5-6.
2. Cited by Barrington R. White, 'Why Bother with History?', *Baptist History and Heritage*, 4, No. 2 (July 1969), p.85.

Preface

Most writers who have introduced John Calvin to modern readers tend to emphasize the theological issues that form the core of his writings, giving only slight attention to the *pastoral* dimensions of his ministry. Calvin served as a pastor in Strasbourg and in Geneva, and his sermons reflect his benevolent regard for the spiritual welfare of the French refugees who gathered on Sundays and weekdays to worship and hear his sermons.

Readers who imagine Calvin's sermons to be dry, cerebral lectures will be gratified to sense his passionate devotion to God and his warm pastoral concern for his congregation. Calvin was pre-eminently a preacher of the Word of God. Unlike many modern preachers, for whom Scripture functions merely as a starting-point for a light inspirational talk, Calvin stayed with his text, expounding it clearly and exhibiting its relevance to the concerns of sixteenth-century Christians. Although he had deep appreciation for, and wide knowledge of, classical authors, 'Scripture alone' was the guiding principle of his preaching and writing. 'I declare,' Calvin testified in his will, 'that, according to the measure of grace and goodness which the Lord has accorded me, I have endeavoured in my sermons and also in my writings and commentaries to preach his Word purely and chastely, and faithfully to interpret his sacred Scriptures.'

The heart and soul of Calvin's preaching is God's sovereign grace in Jesus Christ, which bears fruit in the believer's life. Although these sermons were preached some 450 years ago, they have not lost their relevance, for, as Calvin states in his prefatory remarks to the readers of his sermons, this book contains the Word of God (Paul's epistles to Timothy and Titus), and the preaching of that Word will benefit all 'to whose hands it shall come, having grace to receive it thankfully, and to use it fruitfully'.

The sermons that follow are a selection from those which Calvin preached in the Church of St Peter's, in Geneva. Taken down in shorthand and translated from the French, his one hundred sermons on the Pastoral Epistles were first published in English in London, in 1579.

Most modern readers find that sixteenth-century English is difficult to comprehend. Many words and expressions that found their way into the early translation of the sermons are now obsolete. In order to make them accessible to as many readers as possible, the present volume is offered as a simplified and contemporary edition of sermons that are representative of Calvin's expository preaching. Obsolete words and archaic expressions have been replaced by suitable modern equivalents; however, care has been taken to employ a form of wording that preserves the essential meaning of the original discourse, without introducing anachronisms into the text. Where possible, long complex sentences have been recast in a modern literary style.

Each sermon has been given a title indicating its principal theme, and headings have been introduced in order to highlight the development of thought within each sermon. In a word, special care has been taken to make the sermons as plain and straightforward to modern readers as they were to the congregation of St Peter's who heard Calvin preach them.

The issues facing evangelical churches today are obviously different from those of the medieval churches. The need for preaching that expounds the doctrines of the evangelical faith, however, is as pressing now as it was in the time of Luther and Calvin. If we remember that 'A church reformed is always reforming,' we may cherish the hope that as the evangelical world moves beyond its fascination with modernity and reclaims the truth of God's grace and glory revealed in Jesus Christ — so passionately proclaimed by Calvin — we may witness a reformation of the church in our time.

To the directors and editors of Evangelical Press, especially David Clark and Anne Williamson, I wish to express my sincere thanks for the many courtesies conferred upon me and for their careful editing of my work.

Scriptural quotations throughout are from the New King James Version: Thomas Nelson Publishers, Nashville (1982). Special mention must be made of my use of English translations of John Calvin's sermons on the epistles of Paul to Timothy and Titus: G. Bishop and T. Woodcoke, London (1579); facsimile edition, The Banner of Truth, Edinburgh and Carlisle, Pennsylvania (1983) and Thomas, Cowperwait & Co., Philadelphia — *A Selection of the Most Celebrated Sermons of John Calvin* (1847).

I offer my sincere thanks to B. J. Moore, whose computer skills made possible instant communication between myself and the publishers, and to Sheryl Breit, who made corrections in the electronically stored manuscript.

I would be remiss beyond words if I were to omit the acknowledgement that is supreme. The sermons are Calvin's. But the subject, Paul's epistles to Timothy and Titus, is, in Calvin's words, 'the Word of the immortal God'. Its theme is the grace of God revealed in Jesus Christ and bestowed upon God's children by the Holy Spirit. And it is because the God of grace has put this treasure in earthen vessels that Calvin was given the task and privilege of exposition. If our efforts to make his sermons heard again in the evangelical world today are met with any success, it is only by the grace of the Holy Spirit, by whose illumination the sermons were preached and by whose prompting they were recast in the language of contemporary readers. It is with humility as well as gratitude that they are presented here, since the power of the Word is not of us but of God, to whom alone be all praise and glory.

Joseph Hill
Geneva College, Beaver Falls, Pennsylvania

Introduction
The life and times of John Calvin

The world in which John Calvin lived was accustomed to conflict and disorder. Religious disputes had drawn battle lines between those who favoured the reform of the church and the defenders of traditional Roman Catholic religion. Calvin, by nature a man of peace and order, did not create the conflict, which was already well underway by the time he was born. Nevertheless, his conviction that God had called him to contend for the truth of the gospel placed him squarely in the front line of the battle.

Family and early years

John Calvin was born at Noyon, in the province of Picardy, in north-eastern France, on 10 July 1509. Christened Jean Cauvin, he adopted, in accordance with scholarly custom, the Latinized form Johannes Calvinus. His parents, Gérard and Jeanne le Franc Cauvin, had four sons: Charles, the eldest, Jean, Antoine and François, who died at an early age. While the boys were still very young, their mother died and their father is said to have married a second wife, who had two daughters. Gérard served as a town clerk and held various positions as a church official in the service of the bishop, Charles de Hangest, whose family had both ecclesiastical and political connections going back over some seventy-five years.

Years of preparation

The town of Noyon in the early sixteenth century was a centre of ecclesiastical power. Since Gérard Cauvin was in the employment of the bishop, he was able to obtain grants to help finance his sons' education. John, in particular, was given a position as chaplain at the altar of La Gésine, a chapel in the Cathedral at Noyon. He also fulfilled a charge at Pont-l'Evêque, a neighbouring town, where he preached on occasion during his early years. John's father intended that he should enter the service of the church, and these positions, along with his schooling, would help prepare him for that calling.

John received his early formal education in preparation for the priesthood at the Collège de la Marche and the Collège de Montaigue, branches of the University of Paris. His Latin teacher was the learned Mathurin Cordier, whose instruction Calvin looked back upon many years later as a special blessing conferred on him by God. It was probably at Montaigu that the young Calvin began to breathe the spirit of humanism[1] which marked his outlook in later years and remained with him, though radically transformed, after his conversion.

Once he achieved his master's degree in arts, he was ready to pursue his theological studies. Gérard, however, considering the steady advance of the Reformation in France and Switzerland, as well as in Germany under the influence of Martin Luther, was determined to redirect his son's career. He insisted on John's giving up philosophy and enrolling in the faculty of law in the hope that he might achieve distinction in a more lucrative vocation than any position he was likely to achieve in the church. The young scholar, ever an obedient son, left Paris and settled in Orleans, where he immersed himself in the life of the university and the study of civil law under an able teacher, Pierre de l'Estoille. At Orleans he gained knowledge of church doctrine and grappled with theological issues as part of his training in law. So extraordinary was his progress that he was treated as one of the regular teachers, rather than a mere student. He frequently lectured as a substitute for the professors and was held in such high esteem that he was offered a doctor's degree in law.

During his student days at Orleans, and afterwards at Bourges, Calvin acquired a knowledge of Greek under Melchior Wolmar, who was sympathetic to the reform movement. While studying law in Bourges, Calvin also found time to read the Scriptures and to engage in some preaching in nearby villages. After his father's death in 1531, John returned to Paris to resume his study of Greek and take up Hebrew. While in Paris he published his first book, a commentary on a Latin treatise by Seneca, *On Clemency*, in which the Roman political leader appeals to Nero to exercise forbearance in his dealings with his subjects. In Calvin's mind, Seneca's tract could have had contemporary application in France, where advocates of the evangelical faith were being persecuted by the king.

Calvin's association with Nicholas Cop, the newly elected rector of the University of Paris, forced both men to leave Paris in order to escape arrest after Cop announced his support of Martin Luther. Calvin went to Angoulême where he spent a few months in the home of a friend, Louis du Tillet, a cathedral canon of that district. The du Tillet family had a large library and Calvin spent time reading and probably writing during his stay there. It is possible that he began at that time to write his major theological work, the *Institutes of the Christian Religion*.

In this book Calvin presented a full statement of evangelical doctrines, which had come under vigorous attack by adversaries of the reform movement. He dedicated the *Institutes* to the king, Francis I, insisting that the allegations that were circulating — that the intention of the Reformers was to overthrow the government and throw everything into confusion — were utterly false. Written originally in Latin and later translated into French and other languages, the *Institutes* quickly became a standard textbook for students of theology. It was, however, intended as a manual for general readers, for instruction in the doctrine of salvation and the way of godliness. The first edition contained detailed expositions of the Ten Commandments, the Apostles' Creed, the Lord's Prayer and the sacraments, baptism and the Lord's Supper. To this body of doctrine Calvin later added a chapter renouncing the 'false sacraments' of the Roman Catholic Church and another, 'On Christian Liberty, Ecclesiastical Power and Civil Administration'. In the following years, he elaborated and reorganized his work in as many as five editions.

Conversion to the evangelical faith

Following his sojourn with Louis du Tillet, Calvin returned to his native Noyon in May 1534, marking what may have been a decisive moment in his journey from humanist to reformer. While at Noyon he resigned the chaplaincy of La Gésine, giving up income from the benefice of that post. This resignation probably indicates his breaking his ties with the Roman church, which he had come to consider corrupt in doctrine and practice. Calvin's movement away from humanist ideals and loyalty to the Roman Catholic Church towards a life devoted to God and the reformation of the church occurred gradually as he advanced in his study of the Scriptures and became acquainted with persons devoted to the cause of reformation. In God's own time, however, the change in Calvin's life was decisive. In the preface to his commentary on the Psalms, he recounts how God called him to 'the honourable office of a preacher and minister of the gospel'. He was diligently studying law, in obedience to his father's wishes, 'but God, by the secret guidance of his providence, turned my course in a different direction'. He describes the turnabout as 'a sudden conversion' by which God subdued him and made teachable his mind, which had been obstinately devoted to 'the superstitions of the papacy'. At that turning-point, he writes, 'I immediately had such a burning desire to progress that, although I did not entirely give up other studies, I pursued them with less fervour.'

God's providence had been moving John Calvin towards his unexpected conversion since his early student days in Paris and afterwards in Orleans. His father's change of mind diverted him from the priesthood. His study of law then brought him into contact with fellow scholars who were committed to the evangelical faith. Among them was his Greek teacher, Melchior Wolmar, whose evangelical faith may have had a profound influence on his student. Theodore Beza states that it was through Calvin's cousin, Pierre Robert (also known as Olivétan) that he was 'made acquainted with the reformed faith'.[2] Calvin assisted Pierre Robert in his French translation of the Bible, and while engaged in this project he 'began to devote himself to the study of the Holy Scriptures, and, from an abhorrence of all kinds of superstition, to discontinue his attendance on the public services of the church'.[3] Beza also mentions Etienne de la Forge, a merchant with whom Calvin lived in Paris and whom he held in high esteem for his piety. Forge later suffered martyrdom in the cause of Christ. Through his association with these and other friends of the Reformation, God was preparing John Calvin for a distinctive role in the evangelical movement. His 'sudden conversion' — probably while he was studying law at Orleans and Bourges — was only a beginning, a turning of his course in a different direction. He did not immediately possess the fulness of the evangelical faith; but having had a taste of godliness, he 'was set on fire with a desire to increase in the knowledge and love of God'.[4] His conversion and subsequent commitment to the service of God are aptly represented by an emblem which he used as a signet: an extended hand holding a heart aflame, encircled by the words: 'I offer my heart to you, Lord, promptly and sincerely.'

Calvin the Reformer

Calvin's first theological tract was written, not against the Roman Catholic Church, but against the Anabaptists,[5] who insisted that only adult baptism was valid and held, among other doctrines, that the soul, after death, sleeps until the resurrection. To refute this belief Calvin wrote a tract which was later given the title *Psychopannychia*, in which he asserted that the souls of believers are awake after death, living in union with Christ.

Calvin left France suddenly when he was implicated in an incident involving the posting of placards in several towns denouncing the mass as a horrible abuse of the Lord's Supper. The French authorities arrested those responsible for this demonstration and executed about twenty of the offenders, including Calvin's friend Etienne de la Forge. Calvin escaped to Basle, a town friendly to the Reformation. While there, he wrote the preface to Pierre Robert's French translation of the Bible and continued his writing of the *Institutes of the Christian Religion.*

After his banishment from France, Calvin spent a year or more in Basle, and returned to France. The French government at that time had offered an amnesty to evangelicals, on condition that they would return to the Roman church within six months. Unwilling to do this, Calvin left France for good, taking his brother Antoine and their half-sister Marie, and set out for the free city of Strasbourg. At that time troop movements forced them to detour through what we now call Switzerland. They stopped for the night at an inn in Geneva. The word spread quickly that John Calvin was in town. William Farel, the fiery evangelical pastor of Geneva, hurried to the inn and demanded that Calvin remain there and help him with the work of ministry. Calvin refused. He was going to Strasbourg to continue his studies and his writing. Farel persisted. Frustrated and impatient, he swore an oath that God would curse all Calvin's studies if he did not remain. Calvin reluctantly agreed to stay, believing that God had intervened to keep him there. Later he wrote, 'I felt as if God from heaven laid his mighty hand upon me to stop me in my course.' At Geneva Calvin served as a lecturer on Paul's epistles in the St Peter's Church and later as a pastor.

Under the leadership of Farel and Calvin, the Council of Geneva adopted ordinances regulating the church and its worship, and all citizens of Geneva were required, under threat of expulsion, to submit to the church's discipline. Moral laws had long been imposed in Geneva, but their enforcement by the church was not well received by many of the fun-loving citizens. Opposition to the policies of Farel and Calvin came to a head in a dispute between the leaders of the church and the city council, and the upshot was the expulsion of Farel and Calvin from the city.

The two ministers, now banished from Geneva, went to Basle, seeking God's will for their future ministries. After a time, Farel was called to be the pastor of the church in Neuchâtel, and Calvin was persuaded by Martin Bucer, an evangelical leader in Strasbourg, to become the minister of a church of French refugees in that city. While in Strasbourg he wrote musical versions of Psalms and canticles to be sung in worship. He also wrote a commentary on Romans, the first of his many commentaries on books of the Bible, and a revised edition of the *Institutes*. In 1540 he married Idelette de Bure, a widow who had two children. The couple's only child, Jacques, died in infancy.

Return to Geneva

During Calvin's absence from Geneva, political and religious turmoil raged, and the church suffered serious decline. Official delegates were sent from Geneva urging Calvin to return to put things right. He shuddered at the thought of returning to the city where he had suffered gross indignities. Nevertheless, he was prepared to follow the Lord's leading, and once persuaded that Geneva would take him back on his terms and accept his plan for the church, he left Strasbourg to return to Geneva. On his arrival in September 1541 he was greeted with uncommon courtesy, given a furnished house and a stipend from the government.

Soon after he was settled again in Geneva, the council, at Calvin's insistence, reorganized the church to conform to biblical orders — pastors, teachers, elders and deacons — and drafted new ordinances specifying the details of worship and the procedures for discipline. Along with congregational singing,[6] the preaching of the Word of God was made a central element of worship in the Genevan church services.

Calvin's preaching

The Second Helvetic Confession, drafted by Calvin's older contemporary, Henry Bullinger, in 1561 and adopted by most of the Swiss churches, reflects Calvin's view of preaching: the preaching of the Word of God is the Word of God. Since God speaks in the Scriptures, God also speaks in preaching that faithfully interprets the Scriptures. Preaching, though not infallible, is the authentic speech of God to the assembled church. God expects the church to listen to the pastors whom he sends to preach his Word as if he himself were speaking to the church in person.

Calvin customarily preached through a book of the Bible, expounding one or more verses at a time, in consecutive order. He seldom veered from his text, which he explained phrase by phrase and applied to the congregation in the context of their present situation. Far from dry theological lectures, Calvin's sermons came from a heart aflame with devotion to God and love for the people of God. He preached in the everyday language of ordinary people, illustrating his points with figures of speech and pungent conversations between himself and imaginary opponents.

One can sense, when reading his sermons, Calvin's passion for the doctrine of salvation revealed in the gospel, for the grace of God and its fruit in the believer's life and, above all, for the Saviour whose atoning death and bodily resurrection are the believer's hope of eternal glory. Calvin's 342 expositions on the book of Isaiah are described by T. H. L. Parker as 'sermons born of an infinite passion of faith and a burning sincerity, luminous with theological sense, lively with wit and imagery, showing depths of compassion and the unquenchable joyousness of hope'. [7]

He preached without notes, drawing on his astonishing memory and his intimate knowledge of the Scriptures and literature, both secular and religious. His sermons were taken down in shorthand, then transcribed into full text. Though extempore, his preaching was never without careful preparation. When addressing the 'enemies of the true gospel' he could be fiercely angry, and when appealing to the congregation he was always tender-hearted and compassionate.

Invariably, he appealed to his listeners not only to believe the truth of God's Word, but also to live in obedience to God's commands. The grace that Calvin preached became fruitful when it was rooted in the believer's life. And this rooting was itself a gracious work of the Holy Spirit, who softens the hard heart and opens the closed mind to receive what is preached as the very Word of God.

Fighting the good fight

Calvin encountered fierce and prolonged opposition to his ministry in Geneva. A certain group of people — Calvin called them 'Libertines' — disliked the strict and uncompromising moral code that he had imposed upon them. They saw these reforms as another form of papacy, the concentration of ecclesiastical and moral authority in one man. Calvin, on his part, believed that he had been called to be God's ambassador in Geneva, and he was determined that God's will should be obeyed. And so the battle lines were drawn. On one side were not only the Libertines but also the councils of Geneva, who fought to retain control of the church, particularly in regard to communion and discipline. While struggling with opponents in Geneva, his beleaguered spirit suffered a most grievous blow: in 1549 his beloved Idelette died. Later he described her as 'the excellent companion of my life'.

During Calvin's time in Geneva, the city was constantly threatened by Catholic armies under Emmanuel Philibert, Duke of Savoy, and other adversaries. The threat of conquest made life in Geneva harsh and austere, especially for evangelical Christians, many of whom were expelled and some put to death as disturbers of the peace and heretics. One such man was Michael Servetus, whose books about the 'errors' of the Trinity cost him his life. Calvin wrote letters to him, seeking to win him to the truth, but to no avail. Servetus had been condemned by Roman

Catholic authorities and was on the run, using an alias, M. de Villeneuve. When he turned up in Geneva, he was spotted, arrested and thrown in jail. Calvin agreed with his colleagues, Melanchthon, Farel and Beza, that Servetus deserved capital punishment. The Council of Geneva sentenced him to death and, on 27 October 1553, regardless of Calvin's plea for a more merciful form of execution (decapitation), Servetus was burned at the stake, and as flames consumed him he cried out: 'O Jesus, Son of the eternal God, have pity on me.'[8]

The spirit of the times dictated the fate of Michael Servetus. It had long been the custom in Geneva to proceed with violence against those charged with heresy. The civil and ecclesiastical jurisprudence of the courts that dealt with cases of heresy was grossly inconsistent with the spirit of Christianity as we understand it today. But it was in accord with Calvin's understanding of the purposes of civil government as the guardian and defender of the true religion.[9]

More tranquil times

Opposition to Calvin finally came to an end when elections replaced his opponents with civic officials who were sympathetic to him. Shortly afterwards, many French refugees were granted citizenship, and Calvin carried on a fruitful ministry among them. He continued to preach, lecture, write and publish. He also sought to improve the life of Geneva's citizens in many ways. He supported hospitals, designed a sewage system and encouraged the establishment of new industries. One of his greatest accomplishments, however, was in the field of education. In 1558 the council, with Calvin's help, laid plans for a college in Geneva, and solicited funds from the citizens to construct a suitable building. Five years later, in 1559, the school opened its doors, with Theodore Beza as rector of what was to become the University of Geneva.

Calvin himself taught theology and Old Testament. His lectures were the basis of a number of his commentaries on books of the Bible. Exhausted by his labours and stricken by a recurring illness, he feared that he might die before making final corrections and additions to the *Institutes* and therefore hastened to finish the task. In the preface to the final revision, issued on 1 August 1559, Calvin states its purpose, which was 'to prepare and qualify students of theology for the reading of the divine Word, that they may have an easy introduction to it, and be enabled to proceed in it without any obstruction'.[10]

Finishing the course

Calvin's health continued to decline; he suffered from several afflictions and was often confined to his bed. Despite his failing health, however, he managed to continue his preaching, lecturing and dictating. Even when his body was miserably weakened, his mind remained sharp, and he was able, before his death, to finish the last of his commentaries, on the book of Joshua. The ailing Reformer preached his last sermon early in February 1564. Thereafter he was sometimes carried to the service of worship, but spoke only a few sentences. During these months of suffering, his colleague Theodore Beza, who has given a full account of Calvin's maladies,[11] recounts that, even while tormented by so many diseases, he was never heard to utter a word unbecoming to a Christian. He would only raise his eyes towards heaven and say, 'O Lord, how long?'

Several days before his death, a few of Calvin's friends gathered in his house for a last supper with him. Beza recalls that 'His whole body was so emaciated that nothing seemed left but spirit.'[12] He died on 27 May 1564, just a few days before his fifty-fifth birthday. Throughout Geneva there was great sadness. The republic had lost a wise and loyal citizen, the church a faithful preacher and caring pastor, and the college an incomparable teacher. Almost all the population of Geneva attended his funeral. He was buried without unusual ceremony in a simple, unmarked grave, as he had requested, in a public cemetery in Geneva.

John Calvin, more than any other leader of the Protestant Reformation, created patterns of religious and political thought that would dominate Western culture throughout the modern period. His greatest legacy, however, was his recovery of the doctrines of grace, which he bequeathed to future generations through his commentaries and published sermons. In his will he testifies, 'With my whole soul I embrace the mercy which [God] has exercised towards me through Jesus Christ, atoning for my sins with the merits of his death and passion, that in this way he might satisfy for all my crimes and faults, and blot them from his remembrance.'[13]

The fact that Calvin's life, as well as his faith, was centred in Christ alone is evident in one of the great hymns[14] attributed to him from the Genevan Psalter:

> I greet thee, who my sure Redeemer art,
> My only trust and Saviour of my heart,
> Who pain didst undergo for my poor sake;
> I pray thee from our hearts all cares to take.
>
> Thou art the life, by which alone we live,
> And all our substance and our strength receive;
> Sustain us by thy faith and by thy power,
> And give us strength in every trying hour.
>
> Our hope is in no other save in thee;
> Our faith is built upon thy promise free;
> Lord, give us peace, and make us calm and sure,
> That in thy strength we evermore endure.

Notes

1. Humanism: a way of thinking which affirms the dignity and worth of man and human culture, usually without reference to religious faith.
2. Theodore Beza, 'The Life of John Calvin,' in *Tracts Relating to the Reformation,* translated by Henry Beveridge (T. & T. Clark: Edinburgh, 1860), vol. I, p.xxi.
3. Beza, 'Life of John Calvin', p.xxi.
4. T. H. L. Parker, *John Calvin: A Biography* (The Westminster Press: Philadelphia, 1975), p.23. It is not possible to determine the precise date or circumstances of Calvin's conversion, which probably occurred between 1525 and 1530. For a detailed discussion, see Parker, *John Calvin,* pp.162-5.
5. From Latin, *anabaptisa,* 'one who is rebaptized'.
6. The famous Genevan Psalter (1551), composed by Calvin and his colleague Louis Bourgeois, became a source of much Protestant hymnody.
7. Parker, *John Calvin,* p.92.
8. Kenneth Scott Latourette, *A History of Christianity* (Harper & Row: New York *et al.*, 1953, 1975) vol. II, p.759.
9. Although Calvin did not allow that civil government should 'make laws respecting religion and the worship of God', he did approve of the idea that civil government 'provides that the true religion which is contained in the law of God be not violated, and polluted by public blasphemies, with impunity' (*Institutes,* IV. xx, 3).
10. John Calvin, *Institutes of the Christian Religion*, translated by John Allen (Wm. B. Eerdmans: Grand Rapids, 1949), vol. 1, p.18.
11. Beza, 'Life of John Calvin', pp.lxvi-lxvii.
12. *Ibid.,* p. lxvii.
13. *Ibid.,* p.lxx.
14. Selected verses from no. 457, *Presbyterian Hymnal,* (Westminster/John Knox Press: Louisville, 1990).

Grace and its fruits

Selections from John Calvin on the Pastoral Epistles

Chapter 1

Our election revealed in Christ Jesus

'The sun that shines on us lights up the world no more clearly than Jesus Christ shows himself to those who have the eyes of faith to look upon him, when the gospel is preached.'

I.
Our election revealed in Christ Jesus

'[God] has saved us and called us with a holy calling, not according to our works, but according to his own purpose and grace which was given to us in Christ Jesus before time began, but has now been revealed by the appearing of our Saviour Jesus Christ, who has abolished death and brought life and immortality to light through the gospel' (2 Tim. 1:9-10).

Salvation is the work of God

The verses preceding our text show us that, if we would have a right understanding of the free mercy of our God in saving us, we must begin with his eternal counsel, according to which he chose us before the world began. For there we see that he had no regard to our persons, nor to our worthiness, nor to any good deed we could bring to him. Before we were born, we were enrolled in his register and he had already adopted us as his children. Therefore let us attribute our salvation entirely to God's mercy, knowing that we cannot boast of ourselves without robbing him of the honour which belongs to him.

Some have endeavoured to invent trivial objections, seeking to make the grace of God shine less brightly. They have said that, although God chose people before the world began, it was according as he foresaw that one would be different from another. Now the Scriptures show plainly that God did not wait to see whether they were worthy or not when he chose them. But those who quibble with this doctrine thought they might cast a shadow over the grace of God by saying that, though God did not take account of any past merits, he had an eye to those that were to come. They say that, although Jacob and his brother Esau had done neither good nor evil and yet God chose one and rejected the other, nevertheless, God foresaw (since all things are present to him) that Esau would be an evil man, who made light of all that was good, and that Jacob would in time come to be the kind of man that he afterwards proved to be.

But these are foolish speculations. They plainly make St Paul a liar, for he says that God rendered no reward to our work when he chose us, because he did it before the world began. But even if the authority of St Paul were abolished, the matter is very plain and obvious, not only in Holy Scripture, but also in reason, so that those who would try to evade it in this way show themselves to be totally devoid of skill. For if we search ourselves to the very core, what good can we find? Are not all mankind under the curse? What do we bring from our mother's womb, except sin?

Therefore we do not differ from one another in the slightest; the only difference is that God is pleased to take some, whom he chooses, for his own. And for this reason St Paul says the same thing in another place, when he says that no one has any reason to rejoice, for no one is better than any others, unless it is because God makes a distinction between them. So then, if we confess that God chose us before the world began, it necessarily follows that God prepared us to receive his grace; that he bestowed upon us that goodness which was not in us before; that he not only chose us to be heirs of the kingdom of heaven, but also justifies us and governs us by his Holy Spirit. Christians ought to be so firmly convinced of this doctrine that the matter is beyond doubt as far as we are concerned.

When we see people despise this doctrine, as some do today, who would be glad to reject the truth of God altogether, we need to know that they are fighting against the Holy Spirit. Such men behave like bulls or wild beasts as they set about to undermine the Holy Scriptures. There is, indeed, more honesty in the papists[1] than in these men; the doctrine of the papists is a great deal better, more holy and more agreeable to the sacred Scripture than the doctrine of those vile and wicked men who trample under feet [the doctrine of] God's holy election, attacking it like barking dogs, or like boars rooting up everything with their snouts.

Let us, however, hold fast what is taught here: since God chose us before the world was set in being, we must attribute the cause of our salvation to his free goodness. We must confess that he did not take us to be his children because of any merit of our own, for we had nothing to recommend ourselves in order to win his favour. Therefore we must acknowledge him, and him only, to be the cause and fountain of our salvation, and see that we are firmly grounded upon this foundation. Otherwise, whatever and however we build, it will come to naught.

Grace is given to us in Christ

We must also notice what St Paul joins together here — namely, the grace of Jesus Christ and the eternal counsel of God the Father; and then he brings us to our calling, so that we may be assured of God's goodness and of his will, which would have remained hidden from us unless we had a witness of it. St Paul says in the first place that the grace which depends upon the purpose of God, and is included in it, is given in our Lord Jesus Christ. In other words, since we deserve to be cast away and hated as God's mortal enemies, it was necessary for us to be grafted, as it were, into Jesus Christ, in order that God might acknowledge us as his children. Otherwise, God could not look upon us, except to hate us, because there is nothing but wretchedness in us; we are full of sin and crammed full of all kinds of iniquity.

God, who is justice itself, can have no agreement with us while he considers our sinful nature. Therefore, when he would adopt us before the world began, it was necessary that Jesus Christ should stand between us and him and that we should be chosen in his person, for he is the well-beloved Son. When God joins us to him, he makes us his children, as it pleases him. Let us learn to come directly to Jesus Christ, if we would be in no doubt about God's election; for he is the true looking-glass in which we must behold our election.

If Jesus Christ were taken from us, God would be a judge of sinners, and we could not hope for any goodness or favour from him, but instead we would look for vengeance, for without Jesus Christ, God's majesty would always be terrible and fearful for us. If we hear his eternal purpose mentioned, we cannot but be afraid, as though he were already armed against us to plunge us in over our heads [beneath the waves of his wrath]. But when we know that all grace rests in Jesus Christ, we may be assured that God loved us, although we were unworthy.

The link between God's election and our calling

In the second place, we must notice that St Paul is not simply speaking of God's election — for that would not put us beyond doubt, but we would remain in perplexity and anguish — but he adds the 'calling' through which God has made known his counsel, which previously was unknown to us, and which was beyond our reach. How then shall we know that God has chosen us, so that we may rejoice in him and in the goodness he has bestowed on us? Those who speak rashly against God's election leave the gospel to one side. They leave aside all that God lays before us in order to bring us to him — all the means he has appointed for us and knows to be right and proper to our use. We must not go on in this way but, according to St Paul's rule, we must link the calling with God's eternal election.

It is said that we are called; thus we have this second word, 'calling'. God calls us, but how does he do this? Surely, he calls us when it pleases him to certify to us our election, which we could by no other means achieve. For, as both the prophet Isaiah and the apostle Paul say, who can enter into God's counsel? (Isa. 40:13; Rom. 11:34). But when it pleases God to communicate to us in familiar terms, we receive that which surpasses the knowledge of all men. For we have a good and faithful witness, the Holy Spirit, who raises us above the world and brings us even into the wonderful secrets of God.

So we see, then, that we must not speak of God's election in isolation when we say that we are predestinated; but if we want to be fully assured of our salvation, we must not enquire lightly about it — whether God has taken us to be his children, or not. What should we do then? Let us look at what is set forth in the gospel. There God shows us that he is our Father, and that he has marked us out to bring us to the inheritance of life, and that knowledge is a seal of the Holy Spirit in our hearts, and an undoubted witness to our salvation, if we receive it by faith. For the gospel is preached to a great number of persons who are, nevertheless, reprobate. Yes, and God exposes them [for what they are] and shows that he has cursed them, that they have no part or portion in his kingdom, because they resist the gospel and cast away the grace that is offered them. But when we receive the doctrine of God with obedience and faith, and rest ourselves upon his promises, accepting this offer that he makes us, to take us as his children — this, I say, is a true and certain evidence of our election. We must note, however, that when we have [this] knowledge of our salvation because God has called us and enlightened us in the faith of his gospel, this does not bring to naught the eternal predestination that went before.

Faith is the gift of God

There are a great many in these days who will say, 'Who are those whom God has chosen, if they are not those who have faith?' I grant it is so, but they draw a wrong conclusion from that. They say, 'Faith is the cause, yes, the first cause of our salvation.' If they called it a means, or second cause, it would indeed be true, for Scripture says, 'By grace you have been saved through faith' (Eph. 2:8). But we must go higher; for if they attribute faith to men's free will, they blaspheme wickedly against God and are guilty of sacrilege. On the contrary, we must come to that which Scripture shows us — namely, that when God gives us faith, we in ourselves are not capable of receiving the gospel, but only as he has prepared us for it by the Holy Spirit.

It is not enough for us to hear with our ears the voice of a man [preaching the gospel]. That is merely a sound that vanishes away into thin air, unless God works within us and speaks to us in a secret manner by the Holy Spirit. And it is from this [work of God] that faith comes. Who is the cause of it? Why is faith given to one and not to another? St Luke shows us, saying, 'As many as had been appointed to eternal life believed' (Acts 13:48). There were a great number of hearers, yet only a few of them received the promise of salvation. And who were those few? Those who were appointed to salvation.

Again, St Paul speaks at such length on this subject in his epistle to the Ephesians that the enemies of God's predestination must be lacking indeed in sense and reason, having been blinded by the devil and brought totally under his spell, if they cannot see a thing which is so plain and evident. St Paul says that God has called us and made us partakers of his treasures and infinite riches, which he brought to us through our Lord Jesus Christ. And how was this done? It was according as he had chosen us before the world began. Therefore, when we say that we are called to salvation, and assured of it, because God has given us faith, it is not because there is not a higher cause — that is, the eternal election of God. Anyone who cannot come to this point [in his thinking] detracts from God in some way and lessens his honour, by making a difference between men on the basis of their deserts, or their attitude or disposition. Therefore we must hold fast to the truth that Paul is setting out, which is found, not only here, but in almost every part of Holy Scripture.

The grounds of our assurance

And now, so that we may make a short conclusion of all [we have said], let us see in what order we must proceed in this matter. When we enquire about our salvation, we must not begin by saying, 'Are we chosen?' No, we can never climb so high. We shall be puzzled a thousand times, and have our eyes dazzled, before we can arrive at a knowledge of God's counsel. What, then, shall we do?

Let us hear what is said in the gospel. When God has been so gracious as to make us receive the promise offered, it is as if he had opened his whole heart to us and had registered the fact of our election in our consciences. We must therefore have the assurance that God has taken us to be his children, and that the kingdom of heaven is ours, because we are called in Jesus Christ.

How may we know this? How shall we base our confidence upon this doctrine that God has set before us? We must magnify the grace of God, knowing that we can bring nothing on our part to recommend ourselves to his favour. We must become nothing in our own eyes, that we may not claim any praise for ourselves, but may know in our present experience that God has called us to the gospel, according as he chose us before time began.

It is true that this election of God is, as it were, a letter which remains sealed to us, because it consists in itself and in its own nature; but we may read it, for God gives us a witness to it when he calls us to himself by the gospel and by faith. Then we have, so to speak, a counterpart of it. Now, just as the original copy takes nothing away from the letter or writing that we read, but is rather a confirmation of it (in that a man will not go looking for the copy when he has in his hand the authentic writing), so must we be in no doubt about our salvation. When God certifies to us by the gospel that he takes us as his children, this testimony carries peace with it, being signed by the blood of our Lord Jesus Christ and sealed by the Holy Spirit. When we have this witness, do we not have enough to content our minds? Therefore, God's election is so far from being contrary to this [testimony] that it confirms the witness which we have in the gospel, and does so a great deal better. We must not doubt that God has registered our names among his chosen children before the world was made; but the knowledge of this he reserved for himself. We nevertheless have letters patent confirming our salvation; we have, as I have shown, the written counterpart which is sure enough [for our faith to rest upon].

There is another thing which needs to be said here. We must always come to our Lord Jesus Christ when we talk of our election, for without him we cannot come near God. When we talk of God's decree, well may we be seized with alarm, as those worthy of death. But if Jesus Christ is our guide, we may boldly rejoice, knowing that he has worthiness enough in him to make all his members beloved of God the Father — it being sufficient for us that we are grafted into his body and made one with him.

Thus we must muse upon this doctrine, if we will profit aright by it, as it is set forth by St Paul when he says that this grace of salvation was given to us 'before time began'. We must go beyond the order of nature if we are to know how we are saved, and by what cause, and whence our salvation comes. God would not leave us in doubt; nor did he hide his counsel, so that we might not know how our salvation was secured. He has not only called us to himself by the preaching of his gospel, but has sealed the witness of his goodness and fatherly love in our hearts.

Our response must be to glorify God

So then, having such a certainty, let us glorify God because he has called us of his free mercy. Let us rest ourselves upon our Lord Jesus Christ, knowing that he did not deceive us when he caused it to be preached that he gave himself for us and witnessed it by the Holy Spirit. For faith is an undoubted token that God takes us as his children, and by faith we are led to eternal election and to see that God has called us according as he has chosen us beforehand.

The apostle does not say that God has chosen us because we have heard the gospel, but on the other hand he attributes the faith that is given us to the highest cause, namely, because God has foreordained that he would save us, seeing we were lost and cast away in Adam. There are certain foolish people who, in order to blind the eyes of the simple and such as are like themselves, say that the grace of salvation was given to us because God ordained that his Son should redeem mankind, and therefore this is common to all. But St Paul teaches something else; and one cannot by such childish arguments mar the doctrine of the gospel, for it is said plainly that God has saved us. Does this refer to all without exception? No! He speaks only to the faithful. Again, does St Paul include all the world? Some were called by preaching, and yet they made themselves unworthy of the salvation which was offered to them. Therefore they were reprobate. God left others in their unbelief, who never heard the gospel preached.

Therefore St Paul directs himself plainly and precisely to those whom God has chosen and reserved to himself. God's goodness will never be viewed in its true light, nor be honoured as it deserves, unless we know that he would not have us remain in the general destruction of mankind, in which he left those who were like us. We do not differ from them, for we are no better than they are; but so it pleased God. Therefore all mouths must be stopped. Men must presume to take no credit to themselves, but rather to praise God, confessing themselves to be debtors to him for their entire salvation.

Grace revealed in the appearing of Christ

We shall now make some remarks about the other statements St Paul makes in this passage. It is true that God's election could never be profitable to us, nor could [the knowledge of it] come to us, unless we knew it by means of the gospel — because it pleased God to reveal that which he had kept secret before all ages. But to explain his meaning more plainly he adds that this grace is revealed to us now. How? 'By the appearing of our Saviour Jesus Christ.' When he says that this grace is revealed to us by the appearing of Jesus Christ, he shows that we would be guilty of gross ingratitude if we could not be content to rest ourselves upon the grace of the Son of God. What more can we look for? If we could climb up beyond the clouds and search out the secrets of God, what would be the purpose of it? Would it not be to ascertain that we are his children and heirs? But we already know these things, for they are clearly set forth in Jesus Christ. For it is said that all who believe in him will enjoy the privilege of being God's children. Therefore we must not swerve from these things one bit, if we want to be certain of our election. St Paul has already shown us that God never loved us, nor chose us, except in the person of his beloved Son. When Jesus Christ appeared, he revealed life to us; otherwise we would never have been partakers of it. He has made us acquainted with the eternal counsel of God. But it is presumption for men to attempt to know more than God would have them know.

If we walk soberly and reverently in obedience to God, hearing and receiving what he says in Holy Scripture, the way will be made plain before us. St Paul says that when the Son of God appeared in the world, he opened our eyes, that we might know that he was gracious to us before the world was made. We were received as his children and accounted righteous, so that we need not doubt that the kingdom of heaven is prepared for us. Not that we have it because we deserve it, but because it belongs to Jesus Christ, who makes us partakers with himself.

Life and immortality brought to light by the gospel

When St Paul speaks of the appearing of Jesus Christ he says he has 'brought life and immortality to light through the gospel'. It is not only that Jesus Christ is our Saviour, but that he is sent to be a mediator, to reconcile us by the sacrifice of his death. He is sent to us as a lamb without blemish, to purge us and make satisfaction for all our trespasses. He is our pledge, to deliver us from the condemnation of death. He is our righteousness, our advocate, who makes intercession with God, so that God would hear our prayers.

We must acknowledge that all these qualities belong to Jesus Christ, if we are to have a correct knowledge of how he appeared. We must look at the substance contained in this word 'gospel'. We must know that Jesus Christ appeared as our Saviour, that he suffered for our salvation, that we were reconciled to God the Father through his means, and that we have been cleansed from all our blemishes and redeemed from condemnation to everlasting death. If we do not know that he is our advocate, that he speaks on our behalf when we pray to God — to the end that our prayers may not be rejected — what will become of us? What confidence can we have to call upon God's name, who is the fountain of our salvation? But St Paul says that Jesus Christ has fulfilled all things that were requisite for the redemption of mankind.

If the gospel were taken away, of what advantage would it be to us that the Son of God had suffered death and risen the third day for our justification? All this would have been unprofitable to us. So then, the gospel puts us in possession of the benefits that Jesus Christ has purchased for us. And, therefore, though he is now absent from us in body and is not here on earth with us, our condition is none the worse for that: it is not as if he had withdrawn himself, so that we should seek him and not be able to find him, for the sun that shines on us lights up the world no more clearly than Jesus Christ shows himself to those who have the eyes of faith to look upon him, when the gospel is preached. Therefore St Paul says that Jesus Christ has brought life 'to light', everlasting life.

He says that the Son of God has abolished death. If he had not offered an everlasting sacrifice to appease the wrath of God, if he had not descended even to the bottomless pit to draw us out from it, if he had not taken our curse upon himself, if he had not taken away the burden with which we were crushed down — where should we be? Would death have been destroyed? No, sin would reign in us, and death likewise. Indeed, let everyone examine himself, and we shall find that we are slaves to Satan, who is the prince of death. So then, we are shut up in this miserable slavery, unless God destroys the devil, sin and death. And this has been done, but how? He has taken away our sins by the blood of our Lord Jesus Christ.

Therefore, poor sinners and in danger of God's judgement though we are, sin cannot hurt us. The venomous sting of sin is so blunted that it cannot wound us, because Jesus Christ has gained the victory over it. It was not in vain that he suffered the shedding of his blood; it was a washing by which we were washed through the work of the Holy Spirit — as St Peter shows. And thus we see plainly that when St Paul speaks of the gospel, in which Jesus Christ appeared — and appears daily to us — he does not forget his death and passion, nor the things that pertain to the salvation of mankind.

We may be certain that in the person of our Lord Jesus Christ we have all that we can desire; we have full and perfect trust in the goodness of God and the love he bears towards us. It is true that we can see that our sins separate us from God and cause a warfare in our members, but we have an atonement through our Lord Jesus Christ. And why is this? Because he has shed his blood to wash away our sins; he has offered a sacrifice by which God has become reconciled to us. In short, he has taken away the curse so that now we enjoy the blessing of God. Moreover, he has conquered death and triumphed over it so that he might deliver us from its tyranny, which would otherwise entirely overwhelm us.

Thus we see that all things that belong to our salvation are accomplished in our Lord Jesus Christ. And in order that we may enter into full possession of all these benefits, we must know that he appears to us daily by his gospel. Although he dwells in his heavenly glory, if we open the eyes of our faith, we shall behold him. We must learn not to separate what the Holy Spirit has joined together. Let us observe that St Paul meant to magnify the grace that God showed to the world after the coming of the Lord Jesus Christ by a comparison with the Old Testament saints, who did not have this advantage of having Jesus Christ appear to them, as he appeared to us.

It is true that they had the very same faith, and the inheritance of heaven is theirs as well as ours, God having revealed his grace to them as well as to us — but not in the same measure, for they saw Jesus Christ afar off, under the figures of the law, as St Paul says to the Corinthians. The veil of the temple was as yet in place, so that the Jews could not come near the sanctuary; that is, the material sanctuary. But now that the veil of the temple has been removed, we may draw near to the majesty of our God. We come most familiarly to him, in whom dwells all perfection and glory! In short, we have the substance, whereas they had the shadow (Col. 2:17).

The Old Testament saints submitted themselves wholly to bear the afflictions of Jesus Christ, as we are told in the eleventh chapter of Hebrews. It is not said that Moses bore the shame of Abraham, but of Jesus Christ. Thus the saints of old, though they lived under the law, offered themselves to God in sacrifice and bore most patiently the afflictions of Christ. And now Jesus Christ, having risen from the dead, has brought life to light. If we are such delicate creatures that we cannot bear afflictions for the sake of the gospel, are we not worthy to be blotted out of the book of God and cast off? Therefore, we must be constant in the faith and ready to suffer for the name of Jesus Christ whatever God wills — because life is set before us, and we have a fuller knowledge of it than the Old Testament saints had.

We know how they were tormented by tyrants and enemies of the truth, and how they suffered constantly. The condition of the church is less grievous in these days than it was then. For now Jesus Christ has brought life and immortality to light through the gospel. Whenever the gospel is preached to us, it is as if the kingdom of heaven were opened to us, as if God reached out his hand and certified that life is near us, and that he will make us partakers of his heavenly inheritance. But when we look to that life which was purchased for us by our Lord Jesus Christ, we should not hesitate to forsake all that we have in this world and to come to the treasure above, which is in heaven.

So let us not be willingly blind, since Jesus Christ lays before us daily the life and immortality spoken of here. When St Paul speaks of life and adds 'immortality', it is as if he said that we already enter into the kingdom of heaven by faith. Though we are strangers here below, the life and grace of which we are made partakers through our Lord Jesus Christ will bear fruit at the appropriate time, that is, when he is sent by God the Father to show the effect of the things that we now have preached to us daily, and which were fulfilled in his person, when he was clothed in humanity.

1. Calvin uses the term 'papists' to refer to the leaders and teachers of the church of Rome. As such his often vehement condemnations of them should be seen as directed primarily towards those responsible for promulgating doctrine rather than as sweeping attacks on every individual within the membership of the Roman Catholic Church.

Grace and its fruits

Selections from John Calvin on the Pastoral Epistles

Chapter 2

The one mediator

'Let us not fool ourselves any more by thinking that we can purchase God's favour by any ceremony or trifle of our own devising, for we should have been cast off and utterly condemned, had it not been for the atonement made by the blood of Jesus Christ.'

2.
The one mediator

'For there is one God and one mediator between God and men, the man Christ Jesus, who gave himself a ransom for all, to be testified in due time' (1 Tim. 2:5-6).

At all times and seasons the world has been so far from God that all people have deserved banishment from his kingdom. Thus we see that, in the time of the law, God chose a certain people and gathered them to himself, leaving the rest of the world in confusion. Although people were so separated from God, still they all naturally belong to him, and as he made them all, so he governs and maintains them by his virtue and goodness. So when we see people going to destruction — God not having been so gracious as to join them with us in the faith of the gospel — we must pity them and endeavour to bring them into the right way.

One God over all

St Paul says that there is one God. In other words, since God has made all mankind and put them under his protection, there cannot but be some degree of brotherhood existing between us. It is true that those who do not agree with us in faith are at a great distance from us; yet the order of nature shows us that we must not utterly cast them off, but take all the pains we can to bring them again into the unity of the body — because they are, as it were, members of it who have been cut off. When we see people thus scattered, it may well make the hairs of our head stand on end when we reflect that all of us are of the selfsame nature, and that the image of God was imprinted on them as well as on us. Moreover, that which should have been the strongest bond to hold us together has caused division and made us enemies, namely, the service of God, the religion of Jesus Christ.

One mediator between God and men

Therefore, when we see poor unbelievers wander and go astray from the way of salvation, we must have pity on them and do all we can to reclaim them, remembering the words of the apostle: 'There is one God and [St Paul adds] one mediator between God and men.' By this he means us to understand that our Lord Jesus Christ came, not to reconcile to God the Father a few individuals only, but to extend his grace over all the world. We see set forth through the whole of Scripture that Christ suffered, not only for the sins that were committed in Judea, but also for those that were committed throughout the world.

The office of our Lord Jesus Christ was to make an atonement for the sins of the world and to be a mediator between God and men. Since he has taken upon himself our flesh and so completely abased himself as to become man, we should submit ourselves to him in all that he requires of us. Our Lord Jesus Christ was made like us and suffered death so that he might become an advocate and mediator between God and us, and open a way whereby we may come to God.

Those who do not endeavour to bring their unbelieving neighbours to the way of salvation plainly show that they take no account of God's honour. They try to diminish the mighty power of his empire and set boundaries for him, so that he may not rule and govern all the world. They likewise obscure to some extent the efficacy of the passion and death of our Lord Jesus Christ and lessen the dignity given to him by the Father.

The mediator is a man

In the epistle to the Hebrews the apostle says, 'Therefore … he had to be made like his brethren, that he might be a merciful and faithful High Priest in things pertaining to God, to make propitiation for the sins of the people. For in that he himself has suffered, being tempted, he is able to aid those who are tempted' (Heb. 2:17-18). Those who do not know what adversity means will have no compassion on others who suffer, but are so intoxicated with pleasure that they think poverty is nothing. Our Lord Jesus Christ was a partaker of all our miseries and tasted all our afflictions, sin only excepted. And why was this? To the end that, when we come to him, he may be ready to help us. Having tasted our afflictions in his own person, he entreats God to have pity on us.

When he appears as our mediator, we have nothing to fear; we may come with uplifted hands, calling on God our heavenly Father, not doubting that he will receive us as his children, through the merits of his Son, and make us feel the fruit of our adoption. Having Christ as our mediator, we may come to God on familiar terms, laying before him our needs and making known the grief that torments us, in order to be relieved of it. The papists endeavour to prove that the saints are our patrons, and that they make intercession for us — alleging that we are not worthy to appear before God. But if this is the case, of what use is the office of our Lord Jesus Christ, who is the mediator, and a man?

The mediator is also our Redeemer

Let us notice what is contained in the law. When God commanded the people to pray to him, he immediately showed them in what manner they should perform this service, which was this: the people were to stand afar off in the court of the temple, and neither the king nor anyone else, except the priest, was allowed to approach the sanctuary, for he was a figure of our Lord Jesus Christ. This was the reason why he was clothed in new garments and was consecrated and dedicated to God. The high priest, entering the sanctuary, carried with him the blood of the sacrifice which he had offered. By this we understand that no one can find favour with God, except by virtue of the sacrifice which is offered in the person of our Lord Jesus Christ.

Thus God has shown by this solemn ceremony that we could not call upon him unless there were an advocate to make intercession for the whole body of the church, and that this intercession must be grounded upon a sacrifice offered. This is the reason why St Paul, after he has spoken of the intercession of Jesus Christ, adds, 'who gave himself a ransom for all'. For these things cannot be separated one from the other: the death and passion of the Son of God, and [the fact] that he is our mediator, to the end that we may have access in his name to God the Father.

Christ is the *only* mediator

Has not Jesus Christ appeared to show the truth, the substance and the perfection of the things prefigured by the law? And yet Satan strives to darken our minds so that we may not perceive this mediator that was given. We see in the beginning of the gospel that there were many heretics who believed the angels to be advocates. St Paul, speaking of such people, says, 'Let no one cheat you of your reward, taking delight in false humility and worship of angels, intruding into those things which he has not seen, vainly puffed up by his fleshly mind' (Col. 2:18). St Paul gives such honour to Jesus Christ that all other intercessors and advocates must give way, and he must be received as the only Saviour.

For many years now, one might as soon have heard Mohammed called the Saviour of the world as the Son of God named as a mediator and an advocate by the papists. And today, if any of us calls Jesus Christ a mediator and an advocate, they will immediately begin quarrelling with us, asking whether we mean that Christ is the *only* advocate, or that the saints are advocates as well. If we strive to maintain the dignity of the Son of God, they are displeased with us. Let us, therefore, be armed with the doctrine of the apostle, which teaches us that we cannot come near to God, except through the mediation of Jesus Christ.

The papists are so impudent and shameless — I mean their teachers — that when they wish to prove the matter which they have forged against the pure doctrine of the gospel, they say, 'It is true that there is a mediator, but he is not the only one; for when we call a man "one", it is not understood that he is the only one in the world, and there is none besides him!' But is not what St Paul says in this passage, that there is 'one mediator', as true as when he says that there is 'one God'? It is the just vengeance of God (seeing that they have endeavoured to take away the office of Christ's mediatorship) that they should be brought into shame and contempt, because they have dishonoured the Son of God, the Lord of glory — the one to whom the Father commands both great and small to do homage, before whom all knees must bow, and in whose person we must worship the majesty of our God.

Christ is the only intercessor on our behalf

The papists acknowledge Jesus Christ to be the only mediator of redemption, that it is he alone who redeemed the world; but as for intercession, they say that he is not the only mediator, but that the saints who are dead have this office as well. The apostle says that we were redeemed by the blood of the Son of God, and therefore we must pray for all the world, for there is one mediator who has opened the way whereby we may come to God. Jesus Christ is called a mediator not only because he has made reconciliation by his death, but also because he appears now before the majesty of God, in order that through him we may be heard, as St Paul shows us in the eighth chapter of Romans. There he joins together the two offices [of Redeemer and Mediator]. Jesus Christ has redeemed us by his death and passion, so that there is no hindrance why God should not accept us, and now he still makes intercession for us before God.

When the Scripture exhorts us to pray for one another, this is not in any way to diminish the intercessory office of our Lord Jesus Christ, but [rather] that in his name and through this means we may all be made one together. When we pray for ourselves, we ought also to include in our prayers the whole body of the church, that we may not separate that which God has joined together.

The doctrine of the gospel must be our rule and guide. Does that lead us to [praying to] departed saints? Does God appoint them to be our patrons and advocates? No, no! There is not a syllable in Holy Scripture that makes mention of it. It is true that while we live in this world, there ought to be mutual love between us, and everyone ought to pray for his neighbours; but if I attempt to go beyond what the Scripture has shown me, surely I am like someone going astray across the fields [instead of keeping to the path].

Christ is our High Priest

In the [Old Testament] law it was said that the people should not come near the sanctuary, but should remain in the court and at the entrance to the temple, and that no one should enter into it except the one who offered the sacrifice. In the same way, if we would pray to God aright, let us consider our own unworthiness — knowing that we are not only earthly creatures, but that we are full of sin (having become polluted and unclean in Adam), and that we can bring to God nothing of any value, because we are not worthy to open our mouths before him. Let us, then, acknowledge our miserable state, so that we may come to him for the remedy. And what is this remedy? It is to have our Lord Jesus Christ for our High Priest — the one who shed his blood and 'gave himself a ransom for all'. Therefore, let us not doubt that God is now merciful to us, seeing that Christ has reconciled us to the Father by virtue of his death and passion.

As the high priest bore the names of the sons of Israel on his shoulders and had twelve precious stones fastened on his breastpiece,[1] so Jesus bore our sins and iniquities on the cross, and now bears us, as it were, in his heart. This is the foundation on which we stand. Therefore, let us not doubt that we shall find favour with God, if we come to him in the name of this mediator. We must not devise advocates and patrons after our own notions, but content ourselves with the simplicity of Holy Scripture. Jesus Christ is called the mediator, not only because he makes intercession for us at the present time, but because he suffered for the sins of the world.

We are to come to God through Christ alone

So let us learn to glorify God and thank him with all humility, because it has pleased him to draw us out of such abominations [as devising other mediators or advocates, as the papists do], that we may be stirred up all the more to walk [before him] with fear and carefulness. Since it has pleased God to give us such an advocate and mediator as his own Son, let us not be afraid to come and present ourselves before him, and call upon him in all our needs. Not only must each of us, for our own part, do so privately, but let us all pray to God for the whole body of the church, and for all mankind.

When we pray to God, our prayers must be sanctified and consecrated by the blood of our Lord Jesus Christ. We have no need of the sprinkling of the pope's holy water; but the price of which St Paul speaks must make satisfaction for us before God. We may rest assured that God will not reject the sacrifice with which he is very well content (as he has shown us), and by which he has become reconciled to us and made at one with us for ever. When we pray, if we do not stand upon the ground of the death and passion of our Lord Jesus Christ, we shall surely be in doubt and perplexity; and thus all our prayers will be in vain and unprofitable. The Scripture informs us that if we do not pray in faith, we shall not be profited by our praying.

A ransom for all

When the apostle says that our Lord Jesus Christ 'gave himself a ransom for all', he dismisses anything at all in which men might presume to confide by way of making satisfaction, as they call it [to God]. This point is worthy of note, for the world has deluded itself at all times in seeking to please God with trifles. Think of the heathen! They were aware that they could not call upon God unless they had some mediator. So what did they do? They had their intercessors, devising a thousand ways to find favour with God. The papists followed their example and attempt to please God by washing and purifying themselves. In doing so they were blindly imitating that which God had appointed for the Old Testament saints, when he made use of earthly elements, which will pass away, in order to draw them to Jesus Christ. When they came to the temple of Jerusalem, the water was ready, even at the entrance, so that everyone might purify himself and thus draw near to the majesty of God. This was to show them that they were full of defilement and pollution. But it was not enough for them to know this; they must have a remedy, and this remedy was not in the water, which, as we know, belongs to this passing world, but it prefigured the blood of our Lord Jesus Christ.

Let us not fool ourselves any more by thinking that we can purchase God's favour by any ceremony or trifle of our own devising, for we should have been cast off and utterly condemned, had it not been for the atonement made by the blood of Jesus Christ. Here our whole trust lies, and by this we are assured that our sins are forgiven. The papists say that original sin is forgiven us in baptism; and if a Jew or a heathen should be baptized at the age of twenty, thirty, or forty years, the sins which he had committed during his life would then be forgiven, but if after we are baptized we fall and commit sin, we must not expect to find grace and pardon unless we bring something [to God] by way of compensation.

The papists are constrained to confess that they cannot thoroughly make amends to God as they ought, and that it is impossible for anyone to make payment to him in all things; and so they add another supply, which is the blood of the martyrs and the keys of the church (the power given to priests [to impose penance] in confession as they think good). Thus they tear up as worthless the ransom which was paid on our behalf by the death and suffering of our Lord Jesus, trusting in their own performances and works of supererogation, as they are called; and if anything is lacking, the blood of the martyrs and the keys of the church make up the balance. What horrible blasphemy!

Is St Paul speaking here of a ransom that was made only for little children and for those who were not baptized? No, on the contrary, he includes all faults that make us guilty before God, for the way is open whereby we may come to him by prayer and find mercy. The ransom of which St Paul is speaking extends to all our sins; we must therefore have recourse to it from day to day, and place all our confidence in it. It is not only in this place that Holy Scripture directs us to the death and passion of our Lord Jesus Christ and to the shedding of his blood for the remission of our sins; this doctrine is common throughout the Scripture. Let us understand the necessity for a Redeemer, and that by the price of his blood we are reconciled to God the Father and have free access to him by prayer.

Redemption now testified to Gentiles as well as Jews

Since St Paul has shown us that the grace which was purchased by the Son of God was common to all mankind, and that it was not confined to the Jews only, someone might ask why God chose certain people for his inheritance. Why was it his pleasure that only the Jews should call upon him? Why did he confine his promises to them? Why did he give them figures [of what was to come] and grant them an expectation of this great Redeemer who was promised? It is true that, from the creation of the world, God always reserved some people for himself; yes, and when he made a covenant with Abraham he shut out all the heathen from the hope of salvation, but this does not prevent his calling all mankind at the present time. Although for a time it pleased God to extend a special grace towards the Jews, now it pleases him to make the heathen and the Gentiles partakers of it, and to have his church extend throughout the world, bringing to the fold those who were afar off. This, in brief, is the meaning of the apostle in this passage.

We may notice here that it would have been of little use to us for Jesus Christ to have made the atonement, unless we were assured of this benefit and told that God had called us to enter into possession of this salvation and to enjoy the blessings which had been purchased for us. Think, for example, of the Turks, who cast away the grace which was purchased for all the world by Jesus Christ. The Jews do likewise, and the papists (although they do not do it so openly) do it in effect. All of these are as effectively shut out and banished from the redemption which was purchased for us, as if Jesus Christ had never come into the world. And why is this? Because they do not have this witness, that Jesus Christ is their Redeemer. Although they have enough to give them a little taste, they always remain starved; and if they hear the word 'redeemer' mentioned, it brings no comfort to them, nor do they receive any benefit from what is contained in the gospel.

Thus we perceive that those who are not partakers of the blessings purchased by our Lord Jesus Christ do not receive the witness. Before Jesus Christ came into the world, the Gentiles were not only unbelievers, but God had blinded their eyes to such an extent that it seemed as if Christ came only for one particular people [the Jews]. Yes, one would have thought that, in the time of the law, God had not spread abroad the knowledge of his truth over all the world, but had given it only to one people, whom he held as his church.

St Paul informs us that it pleased God to give his law to the Old Testament saints and set them apart from the rest of the world; that he testified his good will towards Israel, and not to other nations, as it is said in the Psalms: 'Have respect to the covenant; for the dark places of the earth are full of the haunts of cruelty' (Ps. 74:20). Moses likewise says, 'The LORD's portion is his people; Jacob is the place of his inheritance' (Deut. 32:9). We see, then, that God chose for himself a particular people, namely, the stock of Abraham, and set others aside as strangers. This is true, says St Paul, but it is now necessary that this knowledge should be spread over all the world: that God is the Father and Saviour of the Gentiles, as well as of the Jews.

Christ's redemptive work testified to us in the gospel

We may therefore perceive that the death and passion of our Lord Jesus Christ would be unprofitable to us unless it were witnessed by the gospel. For it is faith that puts us in possession of this salvation. This is a very profitable doctrine, for it is acknowledged that the greatest benefit that can be bestowed upon the people of this world is to partake of the salvation purchased by Jesus Christ. There are few, however, who take the right way to obtain it. For we see how the gospel is despised and how men plug their ears and refuse to hear the voice which God has ordered to be proclaimed throughout the world!

We see only a few in these days who become reconciled to God by the death of Jesus Christ, for many deprive themselves of this witness. Others cast it away, or at least profit so little from it that Jesus Christ does not dwell in them by faith, to make them partakers of his blessings. St Paul says, 'But of [God] you are in Christ Jesus, who became for us wisdom from God — and righteousness and sanctification and redemption' (1 Cor. 1:30). This shows us that, being grafted into him, we may have part and portion in all his riches, that whatever he has may be ours. Seeing he was once pleased to become our brother, we must not doubt that in taking upon himself our poor and wretched state, he has made an exchange with us, that we may become rich through his grace.

It is certain that God has always borne witness of himself, yes, even to the heathen. Although they had neither the law nor the prophets, he has declared himself sufficiently to leave them without excuse. If there were nothing but the order of nature (as St Paul mentions in Acts 14), it would be sufficient to convince unbelievers of their unthankfulness to God, who formed them and has nourished them throughout life. For it is said in Psalm 19: 'The heavens declare the glory of God; and the firmament shows his handiwork.' Although they do not speak, yet they set forth his goodness in such a manner that we ought to be convinced without any other instructor. Look at the book of nature; it is written with letters plain enough to make known to us that we ought to glorify God!

But this witness was too obscure for the simplicity and weakness of men. It was therefore necessary that God should reveal himself in another manner, which he has done by means of the gospel. The law and the prophets were like a lamp to lighten the Jews, but they belonged to one people. The grace of the gospel, however, is bestowed generally upon all the nations of the earth. Therefore, it is not without cause that St Paul says that this witness was to be 'testified in due time'.

The gospel was testified 'in due time'

In another place we see how marvellously he sets forth this great secret which God had kept from the beginning of the world but had now revealed by the preaching of the gospel. Why, even the angels marvel at it as they see those who formerly were separated from God, those who seemed to be cut off and banished from salvation, now taken to be his children, made members of Jesus Christ and part of the fellowship and company of angels. This was a wonderful secret, enough to astonish all creatures! St Paul says, 'But when the fulness of the time had come, God sent forth his Son, born of a woman, born under the law, to redeem those who were under the law, that we might receive the adoption as sons' (Gal. 4:4-5). In this way it pleased God to make known to the world that which was previously unknown to the believers in Old Testament times.

The apostle tells the Ephesians that 'At that time you were without Christ, being aliens from the commonwealth of Israel and strangers from the covenants of promise, having no hope and without God in the world. But now in Christ Jesus you who once were far off have been brought near by the blood of Christ. For he himself is our peace, who has made both one, and has broken down the middle wall of separation, having abolished in his flesh the enmity, that is, the law of commandments contained in ordinances, so as to create in himself one new man from the two, thus making peace' (Eph. 2:12-15). Thus the discord between the Jews and the Gentiles was abolished.

Jesus Christ has not only proclaimed the glad tidings, but has also sent forth his apostles and ministers to preach and publish peace to the world — to assemble the Jews, who were near to God by reason of the covenant and by the solemn pledge made to their fathers, but who still needed a reconciliation through Jesus Christ the Redeemer. These glad tidings were afterwards directed to those who were afar off, even the poor Gentiles. They also received the message of salvation and the peace of God, being assured that God loved them, that he forgave all their sins. Thus the dividing wall was broken down and the ceremonies were destroyed, by which God had made a difference between the Jews and the Gentiles. And why was this? Because this salvation belongs to all the world without exception.

We therefore have this doctrine made clear: that it was requisite for our Lord Jesus Christ to make an atonement for sins, and that by his death he has purchased our redemption. We must therefore come to the testimony set forth in the gospel, that we may enjoy the blessings contained in it. We must not say that God is changeable because it has pleased him to hide the witness of the gospel for a season, and afterwards to have it preached throughout the world, for this he had determined in the counsel of his own will. Let us therefore be convinced that it is our duty to worship and reverence him with all humility, for this is the greatest wisdom we can possess.

We must not be too curious in seeking answers to useless and unprofitable questions, for God, who knows what we are able to bear, has made known that which it is proper for us to understand. Let us therefore learn in his school, and nowhere else. Isaiah speaks of 'an acceptable time' (Isa. 49:8). He calls it an acceptable time when the message of salvation is carried throughout the world. Seeing then that God has displayed his goodness and shows that he chose a particular time to call us to salvation, let us not, on our part, be stiff-necked and reveal the corruption of our hearts, saying that all is not well — for this will prevent us from coming to God — but let us heartily content ourselves with, and rest upon, this grace which is offered to us, that there may be agreement and sweet harmony between God and us, and that when he shows us that he considers this to be the fit time to call us to himself, we may come to him gladly acknowledging that it is a fit time because he has chosen it.

If things do not go in the way we think they should, we must not find fault and say that God should have done otherwise. Let us instead restrain ourselves and show implicit obedience to his will. Let us be ruled by his counsel, remembering that it is not for us to appoint a time when he shall do what is to be done. It is not our place to rule and command; that belongs to God alone.

The gospel is the testimony of God himself

When the gospel is called 'a witness', it is to assure us that God is kind and favourable towards us. But if we doubt after having this assurance of his good will, and stand wavering and show ourselves rebellious against him, we cannot do him a greater dishonour. Let us remember that whenever the gospel is preached to us God bears witness to us of his goodness.

Moreover, although those who speak the Word of God to us are mortal men, let us consider in what situation God has placed them: he has made them his witnesses. When a man is sworn in as a notary in any place, all the documents which he draws up must be taken as true and authentic. Now, if magistrates, who have so little authority, can have such authority, and their proclamations are accepted as valid on behalf of the realm, how much more ought we, when God sends his witnesses to proclaim the gospel, to receive the message of salvation which they bring! If we do not, the honour of God is shamefully abused. Let us therefore learn to be more obedient than we have been in the past and listen more intently to the doctrine of the gospel.

If St Paul was driven to fight against the pride and malice of men in his time, what is to be done now? For we see that ungodliness overflows, and the papists endeavour to abolish the remembrance of God's truth from the world. But we need not look so far: many among ourselves are profane; they tread the Word of God, as it were, under foot, yes, and live in defiance of it. We see people who call themselves Christians and wish to be regarded as such, yet they will not be governed by the Word of God, but scorn and scoff at the doctrine of the gospel. I heartily wish these things were not so common among us.

If these scoffers come to hear a sermon once a month, it is to ascertain whether we speak according to their own fancy or not. If not, they immediately begin to murmur and to say, 'It is all nothing; you would make us believe that we are not doing our duty!' But let us mark well the words of St Paul, where he protests that he is God's witness and shows that all who rebel against the gospel and will not submit themselves to it must not think that they have to deal with men, but with God — for the work is his. Let us therefore be careful that we submit ourselves to God and bow our necks in obedience to him, and so honour and magnify his glorious name that he may acknowledge us as his children; and that we may, all the days of our life, call upon him as our Father and our Saviour.

1. These gems represented the names of the sons of Israel (Exod. 28:15-21)

Grace and its fruits

Selections from John Calvin on the Pastoral Epistles

3.

The mystery of godliness

'Who is the God that St Paul is speaking about? It is the son of the virgin Mary. It is the one who has life in him who was subject to death. Who is he that has all power? It is the one who became feeble and weak. It is the one who bore our sins who is the source of life.'

3.
The mystery of godliness

'Without controversy great is the mystery of godliness: God was manifested in the flesh, justified in the Spirit, seen by angels, preached among the Gentiles, believed on in the world, received up in glory' (1 Tim. 3:16).

In the previous verses St Paul exhorted Timothy how to conduct himself in his office [as a minister of the Word], showing him to what honour God had advanced him by appointing him to govern his house. He showed him also that the office itself was honourable because the church upholds the truth of God in this world. He went on to show that there is nothing more precious, or more to be sought after, than to know God and to worship and serve him, and to be certain of his truth, that we might by it obtain salvation. All this is kept safe for us, and thus so great a treasure is committed to our care by means of the church, according to the words of St Paul. This truth is worthy of being esteemed more highly than it is.

A wonderful mystery revealed

What a hidden thing this is, and how wonderful, that God was manifested in the flesh and became man! Does it not so far surpass our understanding that when we are told of it we are astonished? Yet despite our lack of understanding, we have a full and sufficient proof that Jesus Christ was made man, was subject to death, and is also the true God who made the world and lives for ever. Of this his heavenly power bears witness. And we have other proofs: he was preached to the Gentiles, who before were banished from the kingdom of God; and the faith that at that time was confined to the Jews has spread throughout the whole world. Moreover, Christ Jesus was lifted up on high and, having entered into glory, sits at the right hand of God the Father.

If men despise these things, their unthankfulness will be condemned, for the very angels have by this same disclosure come to the understanding of that which they were previously ignorant of. For it pleased God to hide the means of our redemption from the angels, to the end that his goodness might be so much the more wonderful to all creatures. Thus we see St Paul's meaning. He calls the church of God the guardian of the truth; he also shows that this truth is such a treasure that it ought to be highly esteemed by us. And why is this?

Let us observe the contents of the gospel. God abased himself in such a manner that he took upon himself our flesh, so that we have become his brothers [and sisters]. The one who is the Lord of glory and governs the angels made himself of no reputation, [stooping] so low that he joined himself to us and took upon himself the form of a servant, even to the point of suffering the curse that was due to us. St Paul includes everything that Jesus Christ experienced in his person when he says that he was subject to all our infirmities, sin only excepted.

It is true that there is no blemish in him, but all purity and perfection. Yet it is a fact that he became weak as we are, that he might have compassion on us in our feebleness and help us, as it is set forth in the epistle to the Hebrews: 'For we do not have a High Priest who cannot sympathize with our weaknesses, but was in all points tempted as we are, yet without sin' (Heb. 4:15). He who had no sin suffered the punishment due to us, and was, as it were, accursed of God the Father, when he offered himself as a sacrifice, that by this means we might be blessed, and that his grace, which was hidden from us, might be poured upon us.

When we consider these things, do we not have good reason to be astonished? Do we consider what a being God is? His majesty is far beyond our reach. He contains all things in himself; even the angels worship him.

What is there in us? If we turn our eyes upon God, and then make a comparison — alas! — can we approach this exalted majesty which surmounts the heavens? Can we even have any acquaintance with it? No, for there is nothing but rottenness in us, nothing but sin and death. How can it be that the living God, the one who is the author of life, in all his everlasting glory and infinite power, should come and not only approach us in all our misery, wretchedness and frailty, and even this bottomless pit of all iniquity that is in all men, [but should enter into all these human experiences] with the sole exception of sin? How can the majesty of God not only come near to all this, but be joined to it and made one with it in the person of our Lord Jesus Christ? Who is Jesus Christ? God and man! But how is he God and man? What difference is there between God and man?

We know that there is nothing at all in our nature but wretchedness and misery, nothing but a bottomless pit of corruption and pollution. And yet, in the person of our Lord Jesus

Christ we see both the glory of God who is worshipped by angels and the weakness of man. We see that he is both God and man in one person. Is this not a secret and hidden thing, worthy to be expressed in words, and also enough to ravish our hearts? The very angels could never have thought of such a thing, as St Paul here observes. Since it has pleased the Holy Spirit to set forth the goodness of God and show us how precious a jewel it is, and how worthy of our esteem, let us be careful that we are not unthankful, nor have our minds so closed and prejudiced that we will not have anything do with it if we cannot thoroughly and perfectly understand it. For it is enough for us to have some little inkling of it. Each one of us should be content with what light is given him, considering the weakness of our judgement, and should be looking for the day when that which we now see in part shall be wholly and perfectly revealed to us. Nevertheless, we must employ our minds in the study of this matter. Why does St Paul call it 'a mystery' of the faith that Jesus Christ, who is the eternal God, was manifest in the flesh? It is rather like saying that when we are gathered to God and made one body with the Lord Jesus Christ, then we shall know the end for which we were made, namely, that God should be joined and made one with us in the person of his Son.

God manifested in the flesh

Thus we must conclude that no one can be a Christian unless he knows this mystery which is spoken of by St Paul. If we should examine and ask both men and women whether they know what these words mean, that 'God was manifested in the flesh', scarcely one in ten could make as good an answer as would be looked for by a child. And yet we need not marvel at that, for we see what negligence and contempt are to be found among the greatest part [of mankind]. We show and teach daily in our sermons that God took upon himself our nature, but how do men hear them? Who is there that troubles himself much to read the Scripture? There are very few that attend to these things; everyone is occupied with his own business.

If there is just one day in the week reserved for men to come together for religious instruction, on that day, having spent six days on their own business, they will go and spend that time in amusement and recreation. Some go off to the fields, others to the taverns to drink — and there are undoubtedly at this time as many who are to be found drinking as there are here assembled in the name of God. Therefore, when we see so many deliberately avoid and flee from learning doctrine, can we marvel that there is such ignorance and that we do not know even the ABC of Christianity, but are apt to regard it as a strange language when we are told that God was manifested in the flesh?

Nevertheless we cannot remove from God's register this verdict — that we have no faith if we do not know that our Lord Jesus Christ is joined to us, so that we may become his members, with him as our head. It seems that God would stir us up to think upon this mystery, whether we would or not, seeing how sleepy and drowsy we are. We see how the devil stirs up these old troublemakers sometimes to deny either the humanity of Jesus Christ or his deity, and at other times to confuse them both so that we may not perceive two distinct natures in him. Or else they would have us believe that he is not the man who fulfilled the promises in the Old Testament and consequently was descended from the stock of Abraham and David.

Is it indeed the case that such errors and heresies, which were in the church of Christ at the beginning, are still abroad even in these days? Then let us mark well the words that are here used by St Paul: 'God was manifested in the flesh.' When he calls Jesus Christ 'God', he acknowledges this nature which he had before the world was made. It is true that there is only one God, but in this one single essence we must include the Father and a wisdom which cannot be severed from him and an eternal power which always was, and which shall be for ever in him.

Thus Jesus Christ is truly God, for he was the wisdom of God before the world was made, and before eternity! It is said that he was 'manifested in the flesh'. The word 'manifested' implies that in him there were two natures. But we must not think that there is one Jesus Christ who is God, and another Jesus Christ who is man!

Let us so distinguish the two natures which are in him that we may know that the Son of God is our brother. God permits the old heresies, which in times past troubled the church, to make a stir again in our days, in order to stir us up to diligence. The devil goes about to destroy this article of our belief, knowing it to be the main prop and stay of our salvation.

If we do not have this knowledge of which St Paul speaks, what will become of us? We are all Adam's children, and therefore under a curse; we are in the bottomless pit of death. There is nothing but death and condemnation awaiting us, until we know that God came down to seek and save us. Until we have learned this, we are indeed miserable. Therefore, the devil has gone about doing all in his power to abolish this knowledge, to mar it and to mix it with lies, that he might utterly bring it to naught. When we see such majesty in God, how dare we presume to approach him, seeing we are full of misery? We must have recourse to this linking together of God's majesty and the human state.

Do what we can, we shall never have any hope, or be able to lay hold on the bounty and goodness of God, to return to him and call upon him, until we know the majesty of God that is in Jesus Christ, and also the weakness of man's nature, which he has received from us. We are utterly cast away from the kingdom of heaven; the gate is shut against us, so that we cannot enter into it. The devil has employed all his art to pervert this doctrine, seeing that our salvation is grounded upon it. We should, therefore, be so much the more confirmed and strengthened in it that we may never be shaken, but may stand steadfast in the faith which is contained in the gospel.

Christ was God from eternity

First of all, we have this to note: that we shall never know Jesus Christ to be our Saviour until we know that he was God from eternity. That which was written concerning him by Jeremiah the prophet must be fulfilled: 'Let him who glories glory in this, that he understands and knows me, that I am the LORD' (Jer. 9:24). St Paul shows that this must be applied to the person of our Lord Jesus Christ, and in view of that he insists that he takes no account of any doctrine or knowledge, except to know Jesus Christ.

Again, how is it possible for us to have our life in him, unless he is our God, and we are maintained and preserved by his power? How can we put our trust in him? For it is written: 'Cursed is the man who trusts in man and makes flesh his strength' (Jer. 17:5). Again, how can we be preserved from death except by God's infinite power?

We see then that, although the Scriptures bear no record of the deity of Christ Jesus, it is impossible for us to know him as our Saviour unless we attribute to him the whole majesty of God and unless we acknowledge him to be the true God. He is the wisdom of the Father, the one by whom the world was made, preserved and kept in existence. Therefore, let us be fully resolved on this point that, whenever we speak of Jesus Christ we shall lift up our thoughts on high and worship this majesty which he had from eternity, and this infinite essence which he enjoyed before he clothed himself in human flesh.

Christ truly became man

We should also note that Christ was made manifest in the flesh — that is to say, he became man — and was made like us in all things, sin only excepted (Heb. 4:15). When it says that he was 'in all points … as we are, yet without sin', the meaning is that our Lord Jesus Christ was without fault or blemish. Nevertheless, he did not refuse to bear our sins; he took this burden upon himself, that we through his grace might be freed from our burdens. We cannot know Jesus Christ to be a mediator between God and man unless we see him as man. Indeed, when St Paul goes on to encourage us to call upon God in the name of our Lord Jesus Christ, he expressly calls him 'man'.

St Paul says, 'There is one God and one mediator between God and men, the man Christ Jesus' (1 Tim. 2:5). He brings this to our attention so that we may, in the name of Christ and by his means, come familiarly to God, knowing that we are the brothers and sisters of Jesus Christ, the only begotten Son of God. Besides, if we were to seek our salvation [through one who is] without our human nature, where would we be? Seeing, therefore, that there is nothing but sin in mankind, we must also find righteousness and life in human flesh. Therefore if Christ has not truly become our brother, if he has not been made man like us, where does that leave us?

Let us now consider his life and passion. The death of Jesus Christ is called one sacrifice for all time, by which we are reconciled to God: 'But now, once at the end of the ages, he has appeared to put away sin by the sacrifice of himself' (Heb. 9:26). And why is it so called? St Paul shows us the reason when he says, 'As through one man's offence judgement came to all men, resulting in condemnation, even so through one man's righteous act the free gift came to all men, resulting in justification of life' (Rom. 5:18). If we do not know that the sin which was committed in our nature was repaired in the very same nature, where do we stand? What would be the grounds of our confidence? The death of our Lord Jesus Christ would be of no profit to us at all if he had not been made a man like ourselves.

Again, if Jesus Christ were only God, could we have any certainty or pledge in his resurrection that we ourselves should one day rise again? It is true that the Son of God rose again. When we hear it said that the Son of God took upon him a body like ours, came of the stock of David, and that he rose again, we know that our nature, though itself subject to corruption, is lifted up high into glory in the person of our Lord Jesus Christ, and we are made to 'sit together in the heavenly places in Christ Jesus' (Eph. 2:6.) Therefore those who went about denying human nature in the person of Jesus Christ are to be detested all the more. For in former times the devil raised up some individuals who declared that Jesus Christ appeared in the form of man, but did not have man's true nature. In this way they endeavoured to abolish God's mercy towards us and utterly destroy our faith.

Others have imagined that he brought a body with him from heaven, as though he did not partake of our nature. This was declared by that detestable heretic who was put to death here [Servetus]: that Jesus Christ had a body from eternity, which was composed of four elements; that the Godhead was at that time in a visible form, and that whenever the angels appeared, that was his body. What madness it is to make such an alchemy in order to form a body for the Son of God! What shall we do with that passage which says, 'He does not take on the nature of angels, but he does take on the seed of Abraham. Therefore, in all things he had to be made like his brethren, that he might be a merciful and faithful High Priest in things pertaining to God, to make propitiation for the sins of the people'? (Heb. 2:16-17, marginal reading). It is said [in Scripture] that he took on our flesh and became our brother, one of us. Yes, and that he was made like us, that he might have pity on us in our infirmities and help us. In short what was the purpose of his death, except to deliver us? Finally, he was made of the seed of David, that he might be known to be the Redeemer who was promised and whom the Old Testament saints had been looking for all down the ages. All this will come to nothing [if we accept such heretical teachings].

Let us remember, then, that it is written that the Son of God appeared in the flesh — that is, he became a real man and made us one with himself, so that we may now call God our Father. Why can we do this? Because we are members of the body of his only Son. But how are we members of his body? Because he was pleased to join himself to us, that we might be partakers of his substance.

Two natures in one person

Thus we see that it is not empty speculation when we are told that Jesus Christ put on our flesh; for we must reach this point [in our understanding] if we are to have a true knowledge of faith. It is impossible for us to trust in him aright unless we understand his humanity. We must also know his majesty before we can trust in him for salvation. Moreover it is not enough to know that Jesus Christ is God and man; we must also know that he is only one person.

Here again, the devil tries to stir up the coals of strife by perverting or disguising the doctrine which St Paul teaches us. For there have been heretics who have so confused the majesty and deity of Jesus Christ with his humanity that they thought his heavenly essence was immediately changed into flesh and human nature. Thus they say that Jesus Christ was made man. It then follows that God must forego his nature, and his spiritual essence must be turned into flesh. Then they go further and say, 'Jesus Christ is now no longer man, but his flesh has become God.' These are marvellous alchemists, who make so many new natures of Jesus Christ! Thus the devil, in former times, raised up such dreamers to trouble the faith of the church — and they are renewed in our time.

Therefore, let us mark well what St Paul teaches us in this place, for he gives us good armour, that we might defend ourselves against such errors. If we would see Jesus Christ in his true character, let us view in him this heavenly glory which he had from eternity, before all ages, and then let us come to his humanity, which is shown to us in this passage, so that we may distinguish his two natures. This is not idle speculation, but is necessary in order to nourish our faith.

If we seek life in Jesus Christ, we must understand that he has the whole Godhead in him, for it is written in the Psalms: 'For with you is the fountain of life; in your light we see light' (Ps. 36:9). If we are to stand firm against the attacks of the devil and all our enemies, we must know that Jesus Christ is God. In short, if we are to put our whole trust and confidence in him, we must know that he possesses all power, which he could not have unless he were God. On the other hand, when we would seek the forgiveness of our sins and the means to call upon God for help in our infirmities and deliverance from our infirmities, we must find Jesus Christ near to us and must see him as a man. Thus it is easy to see that we must perceive the humanity of our Lord Jesus Christ and distinguish it from his heavenly essence and majesty. And yet we must also join these two natures in one person. Who is the God that St Paul is speaking about? It is the son of the virgin Mary. It is the one who has life in him who was subject to death. Who is he that has all power? It is the one who became feeble and weak. It is the one who bore our sins who is the source of life.

Therefore we must learn to join these two natures together in one person and not separate them. We have two eyes in our head, each performing its function separately; but when we fix our gaze on something, our sight, which is in itself independent [in each of the two eyes], joins together and becomes one, as it is wholly focused on that which is set before us. In the same way there are two diverse natures in [the one person of] Jesus Christ.

Is there anything in the world more different than the body and the soul of man? His soul is an invisible spirit that cannot be seen or touched, which cannot be located in any place and has none of the physical senses. The body is a physical object, subject to decay — a visible thing which can be touched. The body has its own properties, which are entirely different from those of the soul. And so we ask, 'What is man?' A creature that is formed of body and soul.

If God used such workmanship in us, when he made us of two diverse natures, why should we think it strange that he used a far greater miracle in Jesus Christ? St Paul uses these words, 'was manifested', so that we may distinguish his deity from his humanity and may receive him as God manifested in the flesh — the one who is truly God, and yet in the same person has made himself one with us. Therefore we are the children of God, and because he is the one who made atonement on our behalf we are freed from the burden of our sins.

Since he has delivered us from all our misery, we now have perfect riches in him. In short, since he has submitted himself to death, we are now sure of life.

'Justified in the Spirit'

St Paul adds, 'He was justified in the Spirit.' The word 'justified' is sometimes used in Scripture in the sense of 'approved'. When it is said that he was justified, it is not that he became just, nor that he was acquitted by men, as though they were his judges and he was bound to give an account to them. No, no, it is no such thing! He is justified, rather, when the glory is given to him which he deserves, and we confess him to be what indeed he really is. The gospel is said to be justified when men receive it obediently and through faith submit themselves to the doctrine that God teaches. Likewise, in this place it is said that Jesus Christ was justified in spirit.

We must not be content to look only at the bodily presence of Jesus Christ, which was visible, but we must look higher. St John says, in the first chapter of his Gospel, that God was made flesh, or the Word of God, which is the same. The Word of God, who was God before the creation of the world, was made flesh; that is, he was united to our nature, so that the son of the virgin Mary is God — yes, the eternal God! His infinite power was there manifested — which is a sure witness that he is the true God!

St Paul says, in Romans 1, that Jesus Christ was 'born of the seed of David'; and he adds that he was 'declared to be the Son of God'. It is not enough for us to see him with our natural eyes, for in this case we would rise no higher than a man. But when we see that by miracles and mighty works he shows himself to be the Son of God, it is a seal and proof that when he abased himself he did not leave off his heavenly majesty!

Therefore, we may come to him as our brother, and at the same time worship him as the eternal God, by whom we were made and by whom we are preserved.

Were it not for this, we would have no church. Were it not for this, we would have no religion. Were it not for this, we would have no salvation. It would be better for us to be brute beasts, without reason and understanding, than to be destitute of this knowledge, namely, that Jesus came and joined his divine nature with our nature, which was so wretched and miserable. St Paul declares this to be a mystery, so that we may not come to it proudly and arrogantly, as many do who wish to be thought wise. This has caused many heresies to spring up; and indeed pride has always been the mother of heresies.

The practical applications of this doctrine

When we hear this word 'mystery', let us remember two things. First, that we are to learn to keep our senses under control, and not flatter ourselves that we have sufficient knowledge to comprehend how this should be that God should take on him our nature. All human reason must admit defeat in a case like this. Therefore, let us learn to rise beyond our understanding and to reverence that which is beyond our comprehension.

Secondly, we must pay attention when we are told, 'Here is a mystery.' We must not be sluggish or drowsy, but think upon this doctrine and exercise our brains about it. And when we have once begun to enter into what it means, we should endeavour to profit by it all the days of our life.

Once we have come to know that the Son of God is thus joined to us, let us fix our gaze upon that which is so sublimely set forth in him — that is, the virtue and power of the Holy Spirit. So then, Jesus Christ not only appeared as man, but showed indeed that he was Almighty God, as all the fulness of the Godhead dwelt in him! If we once know this, we may well perceive that St Paul had good reason to say that all the treasures of wisdom are hidden in our Lord Jesus Christ!

When we have once laid hold on the promises of this mediator, we shall know the height and depth, the length and breadth — yes, and whatever is necessary for our salvation. In this way we may stay our faith upon him as the only true God, and likewise see him as our brother, who has not only come near to us, but has united and joined himself to us in such a manner that he has become the same substance [with us]. If we have [grasped] this, then we may know that we have arrived at the perfection of wisdom of which St Paul speaks in another place. And having this knowledge, we may fully rejoice in the goodness of God, for it has pleased him to enlighten us with the brightness of his gospel and to draw us into his heavenly kingdom.

Grace and its fruits

Selections from John Calvin on the Pastoral Epistles

Chapter 4

God desires all men to be saved

'We are like birds perched on the branches of a tree, sitting targets for Satan. What assurance, then, could we have for tomorrow, or for the whole of life, or even beyond the grave — were it not that God, who has called us, will complete the work which he has begun in us?'

4.
God desires all men to be saved

'For this is good and acceptable in the sight of God our Saviour, who desires all men to be saved and to come to the knowledge of the truth. For there is one God and one mediator between God and men, the man Christ Jesus' (1 Tim. 2:3-5).

When we despise those whom God would have us honour, it is as if we are rebelling against God; and it is the same if we regard as of no importance the salvation of those whom God has called to be his own. For, in so doing, it seems that we want to prevent him from showing his mercy to poor sinners, who are on the road to ruin. St Paul's reason for using this argument that God desires all the world to be saved is that we may, as far as possible, also seek the salvation of those who appear to be banished from the kingdom of God, especially while they remain unbelievers.

We must always observe what the condition of the world was in the days of St Paul. It was something new and strange to have the gospel published to all the world in those days, for it appeared that God had chosen the descendants of Abraham, and that the rest of the world were to be deprived of all hope of salvation. And, indeed, we see how Holy Scripture sets forth the adoption of the Jewish people. But St Paul commands us to pray for all the world — and not without cause, for he adds the reason, which is that 'God … desires all men to be saved.' It is as if he were to say, 'My friends, it is reasonable that we should consider to what the will of God directs us, and that every one of us should be devoted to serving God aright.' For why are we in this world, if not to promote the will and good pleasure of God as much as we can?

What is meant by 'all men'?

Therefore, since it is God's will that all people should partake of that salvation which God has sent in the person of his only begotten Son, we must endeavour to draw poor, foolish, ignorant creatures to us, so that we may all come together to this inheritance of the kingdom of heaven, which has been promised to us. But we must observe that St Paul is not speaking of every person in particular, but of all sorts of persons and of all peoples. So, when he says that God desires all men to be saved, we must not think that he is speaking of individuals. Rather, his meaning is this, that whereas in times past God chose one particular people to himself, he intends now to show mercy to all the world — yes, even to those who seemed to be shut out from the hope of salvation.

St Paul says in another place that the heathen were without God and devoid of all the promises because they were not yet brought into the fellowship of the Jews. This was a special privilege that God had given to the descendants of Abraham. So St Paul's meaning is, not that God will save every person, but that the promises which were given to only one people are now extended to all the world; for, as he says in this same epistle, the wall [between Jews and Gentiles] was broken down at the coming of our Lord Jesus Christ. God had separated the Jews from all other nations; but when Jesus Christ appeared for the salvation of the world, then this difference between them and the Gentiles was taken away.

So now God will welcome us all — and this is a necessary prerequisite for *our* salvation. For if what God had ordained only for a certain period had always continued, we should all be accursed. The gospel would not have been preached to us, and we would have had no sign or token of the love and goodness of God. But now we have become his children; we are no longer strangers to the promises, as our ancestors were. For Jesus Christ came to be a Saviour to all in general; he offered the grace of God the Father that all might receive it.

As St Paul speaks of all nations, he also speaks of all conditions of men [i.e., men of all ranks and social positions]. In other words, God will save kings and magistrates as well as others. We must not confine his fatherly goodness to ourselves alone, or to any particular group of people. Why not? Because God reveals to us that he will show favour to all. This, then, is St Paul's meaning. And to confirm the matter, he adds that it is God's will that all should 'come to the knowledge of the truth'. We must mark well why St Paul uses this argument, for we cannot know the will of God unless it is made known to us, unless we have some sign or token by which we may perceive it. It is too high a matter for us to know what God's counsel is; but so far as God shows it to us by its effects, so far we can comprehend it.

The gospel is called the mighty power of God to salvation to all who believe. Yes, it is the gate of paradise. It follows, then, that if through the will of God the gospel is preached to all the world, that is a token that salvation is common to all. Thus St Paul proves that God's will is that all people should be saved. God has not appointed his apostles to proclaim his name only among the Jews, for we know that the commission was given to them to preach to all creatures, to be witnesses of Jesus Christ from Jerusalem to Samaria, and from there throughout all the world.

What St Paul does *not* mean

Were the apostles sent to publish the truth of God to all people and to all conditions of people? It follows, then, that God presents himself to all the world, that the promise belongs to both great and small, as much to the Gentiles now as it did before to the Jews. But before we go further, we must demolish the foolish — or rather erroneous — arguments of those who misuse this passage of St Paul. I refer to those who endeavour to make the election of God of no effect, and to utterly take it away. They say that if God desires all people to be saved, it follows that he has not chosen a certain number of mankind and cast the rest away, but that his will leaves the matter open.

They claim that it is left to the choice of people whether to save themselves or not; that God lets us alone and waits to see whether we will come to him or not, and so receives those who come to him. But in the meantime, those who say this destroy the groundwork of our salvation; for we know that we are so accursed that the inheritance of salvation is far from us. If someone says that Jesus Christ has come to remedy this situation, we must examine what human nature is really like. We are so contrary in our nature, and such enemies of God, that we cannot but resist him. We are so given over to evil and wickedness that we cannot so much as conceive a good thought. How then can we become partakers of that salvation which is offered in the gospel, unless God draws us to it by his Holy Spirit?

Let us now see whether God draws all the world to it or not. No, no; for then our Lord Jesus Christ would have said in vain, 'No one can come to me unless the Father who sent me draws him' (John 6:44). So we must conclude that God is pleased to bestow a special grace on those who come to him, in order to draw them and teach them in such a way that they believe the gospel and receive it with true faith.

But why does God choose one, and pass over another? We know that people cannot come to God by their own merits; nor do those who have been chosen deserve to be preferred to their companions — as though there were some worthiness in them. It follows, then, that before the world was made (as St Paul says in the epistle to the Ephesians), God chose those whom it pleased him [to choose]; and we do not know why this person was chosen in preference to that one. Still, we must confess that whatever God does, he does justly, although we cannot comprehend it. Therefore, let us receive that of which we are so thoroughly assured in Holy Scripture, and not allow ourselves to be led astray under a shadow of vain reason by those who are ignorant of the Word of God.

At first sight, there appears to be some weight to their argument. 'God desires all men to be saved'; therefore, they say, it is left to the free choice of each individual to become enlightened in the faith and to partake of salvation. Anyone, however, who reads just three lines will easily perceive that St Paul here is not speaking of every particular person (as we have already shown), but that he is speaking of all peoples and all classes of society. He shows that the case no longer stands as it did before the coming of Christ, when there was only one chosen people, but that now God shows himself to be a Saviour to all the world, according as it is promised: 'I will give you the nations for your inheritance, and the ends of the earth for your possession.'

Moreover, so that no one may deceive himself, or be deceived by the vain and foolish talk of those who pervert Holy Scripture, let us examine the teaching of these enemies of God and all godliness. God desires all people to be saved; that is to say, as they claim, everyone. If this is the will of God at present, no doubt it was the will of God from the beginning of the world, for we know that God does not change his mind, as men do. So then, if today God desires all people to be saved, this was always what he intended; and if this was always his intention, what are we to make of St Paul's statement that it is God's will that all should come to the knowledge of the truth? He chose only one people to himself, as it is said in Acts 14, and left the poor Gentiles to walk in their own ignorance (Acts 14:16). Does that mean he was unable at that time to execute what he purposed?

Even in New Testament times there were some countries where God would not permit St Paul to preach, such as Bithynia and Phrygia (Acts 16:6-7). And so we see that it was not God's will that the knowledge of the gospel should come to everyone at the beginning. Thus we may easily conclude, contrary to the teaching of those who abuse this text, that St Paul is not speaking in this passage of the secret counsels of God; nor does he mean to speak of God's everlasting election, the choice made before the beginning of the world, but is only showing what God's will and pleasure is, as far as we may know it.

It is true that God does not change; neither does he have two wills, or deal with us fraudulently, seeming to mean one thing when he does not intend this. And yet Scripture speaks to us in two ways concerning his will. How can that be? How does it come about that his will is spoken of in two different ways? It is because of our denseness, our lack of understanding. Why does God portray himself as having eyes, ears and a nose? Why does speak of himself as having human affections? Why does he say he is angry, or that he is sorry? Is it not because we cannot comprehend him in his incomprehensible majesty? It is not absurd, then, that Holy Scripture should speak to us of the will of God in two ways — not because his will is twofold, but in order that he may accommodate himself to our weakness, knowing that we are so dense and slow in understanding.

The doctrine of God's eternal election is profitable for us

When Scripture tells us that God has chosen those whom it pleased him [to choose] before the world began, we behold one of the secret counsels of God into which we cannot enter. Why, then, does Holy Scripture inform us that this election, this choice of God, is from eternity? It does not do so without good reason, for this is a very profitable doctrine, if it is received as it ought to be. For by it we are reminded that we are not called to the knowledge of the gospel because of our own worthiness. We are no better than others, for we all sprang from the cursed root of Adam; we are all subject to the very same condemnation; and we are all shut up in the same bondage to sin and death.

When it pleased God to draw us out of the darkness of unbelief and give us the light of the gospel, he did not look at any service we might have performed, or at any virtue we might have possessed (for there was no such thing); but he called us, according as he had previously chosen us. This is the order which St Paul presents to us elsewhere, in Romans 8, to the end that if we know God we must not take the glory for this to ourselves. Instead this came about because our Lord God himself chose us. Thus the calling of the faithful rests upon the counsel of God. We see by this in what way and to what extent our Lord reveals to us what he had decreed concerning us before we were born. He touches us with his Holy Spirit, and we are, as it were, grafted into the body of our Lord Jesus Christ. This is the true down-payment in earnest of our adoption, the pledge given to us to put us beyond all doubt that God takes and holds us for his children when, by faith, we are made one with Jesus Christ, the only begotten Son of God. To him belongs the inheritance of eternal life.

God gives us such a sure testimony of his will that, notwithstanding our ignorance of his eternal decrees, he puts us beyond all doubt of our election and he gives us a hope of which we would be entirely devoid if Jesus Christ did not call us to be members of his body.

Thus we see how profitable this doctrine of election is to us. Firstly, it serves to humble us, seeing that our salvation does not depend on our merits, nor on the virtue that God might have found in us, but on his choice of us before we were born and before we could do either good or evil. Secondly, when we know that according to this unchangeable election God has called us to himself, so much the more is our salvation put beyond doubt. For Jesus Christ tells us, 'No one takes from me what the Father has given me' (John 10:27-29). Who are those whom the Father has given to Jesus Christ? Those whom he has chosen, and whom he knows to be his. Seeing that this is the case — that God has given us to his Son, to be kept and defended by him, and that Jesus Christ promises that none of us shall be lost, but that he will exercise all the might and power of the Godhead to save and defend us — is this not a comfort surpassing all the treasures of the world? Is this not the true ground upon which all the assurance and certainty of our salvation is settled?

We are like birds perched on the branches of a tree, sitting targets for Satan. What assurance, then, could we have for tomorrow, or for the whole of life, or even beyond the grave — were it not that God, who has called us, will complete the work which he has begun in us? How has he brought us together in the faith of his gospel? Is it on the grounds of [something in] us? No, on the contrary; it proceeds solely from his free election. All the more, therefore, we need be in no doubt.

God's will that men should repent revealed in Scripture

We must not strive to know any more of God's counsel than what is revealed in Holy Scripture. The will of God is opened to us as often as we hear his Word preached, by which he calls and exhorts us all to repentance. After he has once shown us that we are all damned in his sight, and that there is nothing but condemnation in us, he shows us that we must renounce ourselves and get out of this bottomless pit, in which we are sunk up to our ears.

From the fact that God exhorts all men in general, we may conclude that it is his will that all men should be saved. He says by the prophet Ezekiel, ' "Do I have any pleasure at all that the wicked should die?" says the LORD God, "and not that he should turn from his ways and live?" ' Or again, he says, 'Say to them, "As I live," says the LORD God, "I have no pleasure in the death of the wicked, but that the wicked turn from his way and live" ' (Ezek. 18:23; 33:11). How will God cause sinners to turn from their ways? And how shall we know God's will? We know it because God will have repentance preached to all the world. When it is said that God will have mercy on sinners, such as come to him and ask for forgiveness, that is a general doctrine. And when it is said that God desires all men to be saved, regardless of what we may devise or imagine, that is as far as we can go, within the limits of our understanding, in comprehending [what is the will of God].

God alone has the power to give repentance

When Scripture speaks of the love and will of God, let us see if people can repent of their own volition and as they are self-taught, or whether it is God who gives repentance. God says by his prophet, 'I desire that all should turn and live.' Can sinners by their own efforts turn themselves round? No, for if it were in our power to do so, it would be more than enough to make us [do so] and experience is enough to show that it is not so. It is undoubtedly true throughout Scripture that our Lord Jesus Christ credits himself with the praise for turning us. He says that he will put a new spirit within us, and take the stony heart out of our flesh and make us bow in obedience to him (Ezek. 11:19). It is his work, not only to give us the ability to obey his commandments, but also the will and desire to do so (Phil. 2:13). In short, there is nothing that the faithful ought so much to do as to give God the glory in this matter, confessing that he alone has the power to turn us, and that it is only because he has adopted us in such a way that he must also draw us [to him] by the grace of his Holy Spirit.

Do human beings have such knowledge that they are able to attain this faith, this wonderful wisdom contained in the gospel — such as the very angels revere? Let us mark well what God says in his Word: that he will open our eyes and unblock our ears, because people in their natural state understand nothing of the secrets of God. It is the Holy Spirit who reveals them to us. It is hardly possible to read three lines in Holy Scripture without finding some sentence or other showing that people are utterly blind by nature, until God opens their eyes, and that they can by no means come to him until he draws them and enlightens them by his Holy Spirit.

God alone has the power to turn people from their wickedness and experience teaches us that God does not give his grace to all. Scripture confirms this: 'The LORD has not given you a heart to perceive and eyes to see and ears to hear, to this very day' (Deut. 29:4). Again, there are many passages which show that God does not, as it were, distribute his grace at random, but that it is only for those whom he has chosen, those who form part of the body of his church, his flock.

God's will as it is revealed in the preaching of the gospel

We see, then, how we are to understand what St Paul means when he says in this passage that it is the will of God that all men should be saved: he is referring to all peoples and all social classes. How do we know that? For he says that God offers his gospel to all, which is the means of drawing us to salvation. But does the offer of the gospel profit all who hear it? No, not at all! Our own eyes bear witness to this fact. For if, when we hear the truth of God preached, we rebel against it, it proves a great condemnation to us. So it is that there are many who do not profit by the gospel, but rather become worse as a result of it — even some of those to whom it is preached, not all of whom are saved. God must go further in order to bring us to salvation. He must not only appoint men and send them to teach us faithfully, but he must operate upon our hearts; he must touch us to the quick; he must draw us to him; he must make his work profitable to us and cause it to take root in our hearts.

It is evident that we have to consider the will of God in two ways. Not that God has two wills (as we observed before), but we must consider it as adapted to our weakness. He forms his speech to us in his Word according to our capacity to understand. If God should speak according to his majesty, his speech would be beyond our comprehension, and it would utterly confound us. For if our eyes are not able to stand the brightness of the sun, would our minds be able to comprehend the infinite majesty of God? Those foolish people who would refute God's election ought not to abuse this passage. Nor should they say that we make God to have two wills, for this is a shameless and contemptible deliberate misrepresentation of our teaching. What we say is that, as far as we can perceive, God desires all men to be saved whenever and as often as he appoints his gospel to be preached to us.

As we said before, the gate of paradise is opened to us when we are called to be partakers of that redemption which was purchased for us by our Lord Jesus Christ. And this is the will of God, as far as we can comprehend it: that when he exhorts us to repentance he is ready to receive us, if we will come to him.

Although we have answered the doubts which might have been raised regarding this subject, it will be good to introduce an illustration in order to make this doctrine easier to understand. By way of illustration I want to draw your attention to the comparison and similarity which God makes between the children of Israel and us.

God says that he chose all the children of Abraham for his inheritance and dedicated them to himself, and that he loved them and took them as his own household (Deut. 7: 6). This is true; he made his covenant with all those who were circumcised. Was circumcision an empty symbol, of no importance? No, it was a sure and undoubted sign that God had chosen that people for his own, regarding as his flock all who came from that race. And yet was there not a special grace for some of those people? Surely there was, as St Paul sets forth when he says, 'For they are not all Israel who are of Israel; nor are they all children [of the promise] because they are the seed of Abraham' (Rom. 9:6-7). For God deprived some of Abraham's descendants of this benefit, so that his grace and goodness might seem all the greater to those whom he called to himself. We see, therefore, the will of God being manifested to us today as it was manifested to the children of Israel.

The gospel shall indeed be preached wherever God has appointed that it shall be, and the same order will apply in all places, yet we see that which was spoken of by the prophet Amos when he said God would make it rain on one city and would withhold it from another (Amos 4:7). In the same way the Lord sends his gospel wherever it pleases him. His grace is poured out, not only on Judea or on one corner of the land, but on all the world. Yet God must work differently and further in those whom he draws to himself. For all of us have blocked ears and blindfolded eyes; indeed, we are deaf and blind unless God works in us so that we may receive his Word. When the gospel is preached to us, it is as if God stretches out his hand (as he says in Isaiah 65:2) and says to us, 'Come to me'. It is something that ought to touch us to the quick when we perceive that God comes to seek us. He does not wait until we come to him, but shows us that he is ready to receive us, even though we were his deadly enemies. He wipes away all our faults and makes us partakers of the salvation which was purchased for us by our Lord Jesus Christ.

So we see how worthy the gospel is to be esteemed, and what a treasure it is! It is, as St Paul says to the Romans, 'the power of God to salvation for everyone who believes'. It is the kingdom of heaven; and God opens the door, so that we, being taken out of the bottomless pit in which we were sunk by nature, may enter into his glory.

What our response should be to the preaching of the gospel

We must also note that it is not enough for us to receive the Word that is preached to us by the mouth of man, but that after we have heard it God must speak to us inwardly by his Holy Spirit, for this is the only means to bring us to the knowledge of the truth. Therefore, when God has dealt so mercifully with us as to give us the light of faith, let us hold it fast, and pray to him to continue it and bring his work to perfection. Let us beware of proudly exalting ourselves above others, as though we were more worthy than they are, for we know that it is God who chose us and set us apart from others, by his mere goodness and free mercy.

We must know, moreover, that people are very much at fault when God offers them his Word, and they do not receive it. Surely this word is in part addressed to us, to the end that all the faithful should, in all humility, glorify the grace of God towards them. It is also said in order that unbelievers and rebels might have their mouths stopped and might not blaspheme the name of God — as though *he* had been lacking in his dealings with them.

Thus we see how God calls to salvation all those to whom his Word is preached. If people reply that they cannot come to God, we cannot argue against that, for we shall always find ourselves at fault. If someone were to say, 'It rests only in the hands of God, and if he would give me repentance, could he not do it?' or, 'If I remain stiff-necked in my hardness and malice, what can I do in that case, since God will not give me repentance to turn to him?' such an objection can by no means be allowed, for God's call is sufficient, and we cannot accuse him of cruelty towards us, or of some lack in his treatment of us. Even if we did not have his Word, we would need to confess that God is just, although we do not know the cause that moved him to deprive us of it.

When we are called to come to God and know that he is ready to receive us, if we do not come, can we deny that we are unthankful? Let us not separate salvation from the knowledge of the truth; for God does not mean to lie or deceive people when he says that if they come to the knowledge of the truth they will be saved. God desires all people to be saved. But how? By coming to the knowledge of the truth. Everyone would like to be saved, but no one will draw near to God. Scripture informs us that if we desire salvation we must use the means which God has appointed — that is, we must receive his Word with obedience and faith.

Christ says, 'This is eternal life': to know God the Father and then to know 'Jesus Christ whom you have sent' and to receive him as the only Saviour (John 17:3). Therefore let us learn, as it is set forth here [in this passage in 1 Timothy], not to doubt the certainty of our salvation, for the kingdom of God is within us. If we wish God to receive us, we must receive the doctrine given to us by St Paul. How are we called to the hope of salvation? By the influence of the grace of God, which makes known to us his love and favour.

Thus we may see what St Paul means when he says that God will have his grace made known to all the world and his gospel preached to all creatures. Since that is God's will, we must endeavour, as much as possible, to persuade those who are strangers to the faith, and who seem utterly deprived of the goodness of God, to accept salvation.

Jesus Christ is not a Saviour of only a few persons, but offers himself to all. As often as the gospel is preached to us, we ought to consider that God is calling us to him. If we heed this call, it will not be in vain, nor will it be lost labour. But can we come to him without any assistance, except what we derive from our own nature? Alas, we cannot! 'Because the carnal mind is enmity against God; for it is not subject to the law of God, nor indeed can be' (Rom. 8:7). When God deals so graciously with us as to touch our hearts with his Holy Spirit, then he causes his gospel to work profitably for our salvation; then he makes a display of the power spoken of by St Paul.

Again, we must remember, when the gospel is preached to us, that it leaves us without excuse, since God has already shown us that he is ready to receive us to his mercy, if we come to him; but our condemnation will no doubt be increased if we are so wicked as to draw back when he calls so mildly and lovingly. Nevertheless (as we are exhorted in the verses preceding our text), let us not cease to pray for all people in general, for St Paul shows that God desires all people to be saved, that is to say, people of all nations.

Although we see a great diversity among people, we must not forget that God has made us all in his own image and likeness and that we are the workmanship of his hand. Since all are made in God's likeness and by his hand, God extends his goodness to those who are far away from him. Of that we have sufficient proof, for when God drew us to himself, were we not his enemies? How, then, does it happen that we are now part of the family of the faithful, the children of God, and members of our Lord Jesus Christ? Is it not because God has gathered us to himself? And is he not the Saviour of the whole world, as well as of us? Did Jesus Christ come to be the mediator on behalf of two or three men only? No, no! He is the 'mediator between God and men'.

Therefore, we may be so much more assured that God takes and holds us as his children if we endeavour to bring to him those who are far away from him. Let us comfort ourselves and take courage in this our calling. Although there is today a great hopelessness — although we seem to be miserable creatures, utterly cast away and condemned — yet we must labour as much as possible to draw those to salvation who seem to be far away from God. And above everything, let us pray to God for them, waiting patiently till it pleases him to show his good will towards them, as he has shown it to us.

Chapter 5

The purpose and grace of God

'The devil has no fitter instruments than those who fight against predestination... The gospel cannot be preached, ... it is a false and profane gospel, and ... there is no such thing as a church or Christianity, if God's election is abolished.'

5.
The purpose and grace of God

'Therefore do not be ashamed of the testimony of our Lord, nor of me his prisoner, but share with me in the sufferings for the gospel according to the power of God, who has saved us and called us with a holy calling, not according to our works, but according to his own purpose and grace which was given to us in Christ Jesus before time began' (2 Tim. 1:8-9).

We must not be ashamed of the gospel

Although God manifests his glory and majesty in the gospel, the unthankfulness of men is such that we need to be exhorted not to be ashamed of the gospel. And why is this? Because God requires his creatures to pay him homage; yet the greater part of them rebel against him. They despise him, and even show defiance towards the gospel by which God would be known and worshipped. Although men are so wicked as to rise up against their Maker, let us remember what is taught us in this passage: that we are not to be ashamed of the gospel, for it is the witness of God and it must be preached in order that he alone may be known and glorified as he ought to be.

If the gospel is not preached, it is as if Jesus Christ were buried [out of sight]. Let us, therefore, do him the honour (since we see all the world so far out of the way) of holding firmly to this wholesome doctrine. St Paul sets his own example before us — not that he wished particularly to be approved, but because we often get into difficulties if we separate ourselves from the servants of God. When a minister of the Word of God is troubled, molested and persecuted, we are apt to forsake him in his time of need, thinking we are only forsaking a mortal man. But in doing this we offend God, because this man who is suffering bears the mark of the gospel, and thus the cause of God is betrayed. Therefore, St Paul says to Timothy, 'Do not be ashamed of me.'

Timothy may well have been shaken in his mind; so St Paul says to him, 'Though the world despise me, though they mock and hate me, yet you must not be moved by these things, for I am a prisoner for the sake of Jesus Christ. Let the world speak as much evil of me as it can; it is not for my offences [that I am suffering these things]. God maintains my cause, for, indeed, it is his own. I do not suffer for my own evil deeds; his truth is always on my side. Therefore, since the reason why I am being persecuted is that I have maintained the Word of God, and continue to maintain it, you must not be guided by the world's judgement, for men are carried away by evil inclinations. Let it be sufficient for you, then, that I am, as it were, a pledge on behalf of the Son of God, that he magnifies my person, so that, however much it may be an object of reproach to the world, it never ceases to be honoured and taken into account in the presence of God and his holy angels.'

Let us learn not to defraud Jesus Christ of the testimony that we owe him, by shutting our mouths when it is necessary to maintain his honour and the authority of the gospel. Yes, and when we see our fellow believers afflicted for the cause of

God, let us join with them in fighting for this good cause as far as we are able. Let us not be shaken by the tempests that arise, but let us always remain constant in our purpose and stand firm as witnesses of the Son of God, seeing that he is so gracious as to use us in so noble a task.

We must share in the afflictions of the gospel

In the meantime let us mark well whether men are suffering for their sins, or for the truth of God. When we see someone suffering oppression, we must be careful not to despise him; we must ascertain for what cause he is suffering, because if we act rashly in this matter we may injure the cause of God. If we can see that people have lived with a good conscience and are suffering blame on account of it, if they are persecuted because they serve God, this is enough to efface completely whatever the wicked world may say against them. Therefore St Paul adds, 'Share … in the afflictions of the gospel.'

There is no one who would not willingly escape affliction — this is according to human nature. And although we confess, without dissembling, that God bestows a singular grace when he enables his children to bear affliction for the sake of his cause, there is not one of us who would not willingly save his own neck from persecution. For we have not learned the lesson taught by St Paul, that the gospel brings troubles. Jesus Christ himself was crucified, and the proclamation of his doctrine is still accompanied by much misery. He could, if it pleased him, cause his gospel to be received without any opposition. But the scripture must be fulfilled which says that he will rule in the midst of his enemies (Ps. 110:2).

We must come to him on this condition, that we are willing to suffer much opposition, because the wicked rise up in rebellion against God when he calls them to him. Therefore, it is impossible for us to have the gospel without affliction. To one degree or another, we must face trouble; we must fight under the banner of our Lord Jesus Christ. So then, does not anyone who wants to escape the cross of Christ renounce his hope of salvation? What is the hope of life? Only this, that we are bought by the sacrifice of the Son of God. Then he will have us made like himself, transformed into his image.

We must not be ashamed of our fellow believers. When we hear evil reports about them and see them cast off by the world, let us always stand by them to strengthen them, for the gospel cannot be without affliction, as I have already said. It pleases God that men should be divided in this way [into two opposing camps]. It is true that he calls all to the unity of faith, and the teaching of the gospel is the message of atonement; but while the faithful are drawn by the virtue of the Holy Spirit, the unbelievers remain in their state of hardness. Thus the gospel kindles a fire [of discord]. As there is bound to be trouble when thunder is generated in the atmosphere, so it is when the gospel is preached.

Now, if the gospel brings affliction, and if it is the will of Jesus Christ that what he himself suffered shall be fulfilled in the members of his body — to be crucified daily — is it lawful for us to withdraw ourselves from that situation? Since we know that all hope of salvation is in the gospel, we must rest upon it. And mark what St Paul says: we must reach out to our fellow believers when we see them in trouble and when they are reviled and abused by the wicked. Let us rather choose to be their companions in suffering the rebukes and scoffing of the world, than to be honoured and to enjoy a good reputation and credit [among the world], while we turn our backs on those who suffer for the cause of the gospel — which is just as much our cause as it is theirs.

God will supply the power we need

We are prone to be weak and to think we shall be swallowed up by persecutions as soon as our enemies assail us; but St Paul assures us that we shall not be destitute of the help and assistance of God. When he sends us out into the conflict, he at once arms us and gives us an invincible power, enabling us to stand fast and unmoved. This is why St Paul adds, 'according to the power of God'. But as I have said, we would all be glad to have some pretext for being exempt from persecution.

'If God would give me grace, I would gladly suffer for his name. I know it is the greatest blessing that I could receive.' Everyone will confess this, but then people will add, 'We are weak and such is the cruelty of our enemies that we shall quickly be defeated and unable to stand up to the trials.' But St Paul takes away this excuse by saying that God will strengthen us, and that we must not look to our own strength. For it is certain that if ever we come into conflict with our enemies we shall be afraid of our own shadows. The very thought of it is enough to make us turn and run. Knowing this weakness, let us come to the remedy.

We must indeed consider our own weakness and how hard it is to withstand our enemies, but this knowledge should stir us up to pray to God to help us. Therefore let us humble ourselves before God and pray to him to reach out his hand and not forsake us when it comes to the crunch, but to help us in our weakness in the way which he knows to be best for us.

If this doctrine were imprinted in our hearts, we should be better prepared to suffer than we are. But we are apt to forget it; indeed, we, as it were, cover our ears and close our eyes when we hear it spoken of. We make a show of wishing that God would strengthen us, but in practice we cannot fix our eyes on the power that St Paul speaks of. We are apt to think that we have nothing to help us, though the Lord has shown us that his power will always be sufficient to uphold us. Therefore, do not let our weakness cause us to withdraw from the cross and from persecution, seeing that God has received us into his hands and promised to supply all our needs.

God will complete the work he has begun in us

St Paul here adds a lesson which should make us ashamed if we are not sufficiently on fire for the glory of Jesus Christ to be willing to suffer persecution when it pleases him [to send it]. He says, 'God … has saved us and called us with a holy calling.' Behold, God has drawn us out of the gulf of hell! We were utterly cast away and condemned; but he has brought us salvation and has called us to be partakers of it. Since God has shown himself so liberal, if we, on our part, turn our backs on him, and disdain to accept the salvation which he offers us, is this not shameful malice on our part? Let us also note that when St Paul accuses them of inconstancy and unwillingness to suffer all the assaults made against them for the sake of the gospel, his intention was undoubtedly also to comfort the faithful and give them a good hope for the future. He therefore shows what God has done for them already.

When God gives us any token of his goodness, it is to the end that we should hope for goodness from his hand again, and wait till he brings to pass what he has begun. Therefore, if God has saved us and called us with a holy calling, do we think that he will abandon us midway? When he has shown us our salvation and given us his gospel, by which he calls us to his kingdom and opens the gates to us — when he has done all this, do we think he will leave us here and mock us and deprive us of his grace, or make it unprofitable to us? No, no! Let us hope that he will bring his work to a perfect conclusion.

So, let us go on with good courage, for God has already displayed his power towards us. Let us not doubt that he will continue to do so, and that we shall have a perfect victory over Satan and our enemies; for God the Father has given all power into the hands of Jesus Christ, who is our head and captain, so that we may be partakers of it.

Thus we see St Paul's meaning. God has witnessed to us, and confirmed it to us in our experience, that he will never fail us in time of need. And why is that? Because he has already saved us, having called us to the gospel and redeemed us from sin. He has called us with a holy calling; that is to say, he has chosen us for himself, out of the general confusion of mankind.

Since the Lord has drawn us to him, will he not uphold us and guide us to the end? This is a sure confirmation of the power of God, that we always find him ready to help us. Therefore we put our trust in him, remembering that we have already experienced his power. In order that we may profit by this doctrine, let us know first of all that, inasmuch as God has given us the knowledge of his truth, it is almost as if he had shown us already that we belong to his heavenly inheritance, that he has chosen us to be his, members of his flock. If we are persuaded of this and resolved in it, we shall always go forward with confidence in the cause [of the gospel], knowing that we are under his protection. Since he has sufficient strength to overcome all our enemies, our salvation is assured.

Let us not be afraid or dismayed because of our own weakness, for God has promised to assist us. This is a topic which is worthy of our contemplation. Let us exercise our minds so that we may receive the truth taught here. The Lord will complete the work of our salvation which he has begun in us. He will assist us in the midst of persecutions and enable us to overcome them. When once we are convinced of this, it will not require much power of rhetoric to strengthen us against temptations. We shall triumph over all our enemies, even though we may seem to the world to be trodden under foot and utterly overwhelmed.

Our salvation was all of God's grace

But we must come to this declaration which St Paul adds concerning the salvation of which we have already spoken, and the holy calling. He says that these things are 'not according to our works, but according to his own purpose and grace'. God did not take our works or dignity into account when he called us to salvation. He did it out of mere grace. Therefore there will be even less excuse for us if we disobey his requirements, since we have not only been purchased by the blood of our Lord Jesus Christ, but God had a care for our salvation before the world was made.

Let us observe here that St Paul condemns our unthankfulness if we are so unfaithful to God as not to bear witness to his gospel, seeing that he has called us to do so. And that he may better express the purpose [of God in saving us], the apostle adds that this was 'given to us in Christ Jesus before time began' — before the world was set in motion, before creation was ever begun.

God's saving purpose and grace were revealed at the coming of our Lord Jesus Christ. When this great Saviour made his appearance, the grace that was previously hidden — indeed, that was beyond the reach of human reason — was made clear and manifest. And why was that? Because the Son of God destroyed death and also brought everlasting life! And we need not beat about the bush to find it, for the gospel leads us to it. When God sends us this message of salvation, we have only to receive the inheritance which he promised us. We do not have to seek far for it; God brings it to us. Let us open our mouths that he may fill them; let us open our hearts and permit this testimony of the gospel to enter, and the immortality of the kingdom shall dwell within us. Though we are poor, frail vessels, having nothing but corruption and rottenness in us, we already do lay hold of this immortality and have a sure witness of it when we can accept the grace that is offered to us in the gospel.

So that we may better understand what Paul is teaching here, let us note that this word 'purpose' signifies the eternal decree of God, which has no cause at all [outside of the will of God]. For when we speak of God's counsels, we must never enter into discussions as to who moved him to act, nor attempt to imagine reasons and say, 'This is the reason why God has determined such a thing; this is the cause behind his will.' No, God would have us approach this topic soberly, acknowledging that his will is itself a sufficient reason for everything. When Scripture says that God has thus appointed it, though our eyes may be dazzled and the matter may seem strange to us, so that we see no reason why things should be as they are, we must conclude that his will alone is just, and we must not find fault with it. It is wisdom in us to receive gladly whatever God appoints, and never ask why.

But because men's minds are always so active and too ready to indulge their curiosity, St Paul brings us to God's purpose and tells us plainly that we must recognize that God has a purpose which is so deep that we cannot enter into it, in order to know who moved him. He was moved by his just will alone; indeed his will is the rule of all justice. By this text we are given to understand that our salvation does not depend on our deserts: God never examined what we were, or what we were worthy of, when he chose us for himself, but he had his purpose; that is, he sought no cause for our salvation outside of himself.

St Paul shows plainly that this word 'purpose' signifies this decree. But because men cannot, because of the pride that is in them, refrain from imagining some worthiness of their own or thinking that they deserved that God should seek them, St Paul says explicitly that it is 'according to his own purpose and grace'. This is as much as if he had said it was '[of his] free purpose'.

This is said to demolish all our works, so that we shall not be so foolish and stubborn as to think that God chose us because there was something in us that was worthy of it. No, no! We must know that God never went further than himself when he chose us to salvation. For he saw that there was nothing but condemnation in us. Therefore he was content, in his grace and infinite mercy alone, to look upon our misery and help us, although we were not worthy. For better proof of this, St Paul says that this grace was given to us 'before time began'.

We perceive by this how devoid of sense people are when they flatter themselves into believing that they are the cause of their salvation, as though there was something in them which was conducive to the goodness of God, or as if they were the first to act and went part of the way to meet him. Upon what does our salvation depend? Is it not upon the election and choice that has been made from eternity? God chose us before we existed. What could we do then? Were we made fit? Were we well disposed to come to God? No, we see that our salvation does not begin after we have knowledge, discretion or any good desires, but is grounded in God's eternal decree, which was before any part of the world was made.

What could we do then? Had we any means to put ourselves forward? Could we give God any occasion to call us and separate us from the rest of the world? Are we not completely out of our minds, then, when we think we have some worthiness of our own, and when we try to exalt our own deserts, casting a veil over the grace of God and supposing that we can be prepared by our own efforts to have access to him?

God's grace was given 'before time began'

We must, therefore, take good note of the reason why St Paul sets out here the doctrine of God's election, saying that grace was given to us in Christ Jesus 'before time began'. Those who think they can abolish this doctrine destroy the salvation of the world, as far as it is possible for them to do so. This is the fittest instrument used by the devil to deface the virtue of the blood of our Lord Jesus Christ and to bring to naught and destroy the gospel — yes, and to put the goodness of God out of people's memory. The devil has no fitter instruments than those who fight against predestination, and cannot in their rage permit it to be spoken of or preached as it ought to be. If we detest the papists — as indeed we ought to — for profaning Holy Scripture and marring and corrupting the truth of the gospel and the service of God by infecting all the world with superstition and idolatry, how much more are they to be detested who go about seeking to bring to naught God's election and endeavouring, by devious and crooked ways, to stop men from speaking of it plainly and openly and from preaching it as it ought to be preached!

In what does the salvation of the faithful consist but in God's free election alone? Are we not willing that men should preach that God has chosen his people, out of his mere goodness, without regard to anything whatever? Are we not willing that this mystery — high as it is and beyond our comprehension — should be explained and declared to us insofar as God is pleased to reveal it? Without a doubt we are guilty of conspiring with Satan, as though Jesus Christ suffered in vain, and the passion that he suffered did not profit the world at all [if we deny this doctrine]. This is the first point that we need to note here: that the gospel cannot be preached, that it is a false and profane gospel, and that there is no such thing as a church or Christianity, if God's election is abolished.

The Holy Spirit who speaks in this passage would of necessity be proved a liar if this doctrine is rejected. Therefore, let us see that we fight constantly to uphold it, for it is the groundwork of our salvation. How can we build, or maintain a building, if the foundation is destroyed? St Paul shows us here the power with which we must fight, and how we shall come into this inheritance, which was purchased for us at so great a cost. He shows us how we shall enter into possession of the glory of God, and bring to completion this building of faith. My friends, we must be grounded upon the grace that was given us, not today or yesterday, but before the world began.

It is true that God calls us today, but his election precedes this; indeed, God chose us without any regard for our works, since we could have done nothing beforehand, but we are debtors to him for it all. He drew us out of the bottomless pit of destruction in which we poor, foolish creatures were all sunk, past all hope of recovery. Therefore we have good reason to submit ourselves wholly to him, and rely on his goodness and be thoroughly enthralled with it. Let us hold fast this foundation, as I said before, unless we would have our salvation perish and come to naught.

Why this doctrine is so important for us

Let us also note in closing that this doctrine is very profitable for us, if we can rightly apply it to our experience. Those who would not have us speak of God's election will say that it is not necessary. But such men never tasted of God's goodness, nor do they know what it is to come to our Lord Jesus Christ. If we do not know that we are saved because it pleased God to choose us before the world began, how can we know that which St Paul is teaching us — namely, that we should give ourselves wholly to God, to be for his use, as he wills, and to live and die in his service? How can we magnify his name? How can we confess that our salvation comes from him only, that he is the originator of it, and that we have not helped him accomplish it? We may say it with our mouths, but unless we believe it as it is here set forth, it will only be hypocrisy.

Therefore, let us learn that the doctrine of God's election — that he predestined us before the world began — ought to be preached openly and fully, even if the whole world were to stand against it. And besides this, we should know that it is a very profitable doctrine for us, because we cannot grasp the infinite goodness of God until we come to know this doctrine. God's mercy will always remain concealed unless this point is made clear to us, that God chose us before we were born and before we could do anything to influence him.

People will readily say that we were bought with the blood of our Lord Jesus Christ, and that we were not worthy that God should show us such great mercy. Yet if they are asked, 'Who has any part and portion in such a redemption as God has made in the person of his Son?' they will answer: 'Those who are willing, those who seek God and submit themselves to him; those who have some good feelings, and whose conduct is not too gross; those who are of good character and practise some form of devotion.' When people make such a mixture, thinking they are called to God and to his grace because of something that is in themselves — that they bring something, however small, to share with God in the work of their salvation — the grace of God is obscured, indeed, torn to pieces.

This is a sacrilege that is not to be countenanced. This is why I said that the goodness of God will never be thoroughly known as it should be until the doctrine of election is set out before us and we are taught that we are called at this time because it pleased God to extend his mercy to us before we were born.

Chapter 6

Strength for the battle

'Why is it that we see so few standing steadfast nowadays? Especially when any trouble is raised, they immediately fall away and turn aside. What is the reason for it, if not that they were never built up as they ought to have been? They only caught a whiff of the gospel in passing, as it were.'

6.
Strength for the battle

'You therefore, my son, be strong in the grace that is in Christ Jesus. And the things that you have heard from me among many witnesses, commit these to faithful men who will be able to teach others also. You therefore must endure hardship as a good soldier of Jesus Christ' (2 Tim. 2:1-3).

We must be strong, but God gives all needed grace

We are sufficiently taught by experience that we are not able to continue in the service of God unless we have a moral strength greater than is to be found in ourselves. For we are ready to fall at every step and we see how Satan assaults us daily, so that we would not be able to resist him unless we had a higher source of strength. But God, who sees our weakness, does not bring us into conflict without giving us sufficient strength to withstand those combats; and our Lord Jesus Christ has received all necessary virtue and power to strengthen his followers, so that they will not find themselves forsaken. Nevertheless, we must prepare ourselves that we might have invincible courage if we are to go on with our vocation, our calling. Those especially who lead others must have this heavenly help, for Satan will assault them more fiercely and dangerously than others.

It is for this reason that St Paul exhorts Timothy to be strengthened in the grace of our Lord Jesus Christ. By these words he gives him to understand that he will not be able to execute the charge that is committed to him unless he has the courage and determination to fight to the end. But let us observe that in speaking thus to one man the Holy Spirit means to teach all of us. So let us not think that we can serve God while we are at ease and resting, for God will test and prove our hearts' desire to be used for him.

And this is how he does it: he gives free rein to wicked and evil men and lets them trouble us. This is the way in which we are so often exercised and tested. But we have the remedy at hand: the grace of our Lord Jesus Christ will be given to us, so that we shall not cast it away through our negligence.

It is a very weighty statement that St Paul makes when he says that grace is in our Lord Jesus Christ. He gives us to understand that it is not so fenced about and locked up that we cannot obtain it. God witnesses to us that Jesus Christ was given to us with the promise that in his strength we shall be conquerors over all our enemies. Thus we see in few words the import of this sentence: it reminds us that if we are to devote ourselves to serve God, it is not enough for us to be lukewarm. And why is this? Because Satan will make every effort to hinder us, as we see plainly [demonstrated] before our eyes. We on our part are weak, and therefore we must gather strength, for without it we shall be utterly defeated.

This is one point. Another is this: we should not be afraid, for God assures us that he will help us in a tight spot. And why is that? Because Jesus Christ is not devoid of strength. If we are weak, let us draw near to him, for he has the means to uphold us. It is true that this teaching is a more suitable subject for meditation than for lengthy discourse; nevertheless, we can easily perceive that St Paul had good reason to exhort Timothy regarding it. For of those who make a show of zeal for God's service, how many actually stand firm in it? The majority forsake it. And why do they do so? Because they reckon that they may serve God by taking their ease; they give no thought to their weakness, nor do they consider that there are nets and snares laid for them on all sides, and that Satan goes about to entrap them as much as he can.

Therefore, those who make no preparation to build up their strength will be taken unawares at every turn — and we should not be surprised at this, for they are not to be excused. God has shown us that he will indeed subject us to trials, and that the life of a Christian is not a pastime or recreation, and we must not live in pleasures, but must fight and engage in combat. Seeing that he has shown us all this, if we faint now through our negligence, are we not to be blamed for it? Let us therefore remember this lesson that St Paul gives us here, that we are to be strong, not weak and retiring. And why is that? Because the service of God requires such a steadiness and constancy that we need heaven's help, since no human strength is equal to it.

And yet, let us comfort ourselves in this: if we have no weapons, if we feel we are on our last legs (as the saying is), our Lord Jesus Christ has the remedy in hand and will not be niggardly in helping us. And therefore if it grieves a man to sustain assaults and endure the heat of the attack because these things are very hard for him, it is because he is ungrateful for the goodness of God and cannot bear to be upheld, when our Lord Jesus Christ reaches out his hand [to support him].

God does not mean to mock us when he permits Satan to oppress us and tread us under foot. It is true that he will have us thoroughly conscious of our weakness. Why is this? So that we may sigh and humble ourselves and be stirred up to run to him. For if we do not face the pressures of adversity, we are so proud and presumptuous. Therefore we must confess and acknowledge our own weakness, and so learn to call upon God and hide ourselves under the shadow of his wings. And we must learn to bow down our heads and to walk circumspectly and in fear.

Nevertheless, this grace and constancy which I have spoken of will always be found in our Lord Jesus Christ, according to his offer in the gospel, so that we shall be fenced about with his strength and thus be conquerors against Satan and all our enemies. And so we see that God does not send us to our free will [for strength]; he does not say, 'See what you are able to do by yourselves,' for he knows that we are able to do nothing at all. Rather, he calls us to himself and, indeed, he directs his only Son to us, whom he has charged to strengthen us. This is why St Paul says elsewhere, 'I can do all things through Christ who strengthens me' (Phil. 4:13). He says this when he rejoices that he was not overcome by a temptation, so that he may not appear to take any of the credit for this to himself, or to glorify himself. It is, he says, 'through Christ who strengthens me' that 'I can do all things'. And he not only states this publicly on his own account, but asserts that as Jesus Christ is the head of all the faithful, his enabling power is likewise poured out upon the whole body of the church.

This is the foundation on which our trust must rest; let us not doubt, even though we may be shaken and though God may cause us to feel that we are mere helpless earthworms, or of no more worth than flies, that he will at length supply our needs. So much for the first thing we must observe regarding this text.

The gospel is a treasure entrusted to us

St Paul also wants Timothy to commit the things which he had heard from the apostle to faithful men, that there may be 'many witnesses' who are 'to teach others also'. Here we see again what a treasure the gospel is, and how highly God regards it. The truth is that the unthankfulness of the world is such that many pass it up. There are a number of people these days who have had a surfeit of the doctrine of salvation, while there are others who have never tasted of it; and though they understand it, they never felt any work of it in their lives, or experienced any of its power. The gospel and papistry are all the same to them — so foolish and dull-witted they are! Others have become so hardened in ungodliness that they are utterly devoid of reason and have no more religion in them than dogs and brute beasts. And, what is even worse, others are so full of bitterness that they gnash their teeth and wish with all their hearts that God might never be remembered again. We see all this before our very eyes.

So, let us take away from this passage this lesson: that, seeing that God has given us so inestimable a treasure as his Word, we must exert ourselves as much as we can to ensure that it may be kept safe and sound and may not be lost. Those, in particular, who are appointed to preach the gospel must value it highly and take great care that the doctrine of salvation does not fall to the ground or be extinguished, but that it be received and safely preserved. Indeed everyone, to a greater or lesser degree, should have the same care and devote all his attention to the same object. This is what St Paul has in mind when we says, 'The things that you have heard from me … commit these to faithful men.'

How true it is that first of all everyone must have this treasure locked up within his own heart! Moreover, the key to keeping it safe is a good conscience. As we have seen before, those who had no fear of God were perplexed, as though sent forth to be a prey for Satan. (Indeed, there is good reason that God should be avenged of such profane men as mock his holy Word and shamefully abuse it.) Well then, will we have this treasure remain safe and sound in our custody? First of all, let each one of us see that we lock it up securely in our hearts.

Yet it is not enough for us to have an eye to our own salvation; the knowledge of God must shine generally throughout all the world, that everyone may be a partaker of it. We must take pains to bring to the way of salvation all those who are wandering out of the way. And we must think not only about our own lifetime, but also about the time after our death, as St Peter also sets down in his second epistle. Because he sees his death at hand, and knows that he must change his lodging, he says that he takes pains and labours to the end that the remembrance of what he taught during this life may live on when God has taken him from this world, and that when he is no longer among men, they may nevertheless still remember what he preached to them (2 Peter 1:12-15). This is also what St Paul means in this passage. Let us learn, therefore, how to receive the gospel, so that our children's children may be able to have the same grace as we have; and so that when God has revealed himself to a people, those who come after them, who are raised up from the line of those who are now dead, may experience that unlooked-for blessing.

So then, we see first of all that the gospel is a precious jewel committed to our charge, and God honours us by making us keepers of it. Thus we may perceive how much we are under a solemn obligation to him. For what are we, that God should put into our hands the most precious jewel, the thing of greatest value that he has? His glory shines in the gospel; it is the sceptre of his kingdom by which he will govern us. Nevertheless, he commits it to us. Let us learn therefore not to be negligent or tread such a precious thing under our feet. If the world counts it as nothing, let us esteem it as of great worth, as we ought to do.

This is one point. Another is this: let those who are charged with preaching the gospel see that they work so [diligently] and are so well grounded in the faith that they never bow or bend [beneath the storms of opposition]. And though the devil never ceases to stir up troubles and place stumbling-blocks in the way, in order to bring all to nothing, let us fight against him as much as we can and cause the gospel to flourish and prosper, not only for this time, but so that after our death there may always be a people to worship God; that the doctrine may continue to hold sway, and that what the prophet Isaiah says may be seen among men — that the truth of God endures for ever, and shall never fail.

What the doctrine was that Timothy was to pass on

But so that we may perceive this more clearly, let us observe that St Paul distinguishes between the purity of the gospel and false doctrines when he says, 'the things that you have heard from me'. For we have seen already how Antichrist worked secretly and in underhand ways, and that even in those days there were a great number of false teachings. It was, therefore, necessary to be wise and attentive, and to know the Word of God in its purity and simplicity.

Now St Paul rejoiced greatly, and with good reason, that he was the messenger of Jesus Christ, the instrument of the Holy Spirit, so that what he preached can in no way be called into doubt. And therefore St Paul has here given us the true and genuine doctrine, so that this may be beyond doubt and not open to controversy.

This is a point of which we must take good note. For we see how gullible people are; they accept without thinking whatever they are told; indeed, they have corrupt appetites, for if someone brings them any vanity or lie, they embrace it at once with the warmest affection, because they are so volatile and have such foolish and depraved desires.

St Paul wants us to know precisely what the doctrine of the faith is that we have been taught, and to be fully persuaded that it is a most certain truth. He wants us to know that that this is not something we have received from men, and that we are not wandering aimlessly [in search of the truth], but that God is the true author and keeper of our faith. It is this that St Paul meant to show us.

Now, he is not setting himself up in the place of Jesus Christ, usurping his lordship, for [the apostle] claims nothing for himself except that he was Jesus Christ's servant, and therefore he now takes as read what he had said earlier. And so he means to keep Timothy in true obedience to the gospel — as if to say that we cannot be tossed to and fro and carried about with every wind of doctrine, if we look to the one whom God has appointed to be our Master.

The support of 'many witnesses'

Therefore, let our faith be grounded as it ought to be, as St Paul testifies to Timothy. He says that he has instructed Timothy in the presence of 'many witnesses'. The reason he adds this was not for Timothy's sake, for Timothy knew well enough that St Paul had not given him dregs to drink, but was convinced by the Holy Spirit that the doctrine which he had received from St Paul was truly heavenly and divine. Timothy knew this, and therefore he needed no other witnesses. His own conscience and the seal of the Spirit of God, which was registered in his heart, were enough for him. But St Paul meant to deal with the malicious objections of those who might say that the things Timothy preached to them were the inventions of his own head. That is why he showed that there were sufficient witnesses who could help Timothy to maintain that he was not bringing in any new thing, or strange point, but that he was truthfully and faithfully dispensing what he had received — that which was preached to him by St Paul's own mouth.

It is true that these witnesses must be chosen carefully. We must not take those who turn a blind eye; when they have seen a dozen people slain, you will never be able to make them say one word [about it]. We must not go and seek such infernal witnesses as we see nowadays, nor those who permit the name of God to be blasphemed and torn to pieces, who can see the most obvious contempt of God and his gospel, or witness such shameful destruction of life as would grieve a man's heart, and yet all this is nothing to them; they are so far from setting themselves up in opposition to it that if men should ask them to serve God only with a word, they may look for nothing but treachery at their hands. But St Paul speaks of witnesses who had profited by the gospel as it was preached to them by Timothy. They should also help him to keep the doctrine pure, even though it should be fought against on all sides.

The character of those entrusted with this task

And so we see more plainly St Paul's meaning when he adds these words: 'Commit [this doctrine] to faithful men, who will be able to teach others also.' When he says 'to faithful men', he does not mean ones who have merely believed the gospel, but men who are faithful and upright in God's service, and are not double-hearted. In short, St Paul speaks here of faithfulness and consistency, implying that there are a great number who betray God and his Word, and who disguise matters in such a way that they bring all into confusion. We may see a great number of such people, he says, but you must choose such men to serve God as have integrity in the service of God and zeal to hold and keep the doctrine in its purity, so that it will not become adulterated in any way whatever.

Moreover, he specifically says that this is so that they may be able to teach others — in other words, this seed must spread itself abroad. For indeed, when we have preached, it is not enough for each one of us to think only of himself, but we must labour to make God known throughout all the world. And to bring this to pass we must reach out to one another, as the prophet Isaiah says that every man is to stretch out his hand to his neighbour and say, 'Come, and let us go up to the mountain of the LORD… He will teach us his ways' (Isa. 2:3). And therefore, so that we will not be self-centred, St Paul shows us that we must not choose men who are unable to share what they have received with poor, ignorant souls who need to be taught.

A much-needed exhortation

Now, if ever there were a time to put this doctrine into practice, it is our own age. For God has once again caused so brilliant a light to shine that matters [of doctrine] are known; and though the world has been in such gross darkness that people were like brute beasts and there was nothing anywhere but confusion and desolation, yet today we are enlightened by the gospel, and God shows himself to us face to face, as it were. The devil, knowing that if this brightness lasts he will lose his kingdom, goes about to obscure and disguise this pure truth as much as he possibly can, in one way or another.

We see how among the papists these vile friars are hired to set themselves against the true doctrine, and to do so in the most rebellious and devilish ways. For their consciences bear them so plain a witness that they are not able to resist it; and yet they have grown so impudent, spewing out whatever [false teaching] they can in order to hold the poor, simple people back and keep them in superstition. And when they cannot turn the doctrine of God completely upside-down, they bring it into hatred and cause it to be an object of suspicion. They disguise it in one way or another.

We see all this, and, indeed, even among ourselves, does Satan not strive so hard that if the zeal of God's servants were not sharpened, the knowledge we have now would at once be abolished? For we know what slanderous reports are raised up against the doctrine of God. It is true that it is men who are attacked, or at least so it is claimed; but however that may be, we know that God is openly assaulted and that the world cannot abide the preaching of the gospel as it ought to be preached, in all its purity. People have gone so far that they seek to bridle the Holy Spirit; otherwise we would not see teachings which are not palatable to them or in keeping with their ideas being removed from Holy Scripture by people who take upon themselves more authority than God himself. We see all these things; we see rascals who unceasingly spew out their poison and malice in order to stir up hatred against the doctrine of God. We see a great number of them carried away with ambition, who never stop making a stir.

But how many are there who walk sincerely and seek to have God honoured, so that his face may shine upon us and that we may be transformed into his image? The number of those who walk uprightly is very small, and they are spread very thinly. Therefore we must take all the more pains to keep this deposit of truth, this excellent and holy treasure that God has entrusted to us. And at the same time, let us be firmly resolved in our minds that we will not waver or be shaken by every blast of wind. Why is it that we see so few standing steadfast nowadays? Especially when any trouble is raised, they immediately fall away and turn aside. What is the reason for it, if not that they were never built up as they ought to have been? They only caught a whiff of the gospel in passing, as it were.

They make out that they are mighty champions, and yet they are not able to give an answer on one point of religion — not even as much as little children can. If someone were to ask one of these fellows who are so zealous [to tell you] who God is, and how we must pray to him, or who Jesus Christ is, you would find them like dumb animals; and we should not be surprised, for they have abused too much the knowledge that was given them. They are drunkards, fornicators and very vile persons, betrayers of the truth, full of envy and malice, given to all sorts of wickedness; and they never stop showing malice against God, not only in private, but they would be glad if there were no discipline or honesty at all among people. They profane and pollute the church of God with their filthiness. Wherever they go, they bring nothing but infection; we see this before our very eyes. Let us, therefore, take heed that we have nothing to do with men of this kind.

What, then, must we do, if not to provide good witnesses who may help us maintain the doctrines of the faith? And in the meantime let us be confident that we are living in those times of which the prophet Isaiah spoke when he showed how God commanded him to seal up his law among his disciples. It is true that the prophet was sent to preach the doctrine of God to people in general, both great and small, for all those who were of the stock of Abraham were brought up by virtue of the promise. But what then? After the prophet had taken great pains, he saw that the greatest part of them were rebels — yes, and so hardened that his preaching only made them worse. They became more and more blind, and seemed to have plotted together against God. Isaiah might then have become discouraged and forsaken all; but our Lord commanded him to seal up his law among his disciples [i.e., confine his teaching to them]. We are, I say, living in such a time today, for do we not see that the world has plotted together against God? As for the papists, we see their rage, and not only their stubbornness.

But among us who make a profession of the gospel, where is the fear of God? Where is this humility to receive the Word of God with all lowliness and meekness, as St James says? (James 1:21). We can perceive a certain lion-like stout-heartedness in a great number; in others we see less honesty than we find in pigs. In short, we see so many wolves and foxes, and so few sheep. Look whichever way you will, you will see that there is nothing but a horrible falling away everywhere.

What we must do

Now, when God once sends us his Word, he intends only to gather us to himself, and yet we see how few there are who cleave to him. What must we do, then, but follow the example of the prophet Isaiah? For be that as it may, the world is heading for ruin, seeking only to entangle itself in Satan's snares. Yet God will always have his disciples; God will never be without some seed. It is true that it will not be as much as we might wish, but let us be content with it, and let us seal up the law of God, keeping it like so many letters that are sealed so that the world — not only the ignorant and fools, but also the wisest and best thinkers among them — cannot understand them. But for our part, though the law of God should be to us like letters that are sealed up, let us not be ignorant of what is contained in it. For indeed it is directed to us. Those especially who are charged with preaching the Word of God must be able to say with the prophet Isaiah, 'Here I am, Lord, with the servants whom you have given me' (cf. Isa. 8:18). For it is not enough for us to approve the doctrine of God as being true; we must also come and present ourselves as a sacrifice to him. And he who has the office of preacher must make his offering, for indeed he is called on condition that he should say, 'See, Lord, here I am with the children whom you have given me.'

And in order that we may be encouraged to do this, let us observe that it was not written for Isaiah's time only. For the apostle shows in the epistle to the Hebrews that it must be fulfilled in the time of our Lord Jesus Christ and in his reign. Yet today, though the trumpet is sounding everywhere and our ears are subjected to a constant onslaught, yet Jesus Christ has only a small audience; as it is said in another place: 'Who will hear our preaching, and to whom has the arm of the Lord been revealed?' So then, Jesus Christ will be despised and cast aside, and men will mock at his doctrine. Nevertheless, he will always have his people, whom he will keep for God the Father.

Therefore, let us be content to be bound up under this blessed seal, which God has appointed for our salvation; and let us not be like those who deliberately cast themselves away because they cannot abide the message of the Son of God. Let us, instead, follow those who show us the right way. Since we see that the doctrine of God is under attack on all sides these days, and that everything is so far out of order that one would think that all would come to naught, we need to pull ourselves together and follow that which is taught here. For we see that those who profess to stand for the gospel have as much good nature in them as brute beasts have. There is no talk nowadays of Christian brotherly love. Even among ourselves we may find such people — yes, and some a great deal worse than we would find among heathens and infidels. Indeed, it can only be that the bewitching of which the prophets spoke is being manifested in those who scorn the gospel so.

We shall see these villains who would mix their vile teaching with the holy doctrine of salvation — we shall see that they have falsely cloaked themselves with the name of God, that they have caused the name of our Lord Jesus Christ to be evil spoken of — yes, and among the papists at that! It can only be that they are thoroughly bewitched, that God has given them over to a reprobate mind, so that the world may see that they are wholly in the possession of Satan, that there is nothing in them of the true nature of man, but only the bare shape of a human being, an outward show. Indeed, God has imprinted the marks of his wrath and vengeance upon them.

And so, let us profit by all of this, following St Paul's exhortation, and let those who are appointed to preach the Word keep this treasure, and make others partakers of it, who are suitable and able men, that they may share it with others. And let us at least have as much courage to maintain the kingdom of our Lord Jesus Christ, as we see these miserable and mad creatures going about to destroy it and bring it to naught.

Encouragements to persevere

Let us also remember that this doctrine comes from God, and that we may confidently assert that we have our faith from him, and not from men; for unless we are fully persuaded of this point, we shall always be wavering, and the least thing in the world will turn us aside. As we see, nowadays the smallest offences are sufficient to make half of those turn back who seemed to show some promise as though they would have persevered to the end. It is not as if they even hold out until the fiercest attacks; the slightest blast of wind blows them away completely. And why is this? Because they were never thoroughly grounded upon the truth of God.

Let us, therefore, learn to recognize those who serve God faithfully, having this touchstone of truth, the Holy Scripture, by which we may test the doctrine that is preached to us; and let us never be shaken, since we know that it is from God.

Let us also note that when God has a small number of people who stick with us and agree with us in the unity of faith, that is a great help to us. It is true that even if a man were alone in the world, without any company, God still deserves our loyalty, and that we should remain faithful to him, forsaking all men. But even though we are scattered apart, we have some who agree with us and we see how the gospel brings forth fruit, so that those who have made a profession of faith in the gospel show by their lives that they have not been taught in vain. When we have such fellowship among us, it is to confirm us in our constancy and help us to follow God. And therefore let us profit from the means of grace which God gives us when we have good witnesses.

And again, let us look higher, for the angels of paradise are witnesses of that teaching which we have received. They are our brothers and companions, as it were, and when we magnify Jesus Christ with open mouths, we are in harmony with them, as the Scriptures show us.

We are to endure as faithful soldiers of Christ

But to conclude the matter, let us observe also what St Paul says at the end of this text: we must bear afflictions patiently, as good soldiers of Jesus Christ. For without this we cannot complete our course. And, indeed, for this reason St Paul exhorted Timothy to be strong. If there were no warfare, no afflictions, it would cost us nothing to serve God, and that strength would then be unnecessary. But because we must bear affliction, and God by that means proves our zeal and our desire to stand firm to his Word, St Paul tells us flatly that we must be Jesus Christ's soldiers. In other words, God does not leave his people in idleness. No, we cannot have an angel's life in this world, but because we are mixed with despisers of God, with God's mortal enemies, and live among hypocrites, among incarnate devils, we must fight. But in the meantime God comforts us when he says that Jesus Christ is our Captain.

So then, there are two points we have to note and carry away with us from this text. The one is that, if we love God we must not expect to live a quiet life, but to be grieved and troubled; and moreover, that we must overcome trouble patiently, and not busy ourselves in doing evil, but bow our shoulders [to the yoke] and show a humble spirit.

So much for the first point. The second is that, since Jesus Christ is our Captain and we are under him, we need not fear in the slightest. Even if our enemies are imbued with a murdering spirit and are full of madness, malice and betrayal, let them do the worst they can; we will still go on boldly. And why is this? Because we shall be safe in the hands of the one who has promised that he will not lose even the smallest part of that which the Father has given him, but will keep it so well and so securely that he will give the Father a good account of it at the last day.

If we carry away with us these two points, it will be easy for us to bear patiently anything at all with which it may please God to try us. And we shall stand firm, though we see such arrogance as is known throughout all the world — yes, even among us — where we see the devil reigning to the fullest extent, as if we had never heard one word of the gospel. Therefore, when we see such shameful crimes perpetrated that a man would think all the fiends of hell had been let loose, and that all would be utterly brought to naught — when we see this, well, we must be content and bend our shoulders [to the yoke]. But we have a good protector in heaven, so let us defy them and not spare those who set themselves up [against God] in this way.

They really think that they have won the battle, and that they should now celebrate their triumphs against God. But we may be assured that victory will be on our side, and that we shall go away conquerors, whatever may come of it, because we have God on our side, and his hand will be strong enough to defend us. And do we think also that God will tolerate these blasphemies and let them go unpunished when, supposedly under the colour of his name, men go about to cut the throats of Christians?

Do we think that Jesus Christ is above in heaven and, as Judge, does not see whatever is done in the world? And does he not see when men abuse his name so falsely, and will he not exercise vengeance for God's honour and for the maintenance of the gospel? Do we think that his eyes are hoodwinked or blind, that he does not see the cruelty that his people suffer and the shameful way in which his Word is despised? No, no, let us be bold about it: God will work so that our patience shall get us the victory when we fight — yes, every one of us to a greater or lesser degree — and we shall know what it is that the Son of God has called us to. And because we are his, let every one of us dedicate ourselves to him, and meanwhile let us take heart.

The truth is that the temptations are great when we see that righteousness is locked up, as it were, in a room, so that it dares not to come out, while robbery is rampant in the streets and in open places. It is as if a man were inside his house and had his tools with him, and thieves come and rob him and take away his goods. One mows his meadows, another cuts his corn and another gathers his grapes, while he stands there as a prisoner, having nothing but the tools in his hands. When we see that there is only a small token of justice, and meanwhile the devil rules mightily, and that these dogs and swine seek only to make havoc of everything — these are great temptations, enough to cast down those who are weak in faith.

But let us come again to what is said here, namely, that we shall not be destitute of aid, so we should wait patiently until it pleases God to bring order to things, and in the meantime walk uprightly in our calling. And though all the world should rise up against us and we see that the devil and all his minions seek only to ruin everything, let us see in those things a just vengeance of God, in that the devil carries [God's enemies] away because they scoff at God and his Word and dare to spew out of their stinking mouths such villainy as to say that they do it for God's honour. Indeed, [they speak] as though they bore the standard of the gospel; but all the world can see that they serve the devil openly. Even little children know it, and the very pavements of the streets and the walls cry out about it. When we see this, let us pray to God to put things in order.

And meanwhile, let us remember what St Paul says — that if we are true soldiers of Jesus Christ we must suffer until he stretches forth his mighty arm to overcome all our enemies. For as it is said, not only is he the Shepherd of the sheep, who has a rod to guide us gently and to gather us unto him, but, on the other hand, he has a rod of iron (as it says in Psalm 2) to bruise and break the heads of all who will rise up against him — not only these little puppets, but kings and princes, as it says in Psalm 110. Let us pray to him, I say, that we may see this fulfilled; and we shall see it, if we have patience to wait for it, and honour him by committing ourselves wholly into his protection.

Chapter 7

God's firm foundation

'There is a great difference between the assurance of the faithful, who are thoroughly persuaded that their salvation is secure, and the thoughtless attitude of those who are negligent and careless, thinking no harm can overtake them.'

7.
God's firm foundation

'Nevertheless, the solid foundation of God stands, having this seal: "The Lord knows those who are his," and "Let everyone who names the name of Christ depart from iniquity"' (2 Tim. 2:19).

In the verses preceding the one to which we now come St Paul has been speaking concerning those who had fallen away. He does so in order to stir up the minds of the faithful, so that they should not be troubled by these things. He now goes on to say that even if we see those fall who seemed to uphold the church, as it were, we must not be shaken. For if men prove frail, if they go astray out of the right way, if they are obstinate, it is no new thing, for such is their nature. Therefore we ought not to be surprised if they fall into wickedness rather than godliness. But in the meantime, our salvation is securely founded upon the grace of our God, inasmuch as it pleased him to choose us before time began, and to count us among his chosen ones, as his children.

But we are grieved to see those turn back who have shown some good tokens [of a work of God in their lives], for we ought to possess a zeal to see the church of God enlarged, and increased rather than diminished. We ought also to care about our brethren and to be sorry to see them perish. It is no small matter to have any souls perish who were bought by the blood of Christ. Nevertheless, we must always comfort ourselves with this doctrine, that God will maintain his church, though the number may only be small. Though it may not be so large as we should wish, we must be content and believe that God will safely keep all those whom he has chosen for himself.

God's church is on a solid foundation

As for those who fall away and those backsliders who renounce Jesus Christ, although they were joined with us, we must conclude they were not of this number, seeing they have departed from us, as St John says (1 John 2:19). For it would be easier for the world to be turned on its head a thousand times than for one of God's chosen children, one of those whom he holds fast, to perish! Such a thing cannot be! For God is the guardian of our salvation, as he himself has declared; yes, and this responsibility is given to our Lord Jesus Christ, to preserve and keep all whom God the Father has chosen. This is what St Paul means by these words: 'The solid foundation of God stands, having this seal: "The Lord knows those who are his."'

St Paul sets down here two articles, which we need to take good note of. In the first place, when we see such instances of turning, when those who seemed to be the most advanced in religion turn back and fall away from us and become so estranged from the kingdom of God that they become unbelievers, we must not think that the church is falling. It is true that the number of those whom we thought to be faithful is lessened by such means. But however unstable the world may be, the church is on a firm foundation. In other words, God will always keep his church and there will always be some to call upon him and worship him. Let this be sufficient for us. For God has declared that so long as the sun and moon endure, he will have some people to worship him, throughout all generations (Ps. 72:5).

If we see the devil scattering the flock of our Lord Jesus Christ, if we see those who have given us some good grounds for hope fall away and at length be completely cut off, we may nevertheless be assured that the building remains, even though it may be hidden and driven underground. As we have seen from experience, the spark of life has endured even at times when there was scarcely a single Christian to be found in all the world. Indeed, what was our own situation before God gave us the light of the gospel? Would one not have thought that Christianity had been totally banished from the world? One could have seen from afar that there was no sign of a building. Yet there was a foundation, albeit hidden; that is, God reserved for himself in a remarkable way, which is beyond human understanding, those whom he chose, even though they were few in number. And so we see the first point St Paul is making here — namely, that 'The solid foundation of God stands.'

When we see such troubles that we think all must come to naught, let us look by faith at this foundation, which cannot be seen by the human eye. For if we have not faith to discern the church of God, we may well think that it is utterly abolished. We remember what happened in the days of the prophet Elijah: how he thought that there was none left in the world beside himself who worshipped God (1 Kings 19:14). But the Lord reproved Elijah, telling him that he still had seven thousand whom he had reserved to himself and who had not bowed down to Baal. And so it will be at all times and seasons; we may think that the church of God is utterly wiped off the face of the earth, yet God will keep his foundation firm, though hidden from view.

The Lord alone knows those who are his

Secondly, we need to note the imagery of the seal. St Paul informs us that although the foundation of God stands firm, it is like a letter which is sealed up. Why is it sealed? Because only 'The Lord knows those who are his'. We cannot pick them out and say, 'This man is one,' nor can we shut people out. God humbles us and makes us blind, as it were, in this respect, or at least blindfolded. We must be content with the knowledge that he has made his election sure, though it is hidden from us. Though he will not make it known at first, it nevertheless remains true in his secret counsel. So then, if God alone knows those who are his, we must not think it strange if we are deceived when people rebel. Why? Because we did not know [whether or not they were God's chosen ones]. But God will not be deceived; he will complete whatever he has determined in the counsel of his own will. So much for the second point.

A word of warning

St Paul exhorts us not to be negligent when we see those who were like angels among us fall from the right way, but to walk in fear and trembling; and he charges us to beware that we do not abuse the name of God by falsely assuming the name of 'Christian', as the hypocrites do when they take the name of God in their mouths but at the same time demonstrate that they make a mockery of him and discredit this holy name that they have been given. Let us put into practice the admonition of our text — that, if we call upon the name of our Lord Jesus Christ, if we make a profession to be his, we must 'depart from iniquity'. For we are not true members of the church of God unless we separate ourselves from the world and from its cunning wiles.

Let us therefore consider the purpose for which we have been called, and what our condition is; and then let us be faithful and conduct ourselves aright; for God can easily cut us off from his church, seeing that he has shown us examples of such things and that we have failed to profit by them.

The foundation is God's eternal decree

But now, so that we may apply this text better, for our instruction, let us enlarge upon a point we have already mentioned, namely, the eternal counsel of God, upon which our election is grounded and upon which our salvation is firmly settled. It is true, as Scripture says, that we are saved by faith (Eph. 2:8), for we do not know that God is our Father and that we are reconciled to him, except by faith, and by laying hold of the promises contained in the gospel, in which God shows us that he accepts us and is pleased with us in the name of our Lord Jesus Christ.

We must accept this benefit, or we cannot know him. So then, we possess our salvation by faith. This is true; but who is it that gives us faith, except God alone? And why does he give it to us? Because it pleased him to choose us before we were made — yes, before the world itself was made — as St Paul shows us, especially in the first chapter of Ephesians. He sets before us that which we know and which is most familiar to us, namely, that God has made us partakers of his heavenly blessings through Jesus Christ, that after he has forgiven us our sins he shows us that we are acceptable to him, and that he has taken us to be his children. Thus we have all that the gospel offers us.

But St Paul lifts us up higher, saying that all this is given to us because God had chosen us before the world began, because he loved us in our Lord Jesus Christ before we could do either good or evil. This is the point to which we must now turn our attention: although God draws us to himself by the gospel, and we by faith receive the righteousness of our Lord Jesus Christ, who is the cause of our salvation, there was a secret love of God that went before this. And although that love was hidden from us, and God was in no great hurry to draw us to himself, it is certain that we were chosen. This is what St Paul aims to show in the sentence before us: 'The solid foundation of God stands.'

He sets this foundation of God over against any virtue that might be found in us. He sets this solidity of which he speaks against this frail condition of ours. St Paul, knowing that we are inconstant, and that we soon fall and pass away like water, says that we must find our security in God, for we perceive that it is not in ourselves or in our own nature. Therefore, if we find no certainty in things on earth, we must know that our salvation rests upon God, and that he holds it in such a manner that it can never vanish away. This is a very encouraging consideration.

If I see someone become dissolute, what can I say about myself? I am a man like him. But I must come to this conclusion: though I am weak, God is steadfast and sure! Therefore, I must commit myself wholly into his hands, assured that, as our Lord Jesus informs us in John 10, those whom the Father has given to him shall never perish. Why? Because God the Father is stronger and mightier than all those who would oppose him or endeavour to prevent him from carrying out his will.

By these words of our text he warns us that if we put our trust in ourselves we shall be utterly dismayed; and indeed, we should be liable to perish every minute, if we were not upheld and maintained by a power higher than our own. But inasmuch as the mighty power of God cannot be overcome, our salvation remains sure, for God keeps it. Yes, as I said before,

Jesus Christ has taken charge of our souls, and he will not allow us to be taken out of his hands. Although the devil may do what he can, although he may use ever so many means, although it may seem a hundred thousand times as though we were about to be violently snatched out of the hands of our Lord Jesus Christ, yet we shall remain there for ever. And why is that? Because our salvation is settled upon the election of God and his unchangeable counsel.

Those who fall show that they were not elected

Let us beware and be on our guard when we see others stumble and fall from the gospel. Let us observe what St John says in the verse we mentioned earlier. It is true, he says, that 'They went out from us, but they were not of us; for if they had been of us, they would have continued with us' (1 John 2:19). We must know that God allowed hypocrites to remain among us for a while, although he knew they were reprobates.

Our Lord Jesus also plainly shows that the faithful ought not to be troubled by the unthankfulness of those who rebel against the gospel, because they find fault with the true doctrine, and find occasion for defiance against God in some idea that they have dreamed up in their own heads.

Jesus Christ says, 'Every plant which my heavenly Father has not planted will be uprooted' (Matt. 15:13). He compares those who seem to be of the number of the faithful to trees that are planted in a field or garden. Those that are open enemies to God bear no resemblance to trees; but the hypocrites, who make a fair show and want to be taken for God's children, seem like trees planted in a field or garden and to belong to God's house; however, they have not taken root because God did not plant them — that is to say, he did not choose them. In order to test us, he allows them to pretend to be God's children and to use the name of God falsely. But God never adopted them as his children, nor are they chosen to inherit eternal life. Therefore they must be uprooted.

If anyone becomes dissatisfied with the gospel, people will say, 'Look, so-and-so has fallen away.' Such a person is a stumbling-block to others. I am not speaking of those who openly show themselves to be enemies of God, those who plainly show contempt for his Word; but if there are any proud and lofty men who cannot abide sound doctrine, even though for a time they seemed to like it — if such people become dissatisfied with it and find fault with it, they become stumbling-blocks. This is why the disciples asked our Lord Jesus Christ why the scribes and Pharisees were so badly instructed. 'Let them alone,' he told them. 'They are blind. But beware lest you go to destruction with them.'

We must know that *all* are not elected and chosen by God the Father. Some will say there is nothing but holiness in them; but this is all on the surface, for it now becomes evident from the fact that they will not receive his truth that they never had any fear of God, but are hypocrites. So we must not be dismayed if we see rebellion in people, for all are not planted by the hand of God.

The value for us of this doctrine

Thus we see how we may profit from this doctrine. First of all, we must know that faith is given to us from above; we receive the gospel, because God has enlightened us by the Holy Spirit, not by our own intellect or good qualities.

God gives us this grace because he had chosen us to be his children and adopted us before the beginning of the world. This is a singular and inestimable blessing bestowed on us, for he did not do so for all. God was at liberty to choose whom he would; therefore it behoves us to know that we are so much the more under obligation to him, because he has delivered us out of the general destruction of mankind. Let us consider that it is very profitable for us to understand this free election of God, which makes a difference between his children and those who have been cast away.

When we see troubles and offences in the church, when we see those who had begun well turning aside from the true way, we must realize that, although men are frail. we shall nevertheless find in our God security sufficient for our need. Since he has been graciously pleased to adopt us as his children and has charged Jesus Christ with the responsibility of keeping us, we may be assured that he will faithfully carry out what he has promised.

Let us, therefore, have recourse to this doctrine of the election of God whenever we become dismayed at the falling away of any whom we had previously held in high regard. Indeed, if the whole church should seem to come to nothing, it is still true that God has his foundation; that is to say, the church is not grounded upon the will of men (for just as they did not make themselves, so they did not bring about the change in their own lives) but it proceeds from the pure goodness and mercy of God. Even though the upper part of the building should be demolished, as it were — though we may see no pillars and the form and shape of it may no longer be visible — yet God will still keep his solid foundation, which can never be shaken. Thus the world may see whether the doctrine of God's election which we preach is necessary or not.

It is true that we do not presume to enter into the secret counsel of God and that we do not thoroughly comprehend his wonderful secrets. But if the fact that God chose us before the world was made should be hidden from us, would that not be to deprive us of a comfort which is not only profitable for us, but most necessary?

The devil can find no better means to destroy our faith than to hide this article of faith from our view. What situation would we find ourselves in, especially in these days when there are so many rebels and hypocrites in the world — yes, even among those to whom people had looked to perform wonders? Might we not fear that the same thing would happen to us? How can we be constant in resting ourselves upon God and commit ourselves to him with settled hearts, not doubting that he will take care of us to the end, unless we flee to this doctrine of election as our only refuge? For if this is not true, it would seem as if God had broken his promise, which was given to us in respect of his gospel, and that Jesus Christ was being hunted out of the world.

[Concealing this truth] is the principal cause and the best means that Satan can devise to cause us to have a distaste for the gospel. Therefore, let us hold fast these weapons, in spite of Satan and his demons, for these must be our defence. Let us be confirmed in the election of our God, and let us make [the teaching concerning it] available and see that it is not taken from us. If we love the salvation of our own souls, let us attend well to these things and consider those who would hide this doctrine from us as our mortal enemies. For the devil stirs them up to deprive us of a comfort without which we cannot be assured of our salvation.

The call to us to depart from iniquity

We must also remember the exhortation of the apostle Paul when he adds, 'Let everyone who names the name of Christ depart from iniquity.' Just as the election of God is to give us a sure and constant foundation, to make us joyful in the midst of trouble which otherwise might disquiet us, so also we must not cease to call upon God or to run to him and to walk diligently in the way to which he has called us. There is a great difference between the assurance of the faithful, who are thoroughly persuaded that their salvation is secure, and the thoughtless attitude of those who are negligent and careless, thinking no harm can overtake them. These persons are blockheads; they are unaware of the danger that surrounds them, which should induce them to call upon God and flee to take refuge under his wings; nor, after they have once received a moment's instruction, do they pay any more attention to doctrine.

But the faithful do not cease to fear; although they rest confidently upon the goodness of God and are firmly persuaded that no storm or tempest that may come can ever carry them away, they are, nevertheless, constantly on the watch for the assaults that Satan seeks to make against them. Knowing their frailty, they put their trust in God and pray to him that he would not forsake them in time of need, but that he would put forth his hand and preserve them. They consider the way of life to which they are called and stir themselves up to repent and call upon God to increase the graces of his Holy Spirit in them and to take their afflictions from them.

Therefore St Paul says, 'Let him who thinks he stands take heed lest he fall' (1 Cor. 10:12). Not that St Paul meant to put us in doubt, or cause us to waver — as though we were to be left on tenterhooks, not knowing what to do, or whether or not God would guide us to the end. For we must be firmly convinced that God will bring to perfection the work which he has begun, as it is said in Philippians 1, as well as in many other places. However, we must still stir up ourselves daily to prayer and calling upon God. Nor are we to abuse his grace, but must rather dedicate ourselves to him and walk in fear and trembling, taking heed that we do not become entrapped in the condemnation of the wicked.

We need not marvel if poor blind creatures go astray, but seeing that God has enlightened us, is it not incumbent on us to walk uprightly? Since he has adopted us as his children, are we not under an obligation to serve and honour him as our Father? This is what St Paul exhorts us to do when he says, 'Let everyone who names the name of Christ depart from iniquity.' To call upon the name of Christ is to affirm that we are his followers. It is true that often when we speak of calling upon God, it means to pray to him and to flee to him for aid, but this word is often used in a more general sense in Scripture. Therefore, we call upon the name of God when we make a profession of being part of his people and his church. The one who calls himself a Christian is one who calls on Jesus Christ.

Therefore, we cannot take to ourselves the name of Christian, we cannot solemnly affirm that we belong to the company of God's children, that we form part of his church and his household — in short, we can have nothing to do with Christ — unless we are delivered from the defilement of our sin. For otherwise do we not shamefully dishonour him, in a manner that is not to be borne? If a man were to call himself the servant of a prince, and at the same time be a thief, would he not be doubly punished because he abused the name that by no means belonged to him? Now the Son of God is the fountain of all holiness and righteousness! Shall we endeavour to hide ourselves and all our defilement, however shameful it may be, under the cloak of his name? Is this not such horrible sacrilege that it deserves the most severe punishment?

It is true that, whatever pains we may take to serve God in purity, we never cease to be wretched sinners, full of blemishes, and to have many wicked imperfections in us. But if we desire to do well, if we hate sin — even though we only limp along — inasmuch as our intention is good and we strive to go forward in the fear of God and in obedience to his will, our hearts are in the right place and Jesus Christ accounts us as though we were just, and frees us from all our faults by not charging them to our account. Therefore, the faithful, though they are not entirely perfect, but have many sins and may be found to be at fault in many things, do not cease to be accepted as God's children; and Jesus Christ thinks it no dishonour to him that they should be called by his name, for he causes that goodness which is in them, through his grace, to be acceptable to God.

But if we abuse the name of Jesus Christ and use it as a cloak to hide our sins, do we not, as I said before, deserve to have him rise up in opposition against us, seeing that we have dishonoured his majesty and falsified his name, that which marks him out for who he is? So, let us mark well what this word 'Christianity' means; it means that we are members of the Son of God! Since Christ has been pleased to accept us as members of his body, we must cleave to him in all righteousness, for he has received the fulness of God's Spirit, that he might make us partakers of his grace. The Spirit of God must reign in us if we want to be known as his children and as members of the Lord Jesus Christ.

The conclusions we are to draw from this text

Thus we see that all those who devote themselves to wickedness and do not seek to submit themselves to the will of God, or to put to death their wicked lusts, are hypocrites and scoundrels and are guilty of abuse in making pretension to the name of Christians. When we see numbers of people separating themselves from the church of God and those who have begun well not going on [in the faith], we need to know that although men may be weak, God still has his solid foundation. And how is that? It is because God knows those whom he has chosen to be his and he will preserve them. Therefore, let us not doubt that we are of that number, seeing that our Lord has called us to himself; for that calling is a witness that he had singled us out before we were born. Let us, then, be content with this holy calling.

Let us not, therefore, be troubled by any stumbling-blocks that may fall in our way; but at the same time, let us hope in the knowledge that we shall be preserved by the power of God, and that he will maintain his church and not allow all his people to perish, although the world may strive hard to lessen their numbers. In the meantime let us study to walk in fear, not abusing the will of our God in any way, but knowing that, since he has separated us from the world, we must live as children in his household and must belong to him. As he has given us the outward mark of baptism, so we must have the seal of the Holy Spirit. This is the guarantee of our election (as St Paul calls it in Ephesians 1:14); it is the pledge which we have of our being called to the heavenly inheritance.

Therefore, let us pray to God, that he would give us the sign and seal of his free election in our hearts by his Holy Spirit and also that he would keep us safe, as it were, under the shelter of his wings. And if those whom God has not chosen go astray and are lost, and are carried away by the devil, and if they are not raised up again when they fall, but instead cast themselves headlong into destruction — let us, on our part, pray God to keep us under his protection, that we may be in subjection to his will and be kept by his power. Although the world may strive to shake us, let us rest secure upon this foundation: 'The Lord knows those who are his.' Let us never be moved from the foundation, but stand steadfastly upon it, and profit more and more by it, until God takes us to his kingdom, which is not subject to any changes.

Chapter 8

Clay pots and vessels of gold

'Although it is the Lord who works all the good that is in us and our nature can do nothing at all towards it, he does not work, as it were, in lumps of wood, but gives us the will, and also the strength and the inclination, to fight against all hindrances.'

8.
Clay pots and vessels of gold

'In a great house there are not only vessels of gold and silver, but also of wood and clay, some for honour and some for dishonour. Therefore if anyone cleanses himself from the latter, he will be a vessel for honour, sanctified and useful for the Master, prepared for every good work' (2 Tim. 2:20-21).

When we see those who despise God and those who set us a bad example, we are prone to take the opportunity of departing from the right way, and think we have an excuse which will be valid in the sight of God, instead of realizing that such persons are meant to put us to the test, so that our faith may be proved [to be genuine]. St Paul, therefore, exhorts us in this verse not only to separate ourselves from all iniquity, so that we may not be like those who despise God, but also not to be offended, nor to take occasion to go astray, when we see men who are so wickedly inclined. He has already touched on this matter [2 Tim. 2:17-18] but now confirms it by another apt illustration.

A great house with many vessels

First of all, so that we may not think that we have any excuse for doing evil and following those who despise God and fall away from him, St Paul says that in a great house there are different vessels. If the cupboard or table is furnished with vessels of gold and silver, in the kitchen you will find vessels of wood, in which to put the kitchen scraps and other waste, and to throw the sweepings from the house. You will also find vessels made of clay. When we see such a variety, we do not marvel at it. For if someone were to throw the gold and silver vessels out among the refuse from the house, what would we think of that? Would we not say that the man was mad? So then, if none of us would say that there was anything unseemly about there being vessels in a great house that are kept for uses which are not very respectable or pleasant, why should we not be content to find the same thing in the house of God? Shall we allow greater privileges to mortal man, and to creatures, than we are willing to grant to the living God?

However, St Paul exhorts all the children of God, although they are in such close contact with the wicked, not to permit themselves to be corrupted, nor to defile themselves with the evil practices of the others, but rather to be stirred up by this means to take even greater care, shunning evil examples and separating themselves from the company of evil persons. In short, they are to dedicate themselves all the more diligently to God. This, in a few words, is the meaning of this passage.

As we have already shown, in considering the earlier verses, the lesson given us here by St Paul is very profitable: that if there should be in the church of God wicked men and hypocrites who remain among us for a time — and may even be more highly esteemed than others — this must not trouble us. Why not? Because the house of God is great. It is true that some understand this passage to be speaking of the whole world

— and it might well be taken in that way, as we shall see later — but we must note the subject St Paul is dealing with here. He has just mentioned backsliders, who fell away and turned away from the gospel, after having for a time made a profession of believing it. This matter, therefore, brings us great comfort, for he puts it in this way: seeing that the church of God is spread throughout all the world, and many people are being called to the gospel, it is as if in a great house there were vessels of gold and silver to be used in a cupboard or on a table, and there were also vessels of wood and clay, which would be used for a time to carry things up and down in the house and then would be burned or thrown away and not regarded as of any great value. In the same way, although we could wish that there was nothing but purity in the church of God, nor anything that we could find fault with, we must, nevertheless, acknowledge that we shall see stumbling-blocks, which could lead us to think it was all for nothing.

Why is this? Because God assembles a great variety of vessels, of many different kinds. Elsewhere it is said that the church of God is like nets that are cast into the sea, into which come fishes of every kind, both good and bad (Matt. 13:47-48). So it is when the gospel is preached: inevitably there will be a number who will assent to it, and who will even seem for a time to belong to the company of the faithful; but later the fishes will be sorted out [and the bad thrown away].

The church of God is also compared to a threshing-floor, where, until it is threshed, the grain is mixed in among the chaff, and even hidden by it, so that the good grain cannot be distinguished from the chaff which will afterwards be thrown out on the rubbish heap (Matt. 3:12; Luke 3:17). This is all meant to show us that in this life the church of God will never be unmixed; there will always be hypocrites, who will assent to the doctrines of the faith, or at least will have a place in the church, and be taken for Christians. Yet in the end it will be discovered that they are illegitimate children, and therefore they will be disinherited. We have an illustration of this in the case of Ishmael, who for a time was senior to Isaac, as the eldest son; but he was cast out, and Abraham was constrained to cut him off [without an inheritance] (Gen. 21:14).

Must not all vessels in God's house be clean?

Before we go any further, we must answer a doubt that might be raised here. It is said in the Psalms that those who come to the mountain of God and have a place to dwell in his temple must be without blemish, and must walk uprightly (Ps. 15; 24:3-4). This, at first sight, seems to refute the idea that there are vessels for dishonour, for all must be chosen to serve God, and must be sanctified and obedient. To what does God call us but to holiness? Are we not vessels of his temple? Indeed, is not every one of us a part of his sanctuary? Must we not, therefore, be consecrated to him and purified from all blemishes and every taint of pollution? But in these passages to which I have just referred, we are taught what manner of persons those whom God calls to himself ought to be. It is not said that all are in fact like this, for there are many who disregard the will of God and, although they are commanded to dedicate themselves to purity, yet remain defiled and wicked. Indeed, when it is said that those who have clean hands and a pure heart shall dwell in God's holy mountain, we are shown that many who claim that they are the children of God, and boastfully take the name of faithful ones, are in fact not worthy to be counted as members of God's household, and therefore in the end they will be cast away. After they have occupied a place [in the church] under this false title, and have so wickedly abused the name of God, he will banish them, as we have already said in the case of Ishmael.

According to the teaching of these two psalms, it may well be (as we see daily in our experience) that some who dwell in the temple of God for a time and are among those who belong to the household of faith will prove to be vain and wicked. We may see them despise God and act with deceit, malice, violence, extortion and cruelty towards their neighbours. We see all this and yet they continue to grow, as do those who are closest to God, but it will not always be so, for in the end God will separate the goats from the sheep and show who are indeed his people.

What our attitude must be towards evil in God's house

In the second place, St Paul exhorts us to purge ourselves from all the corrupt practices of the wicked, that we should by no means be like them. Why must we do this? Because, if we are partakers of their evil deeds, God will cast us off in disgrace. Therefore, if we wish to have an honourable place in his church, we must not only have this outward title before men, but we must indeed live according to our calling, and show that it is not for nothing that God has chosen us for himself.

Let us also take note of what is said in this text: that if there should be wicked persons mixed in among the good, we should not be troubled beyond measure. We see some who are so scrupulous that if they can spot any fault in the church, or if the reformation is not as thorough or complete as one might wish, they will cry out, 'Well now! Is this the church of God?' and they will separate themselves from it, thinking that they would defile themselves by being associated with a congregation that cannot wholly correct the faults present within it.

We ought indeed to be earnest and zealous, and endeavour to put away stumbling-blocks from among us, as far as is possible. Every one of us should strive to achieve this. If we see any evil, it must be purged away; it must be dealt with speedily and not allowed to grow. We must all earnestly desire that the temple of God should remain pure and well ordered, as it ought indeed to be; nevertheless, we must tolerate many things which we cannot take away and when we cannot remedy them, we must mourn. Whatever the world may do, we ought not to estrange ourselves from the church of God, under the pretext that all its members do not conduct themselves as they ought. Why not? In a great house, if someone goes into the kitchen, he will not be angry if he sees there vessels that are only worth being kicked about and to which no one pays much attention. After all, it is not as if they were to be put on display in a cupboard or on a table; their purpose is only to put kitchen scraps in, and for other domestic uses, and so they serve for the upkeep and cleanliness of the house.

Now would anyone be so churlish and irritable as to turn his back on the whole place, saying, 'I will never go into that house again because I see there vessels that serve no purpose other than to gather up kitchen scraps and leftovers'? Would anyone be so foolish as to be grieved and miserable over this? No, on the contrary, he will see that pains have been taken to serve him better. Therefore, when we see such vessels in the church of God, let us not be grieved and make that a reason for withdrawing ourselves from it, but let us still go on and persevere.

God uses even the wicked for his glory

St Paul meant also to show us clearly that, although the wicked endeavour to bring the name of God into reproach and dishonour, they do not, for all that, cease to serve his glory, in the teeth of their intentions. How can this be? God turns their wickedness into goodness. If we were to look only at the wicked, we should think they were made to dishonour God, to bring shame on his majesty and abolish his justice, to turn everything upside down, that the world should know him no more. This is indeed what they aim at, and the object towards which the devil urges. But, in spite of all this, they are still vessels; that is to say, God will find means to use them in such a way that he will be glorified by them. Not that this excuses them, nor that they can escape responsibility under the cloak of serving him — for this was not their purpose or intention — but that, in some way or other, God will use them.

For our own part, if we cannot gladly submit to the providence of God, we shall have no excuse for being irritable and complaining that 'I see that there is nothing here [for me]; everything is out of order.' Let us wait for our Lord to put right all that we find amiss. Whatever may happen, let us be fully convinced that, in spite of Satan, God will be glorified.

Moreover, let us learn to put this doctrine into practice. When we see that there are many blemishes among us, when stumbling-blocks are not removed as they ought to be, when honesty is in short supply and people shut their eyes so they do not see things, or at least cover up things, and when there is not strict enough discipline to keep people in order as we should wish — when we see all these things, let us sigh over them and, if possible, take pains to correct them. Yet, for all that, we must not think that the kingdom of God is utterly destroyed, or that our Lord Jesus Christ is not able to do anything about it, so that his church is left to perish and fall into complete decay. Rather we should be assured that, although the wicked disfigure the beauty of the church of God, although they defile and pollute it as much as they can, God will nevertheless ultimately be glorified. After they have had their fling and have caused great troubles, God will show himself to be their Judge and bring them to their appointed end. And we shall be confirmed all the more in our faith.

But in the meantime let us be patient, knowing that God works in wonderfully skilful ways and is able to bring glory to himself by the most remarkable means, including even the devil and wicked men. It is true that the devil will always show himself as much as possible a deadly enemy to God's glory, and will endeavour by all means in his power to tread it underfoot; but when he has done his worst, God turns his wickedness into good. The same thing happens in the case of the wicked who go about seeking to bring all things into disorder, and to take the kingdom of God from among us, and erase the very remembrance of his name: when they have done the worst they can, they still remain vessels.

St Paul indeed shows plainly in the ninth chapter of Romans (where he is dealing with a topic of more general application than in this passage) that even the reprobates and castaways — not only those who make a profession of Christianity, but also those who are open enemies of the gospel — are God's instruments and vessels by which he causes his glory to appear, although this is not at all their intention, but quite the reverse. In that passage he speaks as much of those who never acknowledged God or made any pretensions to be part of his household, as of hypocrites, who for a time put on a good show, until God revealed them for what they were. Paul says that *all* are God's instruments. For example, there is a wicked man who tries to mix heaven and earth together, as it were, and to usurp matters that are in God's hand. After Satan has employed him this way and that, and although for a time it may have been thought that he would do great wonders, God will show that he has him bridled and in subjection, and that he was [God's] instrument.

It is true that the wicked are not led by the Spirit of God to do evil — it would be blasphemy to say so, for the Spirit of God leads us to justice and righteousness. However, although the devil prompts people to all kinds of wickedness, nevertheless, God rules over all, and does so in a way that is entirely beyond our comprehension. He knows how to use even the wicked in his service, so that his glory may also be seen in this respect. Seeing this is so, let us learn to be patient when there are stumbling-blocks in the church. Not that we are to encourage the evil; for, as we have already seen, each one of us ought on his own account, and within his own limitations, to take pains to see that the church is cleansed from all manner of pollution. But when it is not in our power to make it better, after we have mourned over it, let us wait patiently while God makes use of the evil and turns it to a good end.

Let us, then, understand what is taught us here: that the wicked are vessels, and they shall be constrained to serve God. They have no inclination to do so, but God can draw them by force and dispose of them according to the counsel of his own will, which surpasses our understanding. Thus they serve in his house, though not for honourable purposes; and yet the name of God does not cease to be glorified; their service in no way lessens his justice, wisdom, virtue or goodness. Thus God keeps all things in order, even though the wicked are mingled with the righteous.

We must separate ourselves from evil

Paul goes on to say, 'If anyone cleanses himself from the latter, he will be a vessel for honour.' This is the second part of the point that we touched on previously. When we see that the church of God is not as well reformed as we might wish, we are apt to think that all is lost and that God no longer rules in the world. But St Paul instructs us not to be perturbed, but to wait patiently till it pleases God to turn the malice of the wicked to his own glory. For the end will always be good, provided that we remain constant, and not shaken, even though we see nothing but confusion in the world.

However, while we have to associate with the wicked, we must not follow their example, or be in league with them in their wickedness, but must separate ourselves from them. St Paul tells us plainly, not merely that we must dedicate ourselves to God, but that we must cleanse ourselves from those of whom he spoke. For it is very hard for a man to walk through mud and dirt without becoming defiled, or to go into a foul and filthy place, and come out spotless. Therefore we must take heed and be careful, when we associate with those who despise God, or with wanton and lewd men and with hypocrites, that we remain unsullied, for nothing is easier than becoming caught up in the pollutions of the world and being infected by them. For this reason, St Paul says, we must be on our guard.

This admonition was not given for one time only, but must be observed to the end of the world. Let us learn, then, that although there ought to be discipline in the church to correct faults, to keep people in the fear of God and induce them to live an honest life, nevertheless, we are bound to see many things that might be hurtful to us, and that would turn us out of the right way, if we are not watchful to guard ourselves.

Therefore, although in this life, until we depart out of the world, we must associate with the wicked, let us take pains to cleanse ourselves from their pollution. While Satan seeks only to jumble us all up together, let us, for our part, pray to God that he would set us apart and keep us in all purity by his Holy Spirit, that his righteousness may always reign in our hearts and be seen in our lives.

This is why St Paul expressly says here that we should cleanse ourselves from those of whom he spoke. He means that, although we have to associate with those who would wish to lead us into bad company and who would urge us to be partakers with them in their evil deeds, we cannot excuse ourselves if we become like them; for God did not sanctify us in vain when it pleased him to choose us for himself.

It is God who enables us to purify ourselves

St Paul says that we must cleanse ourselves, not because we are able to do it by ourselves, but because God will have us make an effort to devote ourselves to his service. On the basis of this passage some have concluded that it is in our power to cause God to choose and predestinate us, but this is to turn the very foundation of our faith upside down. It is the height of absurdity to say, 'We must separate ourselves from the wicked if we want God to choose us.' That is much like saying that before we were born, before the world was made, it was incumbent on us to prepare ourselves that we might be worthy of being adopted by God. This doctrine is so foolish and absurd that there is no need to discuss it at length. For God, who chose us before the foundations of the world were laid, took no account at all of any deserts of ours.

Again, there are others who would establish [from this passage] the existence of a free will, saying, 'We are commanded here to cleanse ourselves, and therefore it must depend on our own industry.' But these people show clearly just how ignorant they are, and that they are not well-read in Holy Scripture. For when God shows us what our responsibility and duty are, he does not say that these things are in our own power, or that we are able to do them; but he exhorts us to do what is good. At the same time he constantly works in us, because he sees us falter and because we are not able of ourselves to perform our duty.

Let us, then, learn from this passage to cleanse ourselves, that we may not be like the wicked. God tells us, through the prophet Ezekiel, that he will sprinkle clean water upon us to wash us (Ezek. 36:25); that is, he will send us his Holy Spirit. We are commanded to cleanse ourselves, but God shows us that it is his work and that it proceeds from the pure grace of the Holy Spirit.

Why, then, does St Paul use this language? Because, although it is the Lord who works all the good that is in us and our nature can do nothing at all towards it, he does not work, as it were, in lumps of wood, but gives us the will, and also the strength and the inclination, to fight against all hindrances. This is why he yields to us [the honour] that is rightly his alone, as he works in us in such a way that it seems as if we do it ourselves.

So, then, the believer takes great pains and labours hard to purge himself from the pollution of the world, so that he may not be infected with the corruptions of the wicked. In this we exert ourselves and fight manfully, but it is God who drives us to it; it is he who gives us the power. In short, he gives us the will and enables us to execute it, as St Paul says — and it is all of his free goodness (Phil. 2:13). It is because we are not to be idle that we are thus exhorted in this text and in other passages — and such exhortations are not needless.

We are to be 'vessels for honour'

Having made some observations regarding what St Paul says about purging, or cleansing, ourselves, we notice that he goes on to say, 'He will be a vessel for honour, sanctified and useful for the Master, prepared for every good work.'

When the apostle speaks of vessels of honour, he shows that it is not enough for us to have a place in the church of God, to bear the name of Christian, but we must be separated [from sin and uncleanness]. It is true that all those who are baptized, all who are partakers of the supper of our Lord Jesus Christ and are joined with the faithful, are already separate from unbelievers — no one will say that they are Turks or heathens. Nevertheless, something more than this is necessary. We must not have the outward mark only, and boast of our baptism and profession to serve God, but our lives must give evidence that we are indeed his children; and when we are governed by his Holy Spirit, this is a witness to us, to assure us of our adoption.

This is what St Paul means when he says that we must be 'vessels for honour'. And why is this? It may be that, although we are in the church of God — perhaps even among its most prominent members — in the end we shall be thrown out like a broken piece of pottery, or discarded like a wooden vessel that no longer serves any purpose or is of any value. That is how hypocrites will end up, who boastfully claim that they belong to the company of God's children. They may indeed be vessels, and God may use them, but they are vessels used for dishonourable purposes, and God will bring them into confusion.

Therefore, let us take heed and make sure that we are vessels who serve an honourable purpose, and that we do not only have an outward, temporal mark (so that we may be taken for children of God), but that we are those who have been chosen and are being preserved for his everlasting inheritance; and let us by this means draw near to him. Then we shall not only be vessels in the house, but also vessels for use in the temple, serving to make holy sacrifices and offerings, and thus God will be served and honoured in us.

When God brings glory to himself by the wicked — as it is said of Pharaoh — this is, as it were, against nature: it is like drawing fire out of water. Indeed, God must indeed work miraculously when he makes the malice of men serve his glory, for their inclination is completely in the opposite direction. It is so great a work that it is difficult to comprehend it. Therefore, we cannot properly speak of the wicked 'glorifying God'; but we glorify God when we give ourselves wholly to his service and seek nothing but the honour and glory of his name. And we do this when we are his true children, who labour to prepare ourselves, body and soul, for his use.

A call to purity

[St Paul] not only says that we are vessels to be used in [God's] temple, but that we are the priests who bear them. So, then, God gives us the privilege of being vessels for honour, who dedicate both body and soul to his service; indeed, he makes us vessels to serve in his temple and to be used for whatever will serve to promote his holiness, and so that he may reign among us. This is why we must take even greater pains to sanctify ourselves — as we read in the prophet Isaiah: 'Be clean, you who bear the vessels of the LORD' (Isa. 52:11).

Again, we know how strictly God has commanded that the vessels should be kept clean and pure, and that nothing unclean should be put in them. Therefore, since we are the vessels of the temple, as well as the stewards and guardians of them, let us take heed that we dedicate ourselves to God's use — and indeed to an honourable use. Since we are also his temples, each one of us, and all jointly, let us take care to keep ourselves completely pure.

Seeing that God bestows on us this honour of receiving us to be vessels for use in his holy temple and of dwelling in us by his Holy Spirit, must we not be purged from all pollution? We cannot expect God to dwell in a polluted and filthy place; his house must be pure and holy; whatever comes near him and into contact with him must be sanctified; otherwise he will not draw near to us. Thus we cannot be fit to serve God (who is the Master of the house) unless we are vessels for honour, that is (as St Paul himself expresses it), prepared for every good work.

If we would be fit to serve God for honourable purposes, let us take heed that we devote ourselves to good works; that is, that we seek only to obey him and to respond to his holy calling. Then we shall not only be instruments in the hand of our God, but also vessels for honour. Being governed by his Holy Spirit, we shall be fit for his service, our own wills being drawn to exalt him. He will not wait on us, but will first of all be served by us, body and soul, because he has called us to this task and does us the honour of making use of us for good purposes, that he may be glorified in us. This is the lesson we are to learn from this text.

Practical exhortations from this passage

Let us learn, therefore, by way of conclusion, not to allow ourselves to be thrown into confusion, even though the devil should cast many troubles in our way, though storms and tempests should arise and though we should not see [in the church] such order and discipline as we could wish. In spite of all this, let us keep on our way and let us not think that this in any way detracts from the majesty of God. Let us rather see these things as being like vessels for domestic use in a great house, for there must be such things. Yet let us not think that there will be an excuse for us if we become contaminated by such pollution, but let us rather be all the more watchful. Since God will test what are our feelings towards him, let each of us keep a careful watch on himself. When we see the wicked rejoice and seek to ruin everything, let us pull in the other direction. When we see sin getting the upper hand, and everyone trying to draw his companion into destruction along with him, let us run to our God and pray that he would keep us under the governance of his Holy Spirit, and let us take pains to model ourselves on this purity spoken of by St Paul.

Seeing that we in ourselves are insufficient for these things, and that besides our weakness there is nothing but corruption in us, let us pray that God would send us his pure waters, spoken of by the prophet Ezekiel (Ezek. 36:25) knowing that we shall be fit to serve God when we desire only to devote ourselves to obeying him — and when we do so freely, and not by constraint or by force, as in the case of the wicked. For when God is glorified through them (as he says that he has kept them for his glory), we must know that this is not of their own volition, but is brought about by a wonderful providence before which we can only bow down in worship, because God is able to draw good out of evil, in the same way as he turned darkness into light when he made the world (see 2 Cor. 4:6).

Chapter 9

The Scriptures: God's profitable Word

'The Word of God is not given to teach us how to talk, or to make us eloquent and skilful in debate, but to reform our lives, so that the world may know that our desire is to serve God, to give ourselves wholly to him and live in conformity with what pleases him.'

9.
The Scriptures: God's profitable Word

'All Scripture is given by inspiration of God, and is profitable for doctrine, for reproof, for correction, for instruction in righteousness, that the man of God may be complete, thoroughly equipped for every good work' (2 Tim. 3:16-17).

Since the Word of God is called our spiritual sword, we need to be armed with it, bearing in mind that in this world the devil continually fights against us, endeavouring to deceive us and draw us into sin. Therefore, in exhorting us to make use of it, St Paul begins by saying that the Word of God deserves such reverence that we all ought to submit to it and listen to what it says unreservedly and without quibbling. He goes on to tell us what profit we receive from it — which is another reason to encourage us to receive it with the utmost reverence and obedience.

The authority of all Scripture

We need to be clear that St Paul is speaking here of Holy Scripture, for there have been at all times some wayward individuals who sought to cast doubt upon Holy Scripture and upon all that is contained in it, although they were ashamed to deny that the Word of God deserved to be received without contradiction. There have always been wicked men, who have at first sight appeared openly and freely to confess that there is such a majesty in the Word of God that all the world ought to bow before it — and yet who constantly blaspheme and speak evil against Holy Scripture. But where is the Word of God to be found, if not in the Law and the Prophets, and in the gospel? To the end, therefore, that there should be no misunderstanding, and that men might not make excuses for themselves by saying that they could believe the Word of God even though they never accepted the Holy Scripture, St Paul plainly shows us that if we will do homage to God and live in subjection to him, we must receive what is contained in the Law and the Prophets.

And since no one is at liberty to choose only what pleases him, and so to obey God only in part, he says that the *whole* of Scripture has this majesty of which he speaks, and that *all* Scripture is profitable. In short, St Paul informs us that we must not pick and choose the portions of Scripture we like, as the fancy takes us, but must receive it in its entirety and without exception, adhering firmly to it, and to it alone, since God has spoken in the Law and the Prophets.

Thus we see what St Paul's meaning is in this passage. When he speaks of Holy Scripture, he does not mean his own writings, nor those of the other apostles and evangelists; for at that time only the Old Testament had been written. So we see that what he had in mind was that the Law and the Prophets should always be preached in the church of Christ; for this is doctrine that must, and will, remain for ever. Therefore, those who would have the law laid aside and never spoken of again are behaving like ignorant and foolish beasts. I have been obliged to speak out plainly on this because of certain false teachers who have made it a common proverb in their synagogues and taverns, saying, 'We need neither the Law nor the Prophets any more.'

But, on the contrary, St Paul imposes a restraint on Christians and tells us that if we want to prove our faith and obedience towards God, the Law and the Prophets must reign over us. We must regulate our lives by them; we must know that this is abiding and immortal truth, neither transient nor changeable. God did not give a temporary doctrine to serve only for a time. He intended that it should still be in force in our day, and that the world should sooner perish, and heaven and earth decay, than that the authority of the Law and the Prophets should be diminished.

Thus we see that St Paul's meaning is that we should allow ourselves to be governed by Holy Scripture and should seek for wisdom nowhere else. Let us also note (as has already been said) that he gives us no liberty to choose what we like, but he will have us to be obedient to God in all respects, approving what is contained in Holy Scripture.

A brief outline of the passage

Now let us turn our attention to the two points which are dealt with in this passage. He says first that 'All Scripture is given by inspiration of God'; and then he adds that it 'is profitable'. St Paul commends Holy Scripture to us in two ways, in order to induce us to love it and to show that it is to be received in all humility.

When he says that it is 'given by inspiration of God', it is to the end that no mortal man should set himself up to control God. Shall creatures dare to make war against God and refuse to accept Holy Scripture? What is its source? It is not something hammered out by men, says St Paul; there is nothing earthly about it. Therefore anyone who does not want to be in blatant rebellion against God, or to set him at naught, must submit to Holy Scripture. So much for the question of authority.

St Paul adds in the second place that — besides the reverence which we owe to God by giving him homage — we must acknowledge that God intended our profit and salvation when it pleased him to teach us by Holy Scripture, for he will not have us occupy ourselves with unprofitable things. Therefore, if we are diligent in reading Holy Scripture, we shall perceive that it contains in it nothing but that which is good and fitting for us and from which we may reap some benefit. How unthankful we should be, then, not to accept the blessings which God, for his part, offers so freely to us!

So, to be brief, after St Paul had extolled Holy Scripture, showing that the majesty of God appears in it, he wanted to develop in us a taste for it, so that we might come to it with an affection and desire to profit by it — knowing that this was God's design, and the end that he had in view.

God is the author of Scripture and this gives it authority

With regard to the first point, let us take good note that Holy Scripture will never be of service to us as it ought unless we are persuaded that God is the author of it. If we read Moses, or any of the prophets, as merely being the history of mortal men, do we feel conscious of the Spirit of God kindling a flame in us? No, no, far from it! So, then, the Scripture will be lifeless to us, and will carry no force, until we know that it is God who is speaking in it, revealing his will to us. This is why we must begin with St Paul's declaration that Holy Scripture 'is given by inspiration of God'. Now it is true that the pope will claim that all the proclamations he has made are from God. In this way the world has been deceived and kept in ignorance from the beginning as men have put forward their own ideas under the cloak of speaking in God's name. For there was never any poison of false doctrine that was not put into a golden cup; that is to say, that was not disguised by being honoured with the title of being what God spoke to man.

However, if we are content to be governed by God, our faith will be rightly sealed, so that we may perceive that these things are not the illusions of Satan, nor fables invented by men — I mean those things which are contained in Holy Scripture — but that they were spoken by God, and that he is the author of them. Let us consider the infinite goodness of our God, in that it has pleased him to seal up his truth in our hearts and cause us to feel the power of it, while unbelievers are left in their ignorance to despise the authority of Holy Scripture.

We may also gather from what St Paul says that there is no reliable authority in the church but that of God himself. If, then, we are rightly to accept a doctrine, it must not depend for its authority on the wisdom of men, but we must know that it came from God, for all that does not come from him is of no value. This is a noteworthy point, for God will use it to test us, to reveal whether we are his people or not. We will demonstrate that he is indeed our King by the fact that we have no laws or ordinances except those we have received from him, and our souls are not guided by random decisions, but that he rules over us, and we are all subject to his yoke. If this is not the case, we show no evidence that God governs us; however much we may claim to own his name, it is all so much hot air.

Let us, therefore, note that, in seeking to show us that we must hold Holy Scripture to be undoubted truth, St Paul does not say that Moses was an excellent man, or that Isaiah was very eloquent. He says nothing about the human authors to raise their credit at a personal level; he says only that they were instruments of the Holy Spirit and that their tongues were guided in such a way that nothing which they uttered was their own ideas, but it was God who spoke through their mouths. We must not give credit to them as mortal men, but must recognize that they were the servants of the living God and be firmly convinced that they were faithful stewards of the treasures committed to them.

All human authority is excluded

If this point had been rightly understood, men would never have fallen into such dreadful confusion as we see today among the papists. On what is their faith grounded, if not on men? For we never hear it said among the papists: 'It is God who is speaking — yes, and this is in order to give us an appreciation of his majesty.' There is nothing but hypocrisy in all that they do. It is true that they claim to speak in God's name, but at the same time they give voice to their own ideas and false teachings, and that is all.

St Paul, on the other hand, tells us in this passage that we must confine ourselves to Holy Scripture. Why is this? Because God speaks in it, and not man. Thus we see how he excludes all human authority. God must have the pre-eminence above all creatures, whoever they may be; both great and small must submit themselves to him and no one may presume to encroach [upon his sovereignty] and say, 'I will speak.'

St Peter also wants us to have this same assurance, when we go into the pulpit, that it is God who sent us and that the message we bring is the one which he committed to us. 'If anyone speaks,' he says, 'let him speak as the oracles of God' (1 Peter 4:11); that is, let him show, and give good evidence to confirm, that he is not rashly putting forward his own thoughts, nor patching together any ideas that he has dreamed up, but that what he is holding forth is the truth of God in all its purity. He must make known the doctrine which he is preaching, so that God may be honoured. Seeing that all teachings of human origin are done away with in this passage, let us exclude and banish them from the church of Christ, so that they may never find their way in again. Let us take care that we hold firmly to the pure and simple Word of God, for our Lord has been so gracious as to reveal his will to us by the Law and the Prophets. Let us, therefore, hold fast to [that which we have received], and not give such authority to men as to allow them to rule our consciences or to devise articles of faith as they please.

How we are to approach Scripture

St Paul goes on to say that 'All Scripture … is profitable…' If Holy Scripture is profitable for us, we are guilty of gross ingratitude if we do not apply ourselves to the study of it. Who, indeed, is there among us who does not naturally desire what is for his own profit and salvation? And where can this be found, if not in Holy Scripture alone? Woe to us, then, if we do not listen when God speaks to us, seeing that he intends only that which is for our profit! Moreover, we are also put in mind of the fact that we must not read Holy Scripture in order to support our own notions, or to give rise to empty speculations.

Therefore, when I expound Holy Scripture, I must always be guided by it alone, so that those who hear me may be able to profit from the doctrine I proclaim, for their edification and salvation. If I do not have this attitude, and do not edify those who hear me, I commit sacrilege and profane the Word of God. Those also who read Holy Scripture, or come to hear the sermon — if they approach it hoping to indulge in futile speculation, or in search of entertainment, they are guilty of profaning that which is holy. If we seek to make Holy Scripture pander to our appetites, or seek questions in it, but do not aim to profit by it, we abuse it.

St Paul has taught us that we must come to God earnestly desiring to learn from him, seeing that his object is only for our profit and salvation. The apostle shows us also that we must not abuse Holy Scripture, by making it serve our own fancies. But, knowing that it is God's intention that it should be profitable for us, we must come to it to be taught — yes, and to be taught that which is profitable for our salvation.

It is profitable for doctrine

Now it remains for us to examine separately and one by one the various ways in which Scripture is profitable to us. For if St Paul had concluded his remarks with this one word, 'profitable', the sense of the passage would have been obscure. But he brings out the meaning so plainly that we do not need to look anywhere else for an explanation of the text. He says that 'Scripture … is profitable for doctrine, for reproof, for correction, for instruction in righteousness: that the man of God may be complete, thoroughly equipped for every good work.'

We need to note, first of all, that St Paul does not lay down a simple means of using Holy Scripture, but, having spoken of the doctrine he adds, 'for reproof, for correction, for instruction'. And why is this? It is not enough for God to show us what is good, because we are so pitifully cold-hearted; so he needs to stir us up to earnestness. We need to know that he means what he says when he speaks to us, and that we should not take his word lightly. Thus we see that there is no such thing as a lifeless doctrine in Holy Scripture, or doctrine presented in isolation; but there are always reproofs and corrections to stir us up, that we may come to God.

Why does St Paul begin with this word 'doctrine'? Because this is the natural order [in which to proceed]. If we are not taught to say, 'This is the truth,' there will be little point in exhorting us. We need first to know that what is taught us is good, true and right. Thus the word 'doctrine' signifies that we must be instructed in the truth, that we must be thoroughly convinced of it and so edified by it that we no longer have any doubts whether or not it is really so.

Now we need to remind ourselves what holy doctrine is, in the sense in which St Paul is using the term. The purpose of it is that we may know Christ and put our whole trust in him and may live godly lives. When we call upon God by prayer and supplication, we must put our trust in him and look to the heavenly life to which he calls us. We are to put to death our evil desires and conform ourselves to his righteousness.

So, then, the doctrine of the gospel is, to put it briefly: to know that it is God's will that we should put our whole trust and confidence in him and should flee to him alone; and also to know how and by what means he reveals himself to be our Father and Saviour — namely, in the person of our Lord Jesus Christ, his only begotten Son, whom he sent to die for us. This is the way by which we are reconciled to God and cleansed from all sin and defilement and by which we are counted as righteous. It is from this knowledge that we have the confidence to call upon God, knowing that he will not cast us off, when we come to him in the name of the one whom he has appointed to be our advocate.

It is profitable for reproof

When we consider that there is nothing but sin in us and that we are all by nature under a curse, we must learn to be dissatisfied with ourselves. Since we know that God deserves to be served and honoured by us, we need to know what he requires of us, and what is acceptable to him, so that we may do our duty. This is the doctrine which is contained in Holy Scripture. But, as we said earlier, even though all the rest flows from the doctrine, yet doctrine of itself does not profit us because of our laziness and coldness of heart. We need to be spurred into action. This is why St Paul's second word is 'reproof'. He means us to understand that if we are to be well instructed in the school of God, we must confess our guilt; we must be pricked to the heart; we must submit to reproof and acknowledge that we are at fault.

As St Paul says in 1 Corinthians 14, when the Word of God is rightly expounded, not only are the faithful edified, but if an unbeliever comes into the church and hears the doctrine of God, he is reproved and judged. Although that unbeliever was previously enveloped in darkness, so to speak, and in his own ignorance lived as he pleased, with no more sense or perception of God than a stick of wood, yet when God enlightens him he comes to realize his miserable state and sees that he is wicked and under a curse; and at the same time he sees the heavens open to him, if only he will give ear to the Word of God, and understands that man was not made for this life only, but to be exalted to a higher realm. This is how the unbeliever is convicted. Indeed, to state it even more plainly, St Paul adds that the secrets of the heart are then disclosed; for we know that while the Word of God is buried, no one looks at his own state, for our hearts are, as it were, entangled.

What then must we do? We must apply the Word of God to our use. We must be woken up out of sleep, so that we take greater care that we no longer forget God, or neglect the salvation of our own souls. We must search to the very depths of our hearts and examine our whole lives, that we may be ashamed of our sinfulness and judge ourselves, in order that we may avoid the condemnation which would otherwise await us in the presence of God. This, then, is how we understand St Paul's use of the word 'reproof': it is not enough for men to set the blessings of God before us, and say, 'This is God's will'; we must be woken up and caused to think seriously about it and to take a hard look at ourselves. Then we must indeed draw near to God, as he has summoned us to appear before his judgement seat, and we must bring all to light, so that we may be ashamed when we see in what a pit of corruption we were formerly wallowing. And then as we breathe with the life [given to us] from heaven, we must be careful not to turn aside from the right way.

It is profitable for correction

It is not enough to be reproved in this way; 'correction' must also be added. We must be chastised, as it were, by the Word of God, to the end that we may reform our way of life. We must forsake our sins; and if we were steeped in them we shall need to be dealt with roughly and sharply, in order that our sins might be plucked out by the roots and that we might be completely rid of them. Thus, when we have been roused to think about God, we must be brought under conviction and condemnation as our sins are laid open to view, and we are brought to such a pass that we do not know what to do to escape condemnation. Moreover, we must be drawn to this by force. If we have been intoxicated with pleasures, if we have indulged ourselves in folly and vanity, and have been greatly deceived by them, the corrections must be swift and severe, that we may give God the honour which is his due and allow him to transform us and bring us to him.

When a father sees his children indulging in lewd behaviour, he does not think it is enough to say to them, 'What are you doing, my children, that is neither good or honest?' Rather he will say, 'You wretched creatures, have I brought you up and cared for you until now, only to have you reward me in this way? Is it becoming for you to bring such shame on me after I have treated you so kindly? Away with you! You deserve to be given into the hands of the hangman, since you will never be any good! Must I bring up worthless creatures like this in my house?' So it is with us, when God sees that, although he has been very patient with us, we are more rebellious against him than disobedient children are against their earthly parents. Does he not have reason to be furious with us and to cut us to the quick when he is angry with us? Not that he is subject to unruly fits of temper, but he adopts such severity with us to break us in, like wild horses that need to be tamed, and bring us into subjection to him, so that we may no longer go astray but may learn to obey him.

Now we may judge from this whether it would be enough for a man, when he expounds Holy Scripture, to hold a discourse on it as if it were mere history; for if that were so, there would be no need for St Paul to say what he does here. It would have been enough for him to have said that to preach the gospel we need only say, 'This is what God says …' However, he says that we need to feel the prick of the spurs. The duty of a good and faithful shepherd is not simply to expound Scripture; he must use earnestness and sharpness to give force and power to the Word of God. This is why St Paul says in another place that the shepherds of the church must be in earnest, even to the point of seeming importunate, and must not only show the people what is good, but must rebuke and reprove them.

It is true, he says it is to be done with meekness, gentleness and patience; but however it is done, correction must be carried out and men are not to say, 'This is too hard to be borne; you must not deal with people in this way.' Those who are not willing to submit to reproof had better look for another master than God, for they are not worthy to hear a single word from his lips. The world would indeed gladly be spared, and we see many who are ready to explode in bitter rage when they are threatened or corrected. Do you say you want to be won by gentleness and to be taught in another fashion? Then you had best go to the devil's school, for he will certainly flatter you — yes, and bring you to destruction!

But as for the faithful, after they have received the doctrine, they must humble themselves and be willing to receive reproof and exhortation when they have done amiss. Their sins and offences need to be brought to light, so that the infection can be brought under the knife and by this means they may be purged of the poison that is in them and restored to perfect health. This is how we must conduct ourselves if we wish to be instructed in the doctrine of God.

It is profitable for instruction in righteousness

St Paul concludes by saying that the Scripture is 'profitable for ... instruction in righteousness, that the man of God may be complete, thoroughly equipped for every good work'. When he says that we have in Holy Scripture all that we need for instruction in righteousness, he excludes anything that men might bring, showing that we shall not become righteous by doing this or that, if it is something introduced by man.

Thus we see how the papists torment themselves in vain, constantly observing whatever is imposed upon them by men. In what does their righteousness consist? Upon what is it grounded? 'This is what the church commands.' But St Paul shows that there is neither religion nor doctrine, except that which is contained in Holy Scripture — yes, and there is no other righteousness to be found [outside Scripture]. Do they then follow what God has commanded? No, they go utterly contrary to it. Therefore, if we wish to have our lives well ordered, let us not take as our foundation things which men have introduced as it suited them, but let us follow that which is acceptable to God.

If we take as our guide the instructions contained in Holy Scripture, we may find justification there; but as for all other teachings, God excludes them and shows that they are but folly and will vanish away like smoke. Let us remember, then, that it is with good reason that St Paul joins these two things together, when he speaks of 'instruction in righteousness'. He wants us to understand that to be truly devout we must live holy lives. The Word of God is not given to teach us how to talk, or to make us eloquent and skilful in debate, but to reform our lives, so that the world may know that our desire is to serve God, to give ourselves wholly to him and live in conformity with what pleases him. If we want to know whether a man has profited by the gospel or not, let us take note of his life. There are some who put on a good show and can talk readily enough, but if we find that their lives are not in conformity with the righteousness of God, as St Paul says here, then we may know that the rest is worthless, because their lives are not based on the Word of God as they ought to be.

It contains all that we need to equip us for every good work

We see, therefore, that St Paul means to show that we must make the Word of God serve for this purpose, that we may model our lives according to it and walk uprightly. So he ends by saying, '... that the man of God may be complete, thoroughly equipped for every good work'. This matter of instruction in righteousness is all the more appropriate in order to show plainly that all the inventions of men are to be excluded; for otherwise everyone would serve God according to his own ideas, but that would make God subject to our whims; or again if we thought up good works to suit ourselves, they would not be acceptable to God.

St Paul, seeing such impudence and boldness in men that they always want to take their own works into account, and are not content to keep within the limits and bounds which God has set for them, points out the disease here, so that it might more easily be healed. He tells us that if we have the Word of God in our hearts, there will be a completeness about us, for we shall lack nothing, but shall be 'thoroughly equipped for every good work'. When he says that we shall be 'complete' [or 'perfect'], he means that we shall be like a body that is in every respect well-formed, well-proportioned and attractive, with no parts missing. The word he uses conveys this sense of lacking nothing. Let us, therefore, note that we are by nature absolutely nothing at all, but God restores his image in us by means of his Word, and this is how we come to the completeness of which Paul speaks.

It is also significant that Paul speaks of 'every good work'. Men may boast as much as they please that they live good and holy lives and perform good works, but when they appear before the heavenly Judge, all will be blown away like chaff before the wind. When we mix our own inventions with that which God has commanded, we only confuse and spoil everything. So we may make the general point from this passage that all things that have been fabricated by men are nothing but corruption. The papists call good works such things as fasting on the eve of a saint's day, not eating meat on a Friday, observing Lent, doing homage to saints, running around from altar to altar and from chapel to chapel in order to hear mass, arranging for masses to be sung, going on pilgrimage, and so on. Indeed, they have devised so many such laws and statutes that there is no making head or tail of them. But we must all appear at last before the great Judge, to give an account of ourselves, and he has already pronounced sentence that this doctrine was given to us to serve as a full and final verdict.

It is said here that we shall be equipped for every good work, if we profit by Holy Scripture. What, then, will become of these traditions and inventions which they have introduced, and which are so numerous that the Word of God seems to have been swallowed up in a flood of papistry? If one were to take a pair of scales and weigh the [place occupied in their teaching by the] traditions of men against [that of] the Word of God, one would not find that the Word of God came to as much as one-hundredth part in relation to all the traditions they have. Even though they say, 'God has commanded this,' and cannot deny that God is to be served, they make far greater account of the traditions of men. Therefore, let us stop consciously and willingly deceiving ourselves, considering that we shall find in Holy Scripture a full sufficiency of all that is required for our completeness and for all good works, and that God excludes anything that might be added to what is prescribed in it, and shows that such things will not be taken into account, nor are they to be laid down as things that are acceptable to him. Men, therefore, draw up all their regulations in vain; it will only serve to double their condemnation.

Someone might ask, 'If the Law and the Prophets are so complete, what purpose does the gospel serve? It would seem at this rate that we do not even need Paul's teaching.' This can easily be answered. The gospel was not given to men to add anything to either the Law or the Prophets. Let us read every page of the New Testament — we shall not find one syllable added to either the Law or the Prophets; it only sets forth more plainly what was taught in them. It is true that God has been more gracious to us than to the Old Testament saints who lived before the coming of the Lord Jesus Christ, in that matters are more clearly set forth for us, but nothing is added.

So, then, when St Paul declares that we shall find completeness and perfect righteousness in the Law and the Prophets, it does not in any way detract from the gospel, for all of Holy Scripture is in agreement, both Old and New Testaments. The doctrine which was contained in the law has been expounded to us so well by the apostles who came after Jesus Christ that we cannot say, we must do this or that, other than that which was commanded from the very beginning. Indeed, God has made so many things clear to us, and has given so many reasons [why we should believe it], that we would have to be perverse indeed not to be convinced of these truths by their very familiarity.

Therefore, if we are to profit from Holy Scripture, we must apply ourselves to study holiness of life, knowing that God will not be served according to our own ideas; but that he has given us a sure and sufficient rule by which we should regulate our lives, and one with which we cannot find fault. Let us, then, direct our every thought and the affections of our hearts towards that which is contained in Holy Scripture. Then the heavenly Judge will be pleased with us. We must pay all the more attention to these things, because we see that our good God draws near to us and has set out his will so plainly for us that we have no excuse, but must cling fast to him alone.

Chapter 10

Rules for ministers and all the faithful

'The one whom God has placed as leader and teacher in his house must be the best pupil of all, showing himself to be more ready and willing to receive doctrine and good instruction than all the rest.'

10.
Rules for ministers and all the faithful

'A bishop must be blameless, as a steward of God, not self-willed, not quick-tempered, not given to wine, not violent, not greedy for money, but hospitable, a lover of what is good, sober-minded, just, holy, self-controlled, holding fast the faithful word as he has been taught, that he may be able, by sound doctrine, both to exhort and convict those who contradict' (Titus 1:7-9).

Those who are called to preach the Word of God are shown in this passage what is their office or duty, so that they may be able to fulfil their responsibilities faithfully towards both God and his church. (This subject needs to be well understood, if we are to profit by this text.) All Christians, in general, also need to note what is required of a good minister, so that they may not choose men without due consideration, or from motives of favouritism or ambition, or as the fancy takes them, but they should have in view the collective profit and salvation of all the children of God. This principle ought also to be observed in relation to those who already hold the office [of minister], and they ought not to be allowed to continue in it unless they conduct themselves according to the instructions given by the Holy Spirit.

The minister's role as a watchman

Besides, since the qualities which St Paul mentions here are necessary for all ministers of the Word of God, [in their capacity] as those who must show the way to others, there is also a lesson here for all of us. For it would be unthinkable that the minister should conduct himself well and in a godly manner, while at the same time the people indulged in all kinds of wickedness and evil. Just as the minister must point out the way and set a good example, so also the whole body of the church ought to regulate their lives according to what is taught in this text. We see that those whom St Paul calls 'elders' in the verses preceding the text, he now calls 'bishops', which means watchmen, or overseers. He gives this name to all who are called to preach the Word of God.

It was an abuse and corruption in the popish church to call one man alone the chief bishop, for that changes what the Holy Spirit said and we are bound to regulate our language by the Scriptures. Thus we see that Satan works hard to turn us away from the pure simplicity of the Word of God. And besides, it is wrong and dishonouring to God for a man to depart from the order that God himself has established by his authority and that may not be broken.

All, therefore, whom God calls to preach his Word and who are appointed to that office must first be mature and have proved themselves as elders, and then they are to serve as watchmen. The prophet Ezekiel uses similar language when he compares them to those who keep watch from a tower (Ezek. 3:17). There is no question here of rank or putting on a brave show: it is a responsibility, and a very heavy one, to watch and take care of the flock, while others sleep. So we see that the title which the Holy Sprit gives to all shepherds shows plainly what it is that God calls them to do and the duty they have towards his church, so that men may not think they can be appointed to office in the church and at the same time devote themselves to rest and sleep and enjoying themselves. God does not choose those whom he appoints to be shepherds in his church because they look good, so to speak, but he binds them to his people. We cannot serve God except by devoting ourselves to the service of his flock, and the greatest honour that ministers of the Word can have is to be diligent in serving the faithful.

The church is the house of God

St Paul goes on to say that there is a good reason why those who serve as watchmen should be without blame, since they are those who rule in the house of God. For elsewhere he said to Timothy, 'Take heed how you conduct yourself in the church, because it is the house of God' (see 1 Tim. 3:14). God rules over it; he dwells there. Seeing that he has set you to rule on his behalf, you need to walk uprightly. He therefore saw the necessity of Timothy's walking uprightly. Is it a small matter to act as God's lieutenant, and to have this responsibility of governing his house? St Paul shows us in this place how carefully all those on whom God has conferred this honour of being ministers of his Word ought to conduct themselves.

On the other hand, we may take great comfort from the fact that God does us this remarkable honour of calling us into his house and admitting us as members of his family, and that he is pleased to dwell among us and is concerned for our nourishment and government. Therefore, when we realize that we are not separated from our God, and are not left to roam about aimlessly like stray dogs, but that he gathers us into his flock — and, indeed, that he is with us and will be with us till the end of the world, we ought to be moved to love him more earnestly and serve him better.

The church is called the house of God in order that we should magnify his inestimable goodness which he manifests when he is pleased to draw near to us and make his abode among the assembly of the faithful, and when he not only intends to join us to himself, but in the meantime makes provision for our salvation, nourishing and governing us as our Master and Overseer — and all this not for his own benefit, but with a view to our salvation. So we see that this text is not only for ministers of the Word, but that it is profitable for all the faithful, if they understand correctly how to apply it to themselves for their instruction.

The faults to be avoided

St Paul now tells us the qualities required of a good shepherd: he 'must be blameless' and 'not self-willed' — that is, opinionated and wanting his own way; he must not be 'quick-tempered', nor 'given to wine', nor 'greedy for money'. St Paul here lists the qualities required by citing the opposite — as if to say that the man who is given to wine, self-willed, contentious and greedy does nothing but infect the place where he is, and ruins the whole church. These faults are so serious that anyone who is defiled with them is not fit to serve God. These things must therefore be purged out from among us.

So then, the first qualification which St Paul requires in a man who is to preach the Word of God is that he must abstain from the faults which are condemned in this passage and must seek to get the better of them, so that nothing may prevent him from doing his duty. As it is the duty of a faithful minister to draw home those who have gone astray, so it is his duty also to keep in peace and unity those who are already in the church. Now if he is too self-opinionated, he will cause offence to the flock of God and disrupt the church. In order, therefore, that he may serve God and keep the church in peace and concord, he must stop being self-willed and must not place too great confidence in his own understanding.

When we teach others, we must also be willing to be taught. For if we are not willing to learn, and to profit [from instruction] so that we may be able to share with others what we have learned, we shall never be able to do our duty. Therefore, the one whom God has placed as leader and teacher in his house must be the best pupil of all, showing himself to be more ready and willing to receive doctrine and good instruction than all the rest. We must also be ready to listen when others give us advice, and willing to be put right and to acknowledge that theirs is the better opinion. Here we have St Paul's meaning in a few words: those who are called to preach the Word of God must take heed that they are not obstinate, but are willing to be taught. They must be of a meek and gentle spirit, seeking only to edify others; they are not to be so puffed up with pride that they think they know everything, but, on the contrary constantly desiring to learn and willing to be taught. In addition, they must be gentle in their behaviour. Indeed, we often see that those who are headstrong and self-willed are liable to cause division at every turn. They introduce sects into the church of God and make trouble for all. So it is not without good reason that St Paul corrects this high-handedness, for we see by experience that it is a great evil.

He goes on to say that the minister must not be 'quick-tempered'; this fault is closely related to the other. If a man is ruled by his passions and allows them to get the better of him, it will be a great hindrance to him in serving God.

Also, since drunkenness increases leads to greater arrogance in those who are prone to it, and is, as it were, a type of insanity, St Paul says that the minister of the Word must be sober, and 'not given to wine'. For if a man is ruled by drunkenness, he will be totally destitute of reason, impartiality and modesty.

So we see what deadly plagues, or errors, St Paul enumerates here, of which the ministers of the Word must beware. He then adds that they must not be 'violent', like soldiers or men who are always on the point of coming to blows, standing, as it were, with swords drawn. This fault must be corrected also.

Nor must they be covetous ['greedy for money']. For there is no doubt that the minister who seeks to enrich himself by holding office will play the charlatan. He will put a false gloss [i.e. a misleading interpretation] upon the Word of God; he will seek to please this man and to tell another what he wants to hear; in short, he will either disguise and falsify every part of it, or he will seek to present the matter in such a favourable light that he can go off on whatever tack he likes. He will seek out whatever is most to his own advantage and seek to bring grist to his mill, as the saying is. If ministers of the Word are motivated by covetousness, they will undoubtedly prove to be false teachers, whose chief study will be to pervert good doctrine and turn the truth into a lie.

The positive qualities required in ministers of the Word

Having begun by making the point that those who do their duty faithfully must edify the church of God and abstain from all crimes and flagrant faults — which are not to be tolerated in their calling — St Paul now turns to the positive qualities required in those who preach the Word of God.

They must be 'hospitable'; they must be kind towards strangers and receive them kindly. This should be observed at all times, but in the days of St Paul there was a particular reason why it was important: the poor Christians were like birds on the wing, compelled to take flight from place to place as persecution broke out. Some would get up and go to another town, or wherever they could find [refuge]. In fact, they were often compelled to risk their lives. We see, therefore, that great compassion was needed in those days; so there were good reasons why the apostle required the bishop [i.e., minister], who ought to be like a father to the church, to be liberal and hospitable to strangers, receiving them kindly.

Secondly, [those who are called to preach the Word of God] must be 'lovers of what is good'. This qualification is closely linked to the one just mentioned. The word Paul uses implies kindliness and love and a disposition to do good to those in need, and to apply oneself to the task of helping them. The one who is unkind and destitute of pity, and who is content to live at ease, never sparing a glance for the condition of others, will not show kindness and hospitality to those who are persecuted and afflicted. For this reason St Paul links these two virtues together.

Next he says that [ministers are to be] 'sober-minded, just, holy, self-controlled'. 'Sober-mindedness' refers to the man's way of life. 'Justice' means upright dealings with others, when a man is concerned to give everyone what is rightfully his due, and would rather die than that he should wrong anyone, or do any kind of violence or injury to anyone at all. This is what St Paul meant by the word 'justice'.

'Holiness' principally concerns our relationship to God; that is, not only must we do no harm to our neighbours, but we are to live in a chaste manner, devoting ourselves wholeheartedly to the service of God and taking especial care with regard to prayer and supplication and the worship of God. We must also learn to withdraw ourselves from the world, so that we are not given to vanities and outward show. We must not live a dissolute life, but humbly and in submission to the will of God.

Just as 'holiness' relates to God, so 'justice' relates to men, since this is the quality which ensures upright and fair dealings on the part of all towards others.

Finally, 'temperance' [or 'self-control'] includes whatever can be understood by the word 'sobriety'. It is not enough for us to be temperate in matters of food and drink; there must also be propriety and honesty in the rest of our lives; our hands, our eyes and ears, our mouths must all be put under restraint. This is what St Paul meant by 'temperance' — in other words, we are to conduct ourselves with propriety and to be characterized by stability; there must be nothing unseemly in our dealings with others, nothing improper about our actions; no frivolity which would make us seem to be lewd and dissolute in conduct; but we must be so governed by obedience to the will of God that others may be able to see that we have renounced the world.

Finally, Paul says that the preacher must '[hold] fast the faithful Word, as he has been taught'. This is the principal thing required of ministers of the gospel. They must not only be instructed in order to teach others, but they must be strong and steadfast in faith and ready if necessary to fight for the maintenance of the true doctrine, that it may be kept safe and sound. This is why St Paul uses a word which means to 'hold' or 'embrace'. We must hold fast the true doctrine, for if we have once taken a firm hold of it, it will never escape from us. Though the devil may strive as hard as he can to make us shake it off, we shall never be turned aside from it. The apostle then explains how we are to use it. We must exhort with wholesome doctrine and reprove those who speak against it, and so be able to teach those who are willing to obey God and who show themselves to be docile and teachable; and also we may have the means needed to fight against those who speak against the truth, against enemies of the Word of God, against rebels, against mockers, against those who go about creating confusion and disturbances in the church — we shall have the authority to reprove all such people, so that they may be compelled to retire from the combat in shame.

This teaching applies to all the faithful

Now, as we have already seen, St Paul wants the shepherds to give an example to all the faithful. Why should the ministers of the Word of God be modest, just and holy? Why should they be sober, 'not given to wine', nor to strife and blows? Why is there this need for propriety and stability in their lives? Firstly, so that the Word of God may not be brought into disrepute by people seeing disgraceful conduct in its ministers. Secondly, so that they may commend the doctrine by their godly lives, and thus reinforce the message in such a way that it may be received more readily. And thirdly, so that the people may follow their example and seek to cultivate all those virtues which they see in their shepherds.

St Paul's meaning was not, therefore, confined to ministers of the Word, when he exhorted them to avoid dissipation, dissolute behaviour, covetousness and pride, and to be kind, just, sober, chaste, and so forth. Using ministers as an example, he exhorted all Christians to conduct themselves in such a way that sober-mindedness, justice, holiness, modesty, and all the virtues mentioned in this passage may be qualities which characterize all of them in general. If we wish to be loyal children of God, let us see that we put right the faults which St Paul condemns in this passage, and seek to cultivate the good qualities which he lays down here.

Although the minister may be the one who rules in the house of God, every member has a duty to serve God faithfully. When God calls a certain number of persons to preach his Word, this does not mean that he ignores the rest and will not use them to serve him; on the contrary, he will use every one of us, without exception. This is the purpose for which God calls us to preach the gospel: so that we may all devote ourselves to his service. When he confers upon us the honour of receiving us into his house and adopting us as his children, he does not do this so that we should be idle; nor does he leave us unchecked, so that everyone is free to do just as he likes; but he will keep us in subjection to him and will have every one of us active in glorifying him. Since God is pleased to use us in his service, we must not be unprofitable. For it is not in vain that God has called us to such a high status and to the dignity of being, not merely members of his household, but included in the company and fellowship of his children.

Ministers of the gospel must, then, watch carefully their own behaviour, and, likewise, all Christians need to know that the instructions given in these verses concern them, and apply to all of them, from the greatest to the least. Let us therefore take care that we have a humble spirit and are sober, just and holy, and that we have ourselves so much in subjection that none of the sins which St Paul mentions may be prevalent among us.

Sins we must avoid

For example, drunkenness is a sin which is totally foreign to the nature of a Christian. When men become drunkards, they blot out not only the image of God, which was restored in us by our Lord Jesus Christ, but also all the decencies of life, and become no better than dogs or swine. If, then, we wish to be taken for the children of God, must we not shun this vice? This is why St Paul excludes all drunkards from the church. He will not have us associate with them, or frequent their company, in order that they may be ashamed and amend their lives; much less ought they to be admitted to the table of our Lord Jesus Christ.

Or again, are not pride and arrogance totally contrary to the spirit of meekness which is the true mark of the child of God? How will the world perceive that we have profited in the school of our Lord Jesus Christ if we are not humble, meek and holy? When high-handedness reigns in a person, it is a sign that he is too reliant on his own ideas and intelligence, and that he has never known what it was to learn in the school of God. It is evident that the qualities of which St Paul speaks in this text apply not only to ministers, but to the whole congregation.

The same may be said of covetousness, for we plainly see that by thinking too much about this world we forget the spiritual blessings and the inheritance to which we are called. What will become of us if we are ruled by covetousness and we become so caught up with the things of this world that we no longer think of the kingdom of heaven? Although we are constantly being warned against this sin, we are still so preoccupied with earthly cares, and so bound to the world, that we cannot raise our thoughts to set our sights on the heavenly life. It will always be true of us, as the scripture says, that where our treasure is, there our heart will be also (Matt. 6:21). Those who are devoted to the things of this world have their minds and affections so fixed upon them that they cannot aspire to the heavenly inheritance to which we are called.

Thus we see that covetousness is a deadly plague; it so blinds people that it deprives them of that which God has promised. Indeed, it is not without good reason that St Paul calls it 'a root of all kinds of evil' (1 Tim. 6:10), for it carries with it all kinds of wicked practices, deceit, treachery, unfaithfulness and cruelty; in short, there is no kind of wickedness that is not a result of covetousness. The person whose chief aim is what he can get forgets all about uprightness in his dealings, as if he were free to do what he liked. He will plunder and rob without restraint, and grab whatever he can get. He will openly mock God, since he is without fear or reverence, and in all his actions there will be nothing but wrongful and injurious treatment of others. We see how covetousness leads men even to murder and poison one another and to commit all kinds of wickedness. In short, it is a kind of madness that takes such a hold on men that they become like demons, when it has them in its grip. Covetousness, therefore, is an evil that is not only to be shunned by ministers of the Word, but every Christian must be on his guard against it.

Moreover, it is said that the children of God are to be, not only peaceable, but *peacemakers*. It is a mark by which our Lord Jesus Christ will have them to be known. He says, 'Blessed are the peacemakers, for they shall be called sons of God' (Matt. 5:9). Now if we are given to revenge and strife, if we love to quarrel, do we not show that the peace of God does not rule in our hearts, and that we have no part in him?

The need to show kindness and compassion

We must also see that we show kindness to strangers, when we know them to be bereft of all help and support, for it is disgraceful for a person to have no compassion or pity towards those who are destitute. Indeed, even among the heathen this was considered important and they had a very poor opinion of those who were not willing to receive those who had been thrown out of their homes. How much more, then, when we see the church of God persecuted by tyrants and enemies of the truth, should we not offer kindness and hospitality to poor Christians who have been forced into exile from their own countries? If we do not do so, is this not a token that we have renounced God? It is the will of God that we should be strangers in this world — indeed, we are his children on this condition (as we are told in Hebrews 11:9). God is in heaven, and yet he comes down here to us, and governs us, giving us an example of the pity that we ought to show to those who flee to us seeking refuge, when they are like poor sheep scattered by ravenous wolves.

St Paul was, therefore, speaking not only to ministers of the Word of God, but in their persons he gave us, as it were, a mirror by which we must all regulate our conduct. It follows that we must all be committed to doing good and to deeds of kindness. If we are so hard-hearted that we have no concern to help those who are in need, and if we are not moved with compassion when we see our neighbours suffer, it is certain that the love of God is not in us. If it is not our duty to help one another, it would have been necessary for God to create as many worlds as there are individual men and women, if he had intended each of us to be concerned only with himself, or to stay confined to his own little corner. But since God has made us to live together in fellowship with one another, each of us must conclude that he was not born for his own sake, and that he is not to live in this world for his own profit, but is to share with his neighbours and serve them. Woe to us if we do not have this attitude!

Let us, therefore, make certain that we are well-disposed to others and that, as far as we can, and as we have the means to do so, we do good to all, that we help those who have need of help and that we relieve their suffering, sharing what we have with them in such a way that our possessions are not ours alone, but that they benefit everyone, as far as this is within our ability. It is true that we cannot lay down precise laws in this case as, indeed, St Paul himself says only that we must go about it with an open and generous spirit. However, if we do not have this love and good will towards those who are in need, we demonstrate plainly that we are not God's children at all. Indeed, if we fail in this respect, we are going contrary to what nature itself would teach us even if we had no faith or religion, nor any knowledge of the Scriptures.

Other qualities which should characterize all Christians

We are also to be 'sober-minded' and 'self-controlled'. This teaches us that, if we are Christians, it is not enough to abstain from injuring others, from extortionate practices, wrong-doing, cruelty, theft, and so on, but we must also conduct ourselves with such propriety that we are not preoccupied with the things of this world, or with vain trifles, like those who seek only to show themselves off to advantage. Those who have their heads filled with such frivolities show plainly that the world still has too great an influence on them and that they are dissolute, seeking only to be ruled by their own appetites.

If, for example, people are intemperate in eating and drinking, they will also be dissolute in their whole life. Will those who make pigs of themselves in eating and getting drunk dare to say that they have received nourishment from the hand of God? Even the heathen know better than that, for nature itself teaches them, as we saw earlier. But we have received much fuller instruction, which should enable us to control our appetites a great deal better than they. We [are taught to] call upon God for our daily bread, and therefore we ought always to remember, when we eat and drink, that we receive all from his hands. If we abuse these good gifts by becoming gluttons and drunkards, are we not in danger of erasing the image of God in us and showing that we have become so attached to the things of the world that we have forgotten heaven? This is what we are to learn from this text.

Now when St Paul says that the bishops must be 'just' and 'holy', we must understand that every one of us is to be characterized by integrity and justice, giving to every person what is due to him. So we are not to be on the lookout for our own profit, but rather to note what is due to everyone, that we may do our duty. We must also see that we conduct ourselves in the sight of God in such a manner that we demonstrate that there is true holiness in us. Indeed there is nothing more plainly taught in all Scripture than that, in order that we should be separated from all the pollutions of this world, God shows us that holiness implies being brought up in his house and being, as it were, part of his household, under the government of his Holy Spirit. So, then, St Paul's intention in this passage is to lay down a rule which concerns all the faithful, and that no one may think himself exempt from it.

How may we attain to these virtues?

It remains now for us to know how we may attain to these virtues, and how we may overcome and eradicate such faults as are condemned here. Alas, it cannot be done by our free will, nor by any ability of ours, but God must work in us! How will he do this? We must be members of our Lord Jesus Christ. It is said that we must be sober-minded, just, holy and self-controlled. And how shall we become so? When the Holy Spirit rules in us, then we shall have these virtues. It is said that we must flee from drunkenness, intemperance, strife, disputes and pride. How shall we do this? By having the spirit of meekness, the spirit of humility, the spirit of wisdom and discretion and the spirit of the fear of God — all of which were given to our Lord Jesus Christ, in order that he might make those who believe in him partakers of them.

Therefore, seeing we are by nature intemperate, full of vanity, lies, ambition and pride, prone to unrighteousness, deceit and robbery; seeing we allow ourselves to be governed by our unruly passions; let us come and submit ourselves to the one who was appointed our Head, knowing that there is no other way for us to be kept in obedience to God and live in accordance with his will than to be united with our Lord Jesus Christ. For then we are strengthened by the outpouring of the Holy

Spirit, who is the fountain of all holiness, all righteousness and, in short, all perfection. This is the way by which we must come to the things which are commanded by St Paul in this passage; and this is the reason why we are taught that we are called to communion with our Lord Jesus Christ.

When the apostle seeks to give a brief definition of the gospel and of the right way of using it, he says that we are called to be partakers of our Lord Jesus Christ and to be made one with him so that we become part of his body, and that he dwells in us, so that we are joined together by an inseparable bond. This being the case, it follows that we are confirmed in this doctrine by the holy Supper which is set before us. When we come to this holy table, we must know that in it our Lord Jesus Christ makes his presence known to us, in order to confirm us in the unity which we have already received by the faith of the gospel; and that we are grafted into his body in such a manner that he dwells in us and we in him. We must therefore take pains to see that we profit by this holy union more and more, and that we cling more closely to the Son of God than we have done in the past.

This is why the holy Supper is so essential for us and why we observe it often — because we are earthly and fleshly while living in this world, and we need to be reminded often of what we have been taught, so that it may bear fruit in our lives. Let us, therefore, beware that we do not profane the grace which God manifests towards us when he confirms to us by this sign that we are indeed partakers of his Son, our Lord Jesus Christ. Let us pray to him to govern us by his Holy Spirit in such a manner that when we come to his holy table we may not pollute it. Instead we need to remind ourselves that we are poor, miserable creatures and to come to our Lord Jesus Christ to be cleansed from all that defiles us, for he is the fountain of all purity. We need to be cleansed, so that we are able to put off all our sins, and no longer be ruled by them, even though they still dwell within us. Instead we are to be ruled by the Holy Spirit in such a manner that the world may perceive that we are indeed united with [Christ] and drawn away from the things of this world to seek spiritual things. May we so fight against the vanities of the flesh and all our evil desires that we seek only to conform more and more to his image, so that we may truly be seen to be children of God and that our heavenly Father may be pleased to own us as those he has made heirs of the eternal inheritance.

Grace and its fruits

Selections from John Calvin on the Pastoral Epistles

Chapter 11

The good fight of faith

'I could wish that I were able to employ myself wholly in praising God joyfully and to be contented and at peace; that I were not troubled by men, but that all my senses were inclined to do well. This would be what I would wish for; yet God will try me, and my fiercest battles must be against my own natural inclinations.'

II.
The good fight of faith

'Fight the good fight of faith, lay hold on eternal life, to which you were also called and have confessed the good confession in the presence of many witnesses. I urge you in the sight of God who gives life to all things, and before Christ Jesus who witnessed the good confession before Pontius Pilate, that you keep this commandment without spot, blameless until our Lord Jesus Christ's appearing' (1 Tim. 6:12-14).

St Paul, in the verses preceding this text, has shown us the remedies for covetousness and the evils that come of it, and has exhorted us specifically to cultivate patience — and that not without good reason. For we are urged on to seek personal gain, because everyone wants to live an easy life. And when we are so set on getting ahead, Satan is bound to get a foothold among us and deceive us, causing us to go far out of the way. And so we shall often be tormented and will have many wrongs and injuries done to us; we shall be harassed by one and robbed by another — and if we are not armed with patience, how shall we stand firm? And how shall we ever possess such modesty and moderation that we shall not covet unlawful gain? But because the patience of the faithful covers so many things and has many aspects to it, St Paul expressed what he wanted to say in blunt terms: 'Fight the good fight of faith.' Faith, he implies, cannot survive without fighting. Anyone who desires that God should approve of his service must prepare himself for battle, for we have an enemy who never gives up.

Thus we see what St Paul is aiming at, which is that we should not think it strange that he spoke about patience. Everyone needs to realize that, since God has called us to his service, he will also exercise us by requiring us to fight. For God could easily hold Satan in check as with a bridle; he could quickly stop him so that we would have no temptations and that we could be left in peace to go on our way. But we know from experience that Satan has many ways to trouble us, and God gives him free rein and grants him permission to do this.

If we are Christians we must fight

It follows, then, that we must be good soldiers, or else we cannot be good Christians. It is true that St Paul need only have said this one word, 'fight'; but because it is so hard to put this teaching into practice, we need to examine it a little further, so that we can understand it better and remember it more often.

Faith, I say, is never without a fight. For if we resolve to do well and submit ourselves to God, the devil will throw many stumbling-blocks in our way to turn us aside. The world is so full of trickery that we are not able to take a single step without meeting up with a cunning person. We walk among thorns; those who ought to help us make progress pull us backward, for the devil uses the malice of those who live with us to fight against us. And when any man does us harm, he gives us occasion to reply in kind; or else we become downhearted, and angry, and we find that people prey on us, stripping the very wool off our backs when we are simply trying to walk aright and only seeking to do our duty.

And even though a Christian keeps himself under control, he must fight in order to stand steadfast in the faith. That is because there is nothing more contrary to our nature than to forgo these earthly things and not to be preoccupied by them, but to seek instead with all our hearts and souls the things that are unseen, which are completely hidden from our eyes and far beyond the reach of our senses. The faithful Christian must look higher than himself when there is any question of thinking about the kingdom of God and eternal life. And yet we know how our minds are inclined towards the things we have in our hands. How, then, is it possible for us to stand firm in the faith unless we resist and strive boldly against all our natural inclinations? And so, when we meet with these temptations and are stirred up to fight, let us take this doctrine of St Paul as our shield — namely, that faith is never without a fight, that we can never serve God without being soldiers. Why? Because we have enemies before us and we are surrounded on every side. And therefore we must get used to fighting, or else we shall be forced to surrender. Since this is so, that no one can serve God without exercising patience in the midst of the afflictions by which the children of God are afflicted, let us beware lest we renounce our faith, but let us still press on.

I could wish that I were able to employ myself wholly in praising God joyfully and to be contented and at peace; that I were not troubled by men, but that all my senses were inclined to do well. This would be what I would wish for; yet God will try me, and my fiercest battles must be against my own natural inclinations. And when the devil mounts many combats against me, when temptations come on all sides, I must beware lest I should be overcome; I must stand firm, and I must be strong and steadfast. And so I must not be weak in this situation, or I shall be in danger of renouncing my faith. And what a thing that would be — to forsake my faith, to which God has called me! So let us go on, and not think it strange that this life is full of so many assaults, and that we must withstand many enemies, and that we need from day to day to get more strength to submit to this situation in which God would place us. This is one point.

The fight is a good one

But St Paul alleviates the pain that the faithful might feel at learning that they have to fight all the days of their lives by adding that the fight is a 'good' one; as if to say that the outcome of our warfare is not in doubt, that, as he says elsewhere, we do not fight like those who beat the air (1 Cor. 9:26). We see how princes will, for the sake of their ambition, risk all that they have; they will place themselves in danger of being deprived of all their might and power. We see soldiers who, in order to take the wages of those who labour in their vineyards and in the fields, will put their own lives in danger. And what is it that prompts them to do it? A dubious hope, for there is no certainty of success. Indeed, even when they have achieved what they set out to do and have overcome their enemies, one can often ask, what profit has it brought to them? But when God calls us to the combat and to be soldiers fighting under his banner, it is not under any such circumstances, but we are assured that the outcome of the war will be good and blessed. Thus St Paul comforts the faithful by exhorting them, as God himself addresses himself to us, when he shows us not only what our duty is, but also that if we do what he commands us, it will have important consequences for our profit and salvation.

It is true that if we were wise, it would be sufficient for us to know the will of God. This is the point we must be convinced of: since God has appointed that this is the way through which we must pass, we are not to waste time in disputing it. But because we are so ungovernable, and on the other hand are unnecessarily squeamish and faint-hearted, so that a very small thing is enough to destroy our courage — which is so fragile that it is pitiful to behold — our Lord shows us (as I said before) that he tests our patience, that he lays a hard law upon us when he permits us to be grieved and tormented with many temptations; but he does it for our good, and the outcome will always be happy and blessed. Although for a time things may be painful, and we shy away from them, and if it were possible for us we would draw back and step aside — nevertheless, God shows that in the end he orders the evil in such a way that he causes it to turn to our profit and advantage.

The eternal reward God sets before us

And therefore we ought to weigh well this word that St Paul sets down here — that the war in which the children of God are engaged is a good one to those who fight in it. For when they fight, it is not a waste of time, because they are not doing something the outcome of which is uncertain. And he adds, moreover, for better confirmation of the matter, that the reward which God sets before our eyes is not wages of gold or silver, but eternal life. And (as I stated before) if men are so set on fire through vain ambition that they do not spare their own lives, what shall we do? What cowardliness is it, and how can it be excused, if any man spare himself, since God does not set before us any temporal wages, any piece of silver, any fleeting and breakable possessions, but gives us eternal life and shows that he wants only to have us to be his heirs, to be partakers of his glory and his immortality, to enjoy all his blessings and, indeed, God himself?

When God lifts us up so high, are we not worse than lumps of wood or blocks of stone if all the sinews of our being do not strive to engage in this fight, the reward of which is so great and inestimable? Therefore we must be convinced of these three points which St Paul sets down here. The first is that faith cannot exist without facing many assaults, and that the life of God's children in this world is a warfare. The second is that we must not be grieved if God tests us, for we do not fight an uncertain battle — we are in no danger of irrevocably losing our lives, nor of being deprived of the spoils and honours of battle. No, the issue of our warfare will be a blessed one, because God reigns over us; it is he who calls us, and he will not permit our fight to be a waste of our time. And the third point is that God is not content with rewarding us in this world, but sets before us something far more excellent, namely, the inheritance of the kingdom of heaven.

So then, since God will have us pass through this world to come to him and to enjoy for ever his glory and everlasting bliss, which he purchased for us at so great a cost by the blood of our Lord Jesus Christ, is there not good reason for every one of us to apply himself wholly to this? And are we not then held back in this world, and by those things which are seen? When we compare the heavenly life with whatever can be desired in this world — honours, riches, goods, pleasures, and whatever else men seek after — even though we might like such things, are they not like refuse and rubbish in comparison with God's glory? For it is not just a question of God showing himself a Father to us in this world and making us feel his grace by giving us some fleeting blessings; but of making us partakers of his nature, as St Peter says (2 Peter 1:4), and of our being joined to him so that he is one with us. Is this not a privilege that surpasses all?

God's calling enables us to persevere

Now as a fourth point St Paul adds the phrase, 'to which you were also called'. This means, first of all, a confirmation of what he has just said: 'Lay hold on eternal life.' For it is not in men to attain to the kingdom of heaven, or to win it in battle. Are we valiant enough to do it? If we should turn all our efforts in that direction, all our energies and wisdom would serve to no purpose. But when our God calls us to it we may go on, for we have a good warrant for doing so; our confidence is not grounded upon any hope which we have foolishly dreamed up in our own brains, or upon any promise made by a mortal man, or upon any appearance that we see with our eyes. For all these things may deceive us, and we know what becomes of those who rely upon them. But when our Lord has reached out his hand to us, we may walk on boldly, for we shall know that we have not run in vain. This should be a great comfort to us, and should prevent us from being sidetracked, whatever should happen to us. When we feel that the whole world is in a hurly-burly, let us look to the calling of our God. Thus we see that St Paul's meaning was to confirm this doctrine when he said that Timothy was called to eternal life.

Now, what he says to one man pertains generally to all. For (as we said before) it is not he who is responsible for bringing us to the way of salvation, but it is God who must guide us to it. And again, we see by this that men do not obtain salvation by their own industry, but the whole of it proceeds from the free goodness of God. And therefore, no one may take occasion from this to magnify his own merits and to say that we can do something, that it is up to us to put ourselves forward in order to obtain everlasting life. St Paul sets a bar against all these foolish dreams, saying that we lay hold of everlasting life because God has called us to it.

It is true that we must take pains and strive as hard as we can — or even beyond our ability, if that were possible — but still, as St Paul says, it is neither of him who wills, nor of him who runs, but of God who shows mercy (Rom. 9:16). It is not on account of our good will, or our running, that we obtain eternal life, for we are not only slothful and unprofitable as far as all goodness is concerned, but we are apt to go in totally the opposite direction, until God has inclined us to run and has set us in the right way. If men follow their nature, what will they do? They are obsessed with wickedness, like pots bubbling over with it, inasmuch as they do not have a single thought that does not fight against God. As for any goodness, I guarantee that we shall never even think of such a thing, for we are incapable of even so much as one thought of doing good, as St Paul says (2 Cor. 3:5). And therefore it is God who prepares us and gives us the inclination to run, and who shows us the way. Even when he has done so much, still this is not enough. For we are prone to come to a halt midway and to fall down frequently, and we even turn aside out of the way. Therefore God supplies what we lack and makes his calling sure in us, strengthening it by the very same grace which gave rise to it in the first place.

God was not moved to give us hope of our salvation on account of any goodness that he saw in us, but because it pleased him out of his mere mercy; so also when he goes on guiding us until we come to the haven of salvation, he does this too because it pleases him. This is the cause of the free calling of our God that comes to us continually; so that men are put in their place here and have no grounds for rejoicing when they hear it said that we work out own our salvation (Phil. 2:12). God will not have us to be idle; nevertheless, our working must be with fear and trembling. And why is that? Because it is God who works in us, giving us both the desire and the end result, and all according to his good pleasure. Let us do the best we can, but do so without presumption or pride. Let us not think of doing well in order to gain merit, or because we are worthy of being exalted against God, for in this way the grace of God would be cast into obscurity and reduced to nothing. Therefore let us beware of such idle dreams, and let us not do as the papists who, whenever anything is said about doing good, immediately start to talk about their free will and their merits. But when we are commanded to act and to strive, we know that our strength comes from another source, the Spirit of God.

We must know that there is neither wisdom nor discretion in us unless God first guides us to it, and when he has begun his work in us he must perfect it and supply all that we lack by reason of our infirmities. If we know this, let us see that we always hate sin and walk warily, and let us call upon the one who once had mercy on us, asking him that he will continue to do so, for otherwise we would surely stumble at every moment. When we manifest such humility, God is glorified as he deserves. And yet, the faithful are not to be like lumps of wood. They are to work, but in such a way that they always know that it is the Lord who works in them. They are to do their best, but they will know that their strength comes from heaven and not from themselves. And in the end they will know that in laying hold on eternal life they have neither strength nor hard work to boast of, but that they owe all to the goodness of God, which has accompanied them throughout their lives.

We must lay hold on eternal life

This, in a few words, is what we have to note at this point. And now we have to observe, moreover, that we are guilty of gross ingratitude if we forsake God's calling. When we consider that our Lord has shown regard for us — us, I say, who are miserable earthworms — to choose us to be numbered among his children, that he has prepared a heavenly inheritance for us, and has given us hope and assurance — if, when all this is so, we despise it and are held back by the world and led away with the fleeting things it offers, so that we are turned away from and deprived of such a blessing by our own irrational stupidity, what excuse is there for us?

And yet we see how the world goes on, for we need no other witness to accuse us and make the case against us. If every one of us claims to be a Christian, to what do we owe that title, but to the fact that God has revealed himself as our Father? And if we are his children, to what does he call us? To eternal life. And we must lay hold on it. But how shall we do that, except by the means that I have already spoken of? We cannot come to the place which God has appointed for us without conflict. And therefore when men see that we are held back by fleeting things, and that the least thing in the world will turn us aside; that there is nothing as easily broken as we are; that as soon as Satan whispers in our ear, we are carried very far away; and when, instead of turning back to the right way, the world sees that every one of us is devoted to these worthless things — what will people say? Does not the world see that we place little value on eternal life, on such a treasure, and even on the eternal nature of God? It is not in vain that Scripture tells us to awake out of sleep and not to slumber as we do.

Moreover, because people are grieved by the passing of time, and though they began by having some zeal, yet when they have to begin all over again, they become sluggish and cold — therefore St Paul says plainly, 'Lay hold'; he tells us, 'You are to come to this point.' And he expresses himself even more clearly in another place, where he says that he himself has not yet attained that to which he aspired (Phil. 3:12). He sets himself up as an example, saying, 'My brethren, though I have taken great pains, yet I have not yet achieved my goal. I must therefore strive harder; I must continue to press on, and not look back to what is behind me.'

Now if St Paul needed to stir himself up in this way, what must *we* do, I ask you? Must not a man, when he has with difficulty limped a short distance on one foot, look at the ground he still has to cover? If St Paul, who had completed a good part of the distance he had to cover and had run so valiantly, nevertheless needed to stir himself up and to exert himself, must not the one who has done no more than come out of the door and gone only a very short distance pay a great deal more attention to himself, and invest all his labours and pains in obtaining what God has set before him? St Paul says specifically that we must not look back at what is behind us. Why not? Because we always want to bargain with God, saying such things as, 'I have done this; I have done that. Haven't I done enough?' Indeed? Is that what you think? On what condition has God called us to his service? Is it to perform one or two deeds, and then does he give everyone leave to rest? No, no! Rather it is that we should dedicate ourselves to him, to live and die for him, and to be his for good and all. Therefore let us beware that we do not use anything that we have done as an excuse to say, 'I have fought; I have taken great pains; isn't that enough?' And must not others run their course? We must not think of these things which are liable to make us slack, but must see what ground remains to be covered and must go on to do what we are commanded to do — otherwise, let us think that we have done nothing. For it would be better for us never to have begun than to faint in the midst of the way.

Our responsibility is greater because others are watching us

Moreover, St Paul adds — continuing with his subject — that Timothy had 'confessed the good confession in the presence of many witnesses'. By these words he meant to encourage him all the more to stand firm in this combat of faith. For (as we have already said) it is a great shame for a man to begin well and afterwards to fall away and shake off all restraint, and for the world to see him totally changed. For people will not marvel at seeing one who never gave any hope [of better things] continuing to do evil and always being a prodigal. They will say, 'Well! Well! That poor man did not know God, or everlasting life. He never knew the meaning of either virtue or honesty — he is a miserable wretch.' That is what the world will say, and how they will speak. 'He is a drunkard, he is a thoroughly immoral person, he is a bad man; he has always been like that — he is dishonest through and through.'

But when a man has made a show of serving God, when he has employed himself faithfully, has been a model of honesty, has set a good example and has edified many people — if afterwards he shows himself under completely different colours and becomes wicked and profane, and if the world sees him to be a totally different man from what he was before, they will regard him as a monster; everyone will hold him in abhorrence. And for this reason St Paul tells Timothy that he had 'confessed the good confession in the presence of many witnesses'. By this we are warned that when God has been good to us, to make us walk uprightly as we ought, we are under a much greater responsibility and obligation, knowing that it is not lawful for us to veer off course, but that we must all the more take heart for what is to come.

There are a great number who think they have paid for the offences which they have committed when they can allege how valiant they have been in times past. We know that even those who never did anything of worth in their lives, except to be seen and to make a show, have had a certain appearance of goodness. And soon afterwards they give themselves up to lewdness and act like demons, yet always want to be regarded as angels. 'What? I have done this! I have done that!' they will say. In short, they will chronicle their doings, which in fact are worth nothing. But let us suppose for the moment that they are like angels of paradise. Then their shame will be all the greater, and there will be even less excuse for them, and so much the greater will be their discomfiture in the sight of God and his children. And why is this? Did not their earlier actions testify that they knew they ought to fear God? And if it grieved them to do so, and if they have become lewd, will any other reason be needed to condemn them? Will not their former life answer that they are no longer sinning through ignorance, that they can have no cloak for their actions but that of malice, since they have become like devils and have fallen away from God and cast off his yoke, which called for their obedience?

And so let us note well this warning that is given us here that when God has bestowed on us a good state of life and we have set our neighbours an example in goodness, we are bound so much the more to stand firm and continue. For if we fall, the offence will be double, and because God has revealed himself to us, we may not pretend ignorance, since he has thus examined us in all kinds of ways. Therefore our fault will be so much the greater if we do not persevere in our course after God has once reached out his hand to us.

And we must note that when St Paul speaks here of the good confession that Timothy has made, he means not only the confession of the mouth, but the testimony of his life; for indeed that is the proof and witness we must give of our faith and of the hope that we have of eternal salvation. If we only talk, it will be sheer hypocrisy. But when a man so conducts himself that the world may know that he is really telling the truth when he claims that he serves God and holds the doctrine, this is a good matter and very sure. Therefore Timothy is praised here by St Paul because he has conducted himself well in his office and calling, so that men might see that he did not serve God like a hypocrite, but that he preached the gospel as being sure that it was the pure and undoubted truth which is the basis of man's salvation. And because he made such a confession, he is commended, but on this condition, that he must persevere.

Also the apostle specifically says that [this confession was made] 'in the presence of many witnesses' — as if to say that

God had set him up on a platform for all to see. In other words, if a man were not known and his life had, as it were, been hidden — if he happened to do something amiss, it would not do so much harm as it would if he had been highly esteemed among the faithful, and had been regarded as a pillar of the church. But if such a man should come to nothing, his fall will be great. If a small bit of the house should fall down, that is of no importance — the house will remain standing well enough; but if any of the principal parts of the structure should fall, the whole house will come down. So it is with those whom God has raised aloft, who are placed where everyone can see them: if they indulge in licentious behaviour, they cause the downfall of a great number of people, and therefore their condemnation is all the more grievous.

Therefore, let us be clear about this, that if God has been good to us in causing us to give light to others, let us know that we shall be placed in the limelight; that is to say, that if we have done evil by going out of the right way, we shall have more witnesses crying out to God for vengeance against us. Look how many we have edified before; we will have that many voices to convict and condemn us. And therefore, seeing that it is so, when any of us has made a good beginning and has walked in a way that was becoming to him, let him be all the more careful to go on running his race, right to the end. For it is far from being the case that, if we have done well for a time that should cause us to grow cold; rather, our former life should act as a spur to encourage us forward, to acknowledge daily the graces that God has bestowed upon us. And when we have made good use of them, this ought to stir us up to well-doing, knowing that God fashions us for himself, and that since he has fashioned us so well, we must be an example to others. It is especially important that those who are highly regarded in the church and have many eyes upon them should not demolish what they have built; otherwise they will have a terrible vengeance of God fall upon them, if they turn away from the goodness that God has done them, and make the grace which they had received to be of no effect.

And though every minister ought to apply this teaching to his own case, nevertheless it also has a general application to us all. For it is said, on the one hand, that the ministers of the Word are like burning lamps, the light of the world (Matt. 5:14). But St Paul also speaks generally to all Christians, saying that they hold a burning lamp when they have the knowledge of the gospel. Therefore we must walk through the darkness of the world knowing that God has raised us upon a platform, as it were, so that we can be seen afar off. Therefore let us beware that we do not turn out of the way, when we have the way made plain before us and when God guides and governs us. Let us, I say, be so much the more careful that we are not the cause of misleading others who, by our example, might be led to do good.

We are to fix our eyes upon Christ

And because men's confession is not sufficient unless it is grounded on something better, St Paul, in order to conclude the matter, brings Timothy and, in his person, all the faithful, to fix their gaze upon our Lord Jesus Christ and the confession he made under Pontius Pilate. It is true (as I said before) that the one who has made a good confession will be all the better disposed for the time to come; and when God has begun a good work in us, that must encourage us to go on to perfection. Yet we must go higher: we must know that the Son of God has led the way, and that we only follow him, and that we are partakers of the confession that he made before Pontius Pilate. It is this that may give us a great deal more courage. And so St Paul says that he enjoins Timothy, 'in the sight of God, who gives life to all things, and before Christ Jesus who witnessed the good confession before Pontius Pilate', to go on and finish the course.

But to make this doctrine more profitable to us, we must observe that St Paul had good reason to express himself with such vehemence, because he knew how hard a matter it is. It is true that he is speaking here to all the faithful. But however that may be, Timothy is also included in it. Even though in the sight of God he has witnessed with zeal and confidence that he has done his duty as well as possible, yet, nevertheless, he still needs to be exhorted; so St Paul, besides the warning he gives him, calls on him to appear before God, sets Jesus Christ before his eyes and gives him a strict charge. Why does he do this? It is certain that if it had been an easy matter, and one that did not need to be insisted on, St Paul would have been content to have said in a few words, 'Look to your duty; you must conduct yourself faithfully, knowing whom you serve. And therefore be of good courage.'

But when he says to him, 'God is your Judge; you must give an account before his throne and before the seat of his majesty,' he means, 'I summon you to appear before our Lord Jesus Christ, who is appointed as our Judge, and if you do not do your duty to stand firm, I may protest that I showed you what was required, and you did not measure up to it.' Let us note well, I say, that if we desire to be used in God's service, we must not do it casually, nor think we have done with it when we have done our best.

And therefore we have to pray to God that it would please him to strengthen us and so enable us that, though no man is sufficient and able to serve God as he should, we may, nevertheless, have some measure of success in it, with his help and assistance. Thus the faithful are first of all warned to fly to him who is able to make them capable, seeing that by nature they are incapable. And if this is requisite for all Christians without exception, what should we say about ministers of the Word of God, who have a far higher, and consequently a much harder, responsibility? Must they not take very good heed to themselves? And yet, we do not need to be troubled by the difficulty of it. We see a great number of people whose hearts fail them when they consider what they have to do — especially if it is too heavy for them to perform and go through with. 'Say, is it possible that I can do this?' [they say]. 'I feel myself to be weak. I see that this is a great burden, a burden that I am not able to bear.' No, we are not to be like that! Seeing that St Paul, while naming things that surpass the strength of men, nevertheless continues to exhort us to do them, we must know that we shall not be able to claim by way of excuse that we were dismayed and overwhelmed when we saw that we were not able and fit to carry out the charge that God laid upon our shoulders — for God well knows what we can do: nothing at all! But he will not leave us wanting, nor will he ever fail us, if we walk humbly and submit ourselves wholly into his hands.

It is God who gives life

This is what we have to note. And because these things might discourage us, if we would look beyond this world let us also note well the circumstance which St Paul adds by way of conclusion on this point, which is that God 'gives life to all things'. For he shows us by this, although it seems that we are poor and miserable wretches; that our condition is accursed; that as touching the world we are despised and reviled; that men mock at us; that they stick out their tongues at us; that others torment us; that we are regarded as castaways — yet, in spite of all these things, we must not faint, for God gives us life.

Therefore, let us fix our gaze upon that life which God keeps hidden with himself, and which he opened to us when he revealed it by his Holy Spirit and gave a good witness of it in his gospel. So then, when the world has conspired a hundred thousand times to kill us, and when we are taken for condemned persons and are reviled, let us go on, for our life does not consist only of what we see here below. It does not depend on men, nor on their reputation or standing. Let us not think so, but let us surmount all the troubles that the devil casts in our way to make us faint-hearted, considering that it is God who gives life to all things. He holds our life in his hand; he will keep it safely and securely, and it is his pleasure that we should submit ourselves to him and be content to do so, knowing that he will not deceive us in that which he has promised us.

This is what St Paul is implying here. It is true that he will deal with the subject in more detail later; but this is, in a few words, what we are to take away with us, so that whenever we find ourselves tossed up and down with the temptations of this world, and with all the troubles that may befall us, we may know that God has not called us to himself in vain, and therefore we must be *always* his. And if we are conscious of many infirmities that incite us to improper conduct, and if we see the unthankfulness and malice of men on the one hand, and it seems, on the other hand, that we profit nothing by well-doing and that all our labour is wasted, we must still (as I said earlier), strive and endeavour to fix our eyes upon God. And then, do we find ourselves held fast and our way blocked, as it were? If so, let us nevertheless climb over such barriers. Even though there may seem to be great mountains [in our path], yet we must have wings, as it were, to fly where we cannot pass, and the faith and hope that we have in God will serve us for that, if we understand the power which he possesses, and which he reserves as his proper office, which is to give life.

Now God does not give life to anything except what seems to be dead. Accordingly, when we walk as we ought, and as we are called, it is inevitable that we shall seem to have been cast away in the eyes of the world, and that death itself will threaten us and surround us on every side. Otherwise, God would not do what he claims in this place, namely, to give us life. But in the midst of death we may hope for life, knowing that no one can molest us when the invincible power of God is for us, and that those who now trouble us will ultimately be confounded, and God will cause us in the end to triumph with our Lord Jesus Christ.

Grace and its fruits

Selections from John Calvin on the Pastoral Epistles

Chapter 12

A crown of righteousness

'Let us persevere ... knowing that God has not enlisted us for a short time only, but to live and die in his service. They who are not resolved ... to live and die setting forth the glory of God do not know what it is to fight.'

12.
A crown of righteousness

'I have fought the good fight, I have finished the race, I have kept the faith. Finally, there is laid up for me the crown of right-eousness, which the Lord, the righteous Judge, will give to me on that Day, and not to me only but also to all who have loved his appearing' (2 Tim. 4:7-8).

When anyone sets us a good example, and we know that he possesses good qualities that no one can find fault with, the very fact of seeing that person does us much good. And we know that the presence of one man, either in a town or even in a country, can do so much good that things are conducted well and in an orderly manner, and that God causes the grace of his Holy Spirit to do good when he distributes [such blessings] to certain ones. And therefore St Paul, in this passage, realizing that his absence might be harmful to some folk, shows that he has finished the race and that others must not faint when they are only part-way through, but must rather press on, knowing that they have done nothing if they do not keep going to the end as he did.

Thus St Paul continued to strive all the days of his life, and his example was a great encouragement and support to a great number of people. When he is about to depart out of this world, he sees that some might go astray, and so he deals with this danger [which he sees]. He says that as they have seen him persevere on his course, and never grow weary until he came to the end of it, so they must do the same and not lose heart until they come to the place to which God calls them.

An illustration from the sports arena

But so that we may grasp more clearly the teaching that is contained in this passage, let us observe that he uses an illustration taken from the contests that were held in those days, of wrestling or some other sport. For in the same way as contests are held in shooting or archery in order to win a prize, so in those days they would hold fights and also there was racing, both on foot and on horseback, and especially in chariots.

Now, St Paul clearly says, first of all, that he has 'fought the good fight'. This means that when he came to offer his services and to show what desire he had to serve God, he devoted himself wholly to this end. He means, moreover, that he was not disappointed in what he undertook, because his combat had a blessed outcome. But in order that we might know that it was not one single confrontation, he adds another image taken from racing, as if to say, 'I have not only taken up my weapons to test my strength, but I have stood firm and continued steadily in the course that was appointed for me.' Now, the racetrack was measured out as it is for competitive sports today: there was so much length and so much breadth. For those who ran on foot, there were a certain number of paces that had to be run, and when they had run the distance, the first to arrive at the finishing-line presented himself and was commended as the most valiant. It was the same with the chariots.

It is not without good reason that St Paul brings us such comparisons. They were, to be sure, exercises full of vanity and folly; yet they should make us all the more ashamed if we are slow to run or to fight when God calls us and presides over the race, to watch us, and promises us a reward of inestimable value. Therefore, if we are idle, or are loath to keep at it, or if we drop out midway, will there be any excuse for us?

He speaks in the same way to the Corinthians. In these contests, he says, in which men put themselves through immeasurable agony, what do they hope for? A crown of leaves, and nothing else. A crown of leaves was considered a great prize. But we have a far better reward; our Lord calls us to the inheritance of the kingdom of heaven. He will make us partakers of his immortality and of his glory; and yet we will not condescend to put one foot forward, or to move an arm, without making a great fuss about it. Do we not show that we give little honour to God, that we put little faith in his promises and, in short, that we are utterly unfaithful?

In those days, when they were preparing to fight, they would eat nothing but dry biscuit, and even then, they dared not eat half their fill. These poor fools, says St Paul (for he uses plain words), for a little worldly praise — so that men should say of them, 'He is a nimble fellow,' or 'He wrestles well' — only for this small commendation they were willing to fast and risk their lives. They pined away all their lives; they dared not eat even a piece of brown bread, or drink their fill, even of water; they abstained from all fancy meats, they kept to a remarkably strict diet, as if they had another life in reserve — and all this was done only for the sake of gaining a little recognition and to have people clap their hands and say, 'Wow! There is a noble lad! He is worthy of a dozen leaves. He has fought manfully; he will be crowned.'

Now see here: our God calls us, not only to receive a word of commendation in this world, but having chosen us for himself, he shows us that our reward is ready. We shall not miss the crown of glory, and we can expect the angels of paradise to clap their hands at us. In a word, the saints of old, the prophets, apostles and martyrs will welcome us on the last day. Ought not this to encourage us to walk faithfully and fight constantly to the end?

This is the reason why St Paul uses such imagery here, when he says that he had fought a good fight. It is as if he had said, 'As for those who labour for worldly ambition, or for covetousness, or for any reason whatever, let them please themselves and boast of their victories as much as they wish; but as for me, I am content when I serve my God. I shall not lose ground by a single foot without his notice. The angels of paradise rejoice because I have been an instrument to fulfil in God's name the task which he committed to me for the advancement of the kingdom of his Son. And I have good reason to rejoice in this.'

And again, looking at the second illustration, let us observe that St Paul says — not without good reason — that he has finished his course; for we shall see a number who would like to quit when they have performed a single action. They think that God should dismiss them, so that they might take their ease for the rest of their lives. St Paul shows, however, that we have done nothing if we do not persevere to the end.

God's judgement is what counts

But at the same time we must note the circumstances in which the apostle found himself. He was in prison; he expected to face execution, and his death was likely to be shameful and ignominious, as the world viewed it. The unbelievers were ready to slander him and spoke all the evil they could against him. The Jews considered him a backslider; and a number of false Christians spread many false tales about him throughout the churches — the whole world was his deadly enemy. In such circumstances a man might be tempted to think that he had spent his time very badly in fighting as he had. For he might have achieved great honours as a learned teacher; he might have sat in the highest place and judged others and got great renown and credit. Or he might have had the name of a holy man in Jerusalem, for there was none whose life was so honourable as his. He might have been rich and welcomed everywhere he went.

Who would not have said that he was a real fool and a complete idiot to go and plunge himself into shame and disgrace and throw away his reputation, to stir up the rage of the whole world against him — that of his own nation and that of other people who knew him — and then in the end to see himself face such a shameful death? Who would not have said that it would have been better for him to have chosen an easier way? But St Paul despised and defied all the judgements of the world. Why was that? Because the one who judges him is in heaven. He was content to be absolved in that way, even though all the world should condemn him. For punishments and death are inflicted on evildoers as well as on the martyrs; there is nothing but the cause that distinguishes them. Therefore, when we see a martyr burned and a thief suffering the same fate, as far as the kind of death is concerned they are the same. But if we examine the cause, the thief suffers for his evil deeds and offences; the martyr, on the other hand, has a witness in himself and, indeed, is able to show to all the world that he has walked uprightly, and that he suffers for God's name.

St Paul accordingly defies here all the judgements of the unbelievers, and does not care in the slightest that he is considered of no account by the world, so long as the heavenly Judge is pleased with him.

The apostle has set us an example to follow

But let us note well that we too must walk uprightly and suffer for the sake of the gospel, if we are to boast as St Paul did. For often it is the most wicked men who are the boldest, and we see that those who deserved to be hanged a hundred times will be loud in condemnation of their judges. We see such things. But we must come to the main point, which is that a person may always declare in the presence of God and his angels that he has walked uprightly, and has showed it in his deeds. If people want to sit in judgement on his life, they will find there such uprightness that all who have their eyes open may bear witness with him that he is suffering wrongfully. Now, St Paul had these two things, and so had all the prophets, and all who ever suffered for the witness of the gospel. And therefore he might say with good reason that he had fought a good fight.

So, then, according to the warning St Paul gives us here, let us beware that we do not suffer for our sins, for murder, or immorality, or theft, or treason, or sedition, or any other wickedness. But when the truth of God is maintained, God bestows honour upon us by making us the defenders of his cause and making a spectacle of us in order to triumph [over his enemies] and to reveal the invincible power of his Holy Spirit in those who follow his Word and cleave to it. Therefore, when God is pleased to employ us for the testimony of his name and to be glorified in us, let us go on boldly and not think our efforts wasted, even though the world may mock at our simplicity and though unbelievers should spit in our faces and detest us. Let us value so highly being in God's favour that we may rise above and, like St Paul, withstand whatever might be done or said to us when we suffer for the truth.

Indeed, we see how he stood up to the Corinthians: though they called themselves faithful and thought highly of themselves, he mocked at their lack of judgement when he saw them boastful and drunk with pride, thinking their wisdom entitled them to sit in judgement on the gospel (1 Cor. 4:5). 'Well,' says the apostle, 'I submit to you that your judgements are formed now in darkness, but the day of the Lord will come, and then matters will be revealed.' If the apostle issued such a challenge to those who through hypocrisy boasted about the name of Jesus Christ, what must we do when faced with the mortal enemies of our salvation — against those who set themselves up, in a great rage and with fanaticism, against the Son of God and openly speak against the religion which we maintain? Shall we be shaken when we must suffer at the hands of these tyrants? Let us learn by the example of St Paul to lift up our eyes on high, so that we may continue to press on when the world casts us off and when we suffer many troubles and are reviled and slandered for well-doing.

Our eyes must be fixed on God

Let us lift up our eyes on high, for otherwise we shall be like reeds shaken by every wind; but if we can once fix our sight upon God, we shall be made firm. The apostle uses that word speaking of Moses: he was enabled to endure, he says, in the face of all danger, after he fixed his eyes upon God (Heb. 11:27). He meant that Moses showed himself as a rock withstanding the waves. What temptations he faced when he was brought up in the king's court! As the adopted son of the king's daughter, he might have been regarded as heir to the crown. Yet he chose instead the reproach of Jesus Christ and fought a hard and difficult fight. He remained a great while in a strange country, all the while fearing for his life. And at length he had to come and challenge the king; he had to hear threats and suffer reviling and taunts. He could not fail to be made firm under such circumstances.

We must do the same. And the apostle shows us the way — namely, that if we can look God in the face, we shall remain constant and never be defeated. Though the devil may do all he can to overturn our faith, he will never accomplish his purpose. We shall regard ourselves as happy while we fight under our Lord Jesus Christ's standard, even though we cannot do so without being mocked and despised by the world when we are committed wholly and fully to God. Despite all, we must be armed for continuing the fight and sticking with it. For if we merely take up arms, what is the good of that? Let us persevere, then, knowing that God has not enlisted us for a short time only, but to live and die in his service. They who are not resolved and disposed both to live and die setting forth the glory of God do not know what it is to fight.

God calls us to persevere

First of all then, we must realize that when God calls us, it is to the end that we should be dedicated to him, not to be active in service and to make an offering to him for one day only, but to continue to do so all the days of our life. Though we may languish, though we may seem to be perishing in our miseries, let us, nevertheless, stick at it. And when the time of our death approaches, we must know that it is the time for us to be more courageous in exerting ourselves, as mariners do when they draw near to the shore. Though they were weary before, yet they rejoice at the mere sight of the haven, for they think, 'Come now, within two or three hours we shall be able to rest and eat our fill.'

When we see these poor men, who are completely exhausted and utterly wasted and broken, take heart only because they have seen the haven, what must we do when we draw near to our finishing-line and can look back and see that while we were running God always held us fast by the hand, and that though we stumbled many times — yes, and sometimes even fell — our God rescued us and lifted us up before we came to grief? Must we not strive earnestly to come to God and to draw all the closer to him? This, then, is what we need to learn from this phrase: 'I have finished the race.'

We must keep the faith with a good conscience

He then goes on to declare how our fight shall be brought to a happy outcome — namely, by keeping the faith. It is true that this word 'faith' may be taken to mean 'fidelity', as if he meant that he was faithful to our Lord Jesus Christ and never gave up, but always did what his office required. But we may also understand 'faith' in its usual sense; in other words, St Paul did not fall away from the pure simplicity of the gospel, but rested himself upon the promises of salvation which were given to him, and in his preaching to others he showed that he spoke the truth. For, indeed, all the faithfulness that God requires of us proceeds from this, that we are to be fully rooted in his Word, holding firmly to it and so well-grounded in it that we shall not be moved by any storm or tempest that may arise.

Therefore, let us note when we have fought well, that if we desire to see a good end to all our conflicts, we must keep the faith. Now, as we have seen before, a good conscience is, as it were, the place where faith dwells. Those who give themselves to wickedness — those mockers of God who have no reverence for the gospel (no more than they have for — I cannot tell what) — fully deserve that God should throw them overboard, and that their fall should not only be fatal, but fearful and terrible. This is why he says that they are plunged, as it were, into the depths of the sea, like a ship that is sunk and lost.

Those, therefore, who do not keep the faith in a good conscience are sunk beneath the waves, and God will have them perish in this accursed manner, in order to show how highly he values the teaching of the gospel. When he pours out such vengeance upon them, this indicates that he will not have men scoff at the doctrine of salvation.

Let us therefore note well that we must have this uprightness and a good conscience, walking in the fear of God and holding fast the promises of his goodness and grace, or else we shall never be determined to keep right on to the end of the race. Let us, then, hold fast a good conscience, so that we may keep our faith; and though we may be held back to some extent by our own feebleness, though we may be dismayed at the fierce assaults and the alarms to which we must be exposed, even though we may be hindered from going forward, nevertheless we shall surely achieve it, because God will not forsake us.

The prize is for all who finish the course

We must remember what St Paul said earlier, with regard to the passage in 1 Corinthians 9 which we quoted, in order to shame those who do not run as eagerly as they should. 'Well now, how is this?' he says to them. 'Those who compete in order to win a prize, or those who come to wrestle, are not even sure that they will carry away any reward.' For in those days two or three hundred persons would take part in a race, many of them coming from as far as two hundred, or even four hundred miles away. And, after all, it was only for a garland of leaves! They were not afraid to go to great expense and to take pains for something of little worth; and when it was all over, only one was crowned, if he was found to have been quick and nimble; or even if there were two or three, or four prizes, the crown was only for the one who was found to be have shown the most mettle. All the rest went away in shame, and people would mock them and make fun of them, saying, 'You see that fellow! He boasted of what he would do, but he did not win for all that.' Also, in these wrestling matches men would sometimes hurt themselves by giving themselves mighty blows. They held heavy objects in their hands to strike and bruise themselves so badly that they went home badly injured.

When those fellows had fought a good while, they might take away a prize, but not all of them — only one, or two, or three, among the whole lot of them. But when God calls us to run, is it to give the prize only to one man, and to turn away all the others that come in afterwards? No, no, but we help one another, so that if I should be the hundredth, and ten thousand should come in afterwards, those who have already reached the goal will reach out their arms to welcome me into the company of the holy martyrs who went before us, and of the holy prophets who have been waiting still longer for us. When God calls us to such a contest, and on such terms, are we not regular villains if we do not take heart and are not keen to march on and to run the race as the Lord commands us? So much for the phrase, 'I have kept the faith.'

The promise of God is our assurance of victory

St Paul goes on from there to say, 'Finally, there is laid up for me the crown of righteousness, which the Lord, the righteous Judge, will give to me on that Day, and not to me only but also to all who have loved his appearing.' Here St Paul confirms the matter which I touched on before — that he had not run in vain, or as he said in another place, that he had not 'beaten the air', meaning that he had not fought in vain (1 Cor. 9:26). He knew that he could not fail to win the crown because the one who had promised it to him is the one whose word is the sure and undoubted truth.

When we have the promise of our God — when in his infinite goodness he binds himself to us — shall we fear? If that does not cause us to take heart, what excuse will we have? Is it not an indication that we do not honour God, but rather do injury to him, by not accounting him faithful and true? There can be no doubt that all those who hold firmly to all that God has said will overcome all the hindrances in the world. So we may conclude that all who faint part-way through the race, or who cannot so much as move an arm or a leg, are unbelievers and infidels. They go about, as far as they are able, to make God a liar. Though they may not utter this blasphemy with their mouths, their lives show that they do not believe God, for they will not do him the honour of relying upon him, as upon one who cannot deceive us.

So then, let us learn that we cannot rejoice and boast with St Paul that we have fought manfully and have arrived at a blessed outcome, unless we are fully persuaded that our God has not called us in vain. We must also have the promises, by which he directs us and brings us into the way and gives us hope of the eternal salvation which is reserved for us in heaven — we must always have these promises before our eyes and in our minds.

St Paul says, 'Finally ...,' as if to say, 'It is true that here I find myself in deep anguish, and know that I am a frail creature. Nevertheless, my God, who has always helped me up to now, will not forsake me, and I trust in him for the future; as I have proved and tried his grace in the past, and throughout my life.' And this is what we must all do. Our faith must not only reach out to look at things of the present, but it must overcome the world. Indeed, it is not for nothing that the apostle says that faith is the evidence of things which are not seen, and the substance of things which we do not yet have (Heb. 11:1). It is true that this seems strange to us. How can we see things that cannot be seen? It is impossible. That is true, and yet God gives us eyes that can see what is not apparent to the world, eyes of faith that can peer into the heavens.

Therefore, although according to man's sense and reason, the hope that God gives us is hidden, yet we do not cease to be assured when we have the looking-glass of the Word and our faith is focused on him. Here we cast our anchor, not just to a hundred feet, or fathoms, but we cast it into heaven itself, as it is said in the epistle to the Hebrews. And, therefore, let us observe that if we are to walk steadily and not turn aside when we are in the right way, but rather go forward, we must be assured that God will never fail us. And though we may be hindered in coming to him to hide ourselves under the shadow of his wings and to call upon him as our Father by the griefs and troubles which we suffer, nevertheless we must have confidence that the crown of righteousness is prepared for us. Why is that? Because when he set us to work, he did not do so to then leave us, and see what we would do, but he promised to give us strength and enable us to persevere.

Let us, therefore, look for the victory at his hands, and let us not fear that it is not already prepared for us, as if we held the outcome in our hands. God will have us do him the honour of hoping for that which we do not see, and which we cannot attain unto.

This is the meaning of the word 'finally'. As we review the graces which we have received from God up to now, we conclude that God, who began the good work in us, will complete it, as St Paul says in Philippians 1. And likewise he tells the Corinthians that God, who has poured out his bountiful blessings upon them, will not see them lack anything necessary for their salvation, even until the coming of our Lord Jesus Christ. Thus St Paul shows us that we must not only thank God that we have already tasted of his goodness, but we must go about in the world and not doubt that, having adopted us, he will guide us on to this immortal inheritance of the kingdom of heaven.

Although we meet with many a hard blow that is liable to discourage us, and although we see wide chasms yawning on all sides and always have one foot in the grave, and though we are troubled with many hazards and we see the devil ruling in the air, let us nevertheless hope in our God and not doubt that he will bring our adoption to its fruition. Then we shall possess those things which we now only hope for because they are not yet present to us.

The crown of righteousness is God's free gift

At first blush, we might think that St Paul is claiming some merits to himself when he says that the crown of righteousness is prepared for him. And indeed the papists, when they want to support their teaching on free will and meritorious works, cite this text. 'See,' they say, 'St Paul says that the crown of righteousness is laid up for him. So it must be that he was justified on account of his works. Thus the world may see that we are not saved by our faith only, but when we have deserved it, God rewards us as those who have taken pains to do good.'

But, first of all, we need to know from whence our ability and courage come. Is there anyone who dares to boast that he has in himself the ability to withstand even one conflict? When St Paul speaks of those who have the same calling as he — that is, those who have the responsibility of preaching the gospel — he says, 'Not that we are sufficient of ourselves…' (2 Cor. 3:5). To do what? He does not say that we are not able to persevere, or to conduct ourselves manfully when facing any persecution, or to build a church, or to resist even one assault of sin, or to risk death and be ready to give up our lives and all our possessions. He says that we are not able to have as much as a single good thought unless we are given the ability from above.

Let men go now and exalt themselves and put on a brave show; let them boast about their free will [if they dare]. For if they are incapable of as much as a single good thought, how will they be able to do any good thing? How can they have the constancy required to hold firmly to the truth of God and overcome whatever the devil practises against them? And if they cannot have a good thought for one minute of one hour, how will they persevere all their lives?

So then, let us note well that when St Paul says in this passage that the crown of righteousness is prepared for him, he is not pointing to noble deeds that he has done, as though he has done them in his own strength; but the righteousness of which he speaks is that which he received from the grace of God.

And this is according to what he says in another place. 'What do you have,' he says, 'that you did not receive? Now if you did indeed receive it, why do you boast as if you had not received it?' (1 Cor. 4:7). Thus St Paul demolishes with one word all the arrogance and pride of men when they seek to claim anything for themselves. 'You have nothing,' he says, 'but what is given to you. Therefore you play the part of a church robber when you vaunt yourself, for you are misappropriating what is the gift of God, which he gives you on condition that his honour may remain intact; that is, that he may receive all the praise that belongs to him. For if he does not, what does that make you, but a thief, and one who robs God of the honour due to him?'

This is one point. And again, the papists should have considered what one of those whom they themselves look up to as an authority says: 'How should God give the crown as a just

Judge, unless he had first given the grace as a merciful Father? And how could there be righteousness in us, unless the grace that justifies us had gone before? And how could this crown be given as something due to us, unless all that we have had been given to us, since it was not due to us?' These are St Augustine's words. And though the papists will not hold to Holy Scripture, at least they should not be so contemptible as to reject what they want to be seen as defending.

Even our best works are flawed

But this is not all. It is true that this doctrine is very worthy of being received — that God cannot be a just Judge to save us, unless he first shows himself to be a merciful Father; and that there can be no righteousness in us unless he puts it in us; and that he cannot reward us, except by crowning his gifts to us. And what is more, though God has given us this grace to serve him, and though we have taken pains and busied ourselves, according to the best of our ability, to do all that we can, we can never do so well that we shall be thoroughly acceptable to God. No, he may justly find fault with even our best works. What we might single out as the greatest of our good deeds is deserving of blame, for when we think we are fully inclined to serve God, there is always something — I cannot tell what — that holds us back. We turn our eyes on the world, or there is some temptation or other passing before our eyes; we do not call upon God as we ought; we are not so fervent and zealous as we ought to be; nor is there such a desire and love in us as there should be; we do not try to please and do good to our neighbours, as we are bound to do, but instead we labour for ourselves, and look to our own profit.

Therefore, because there are always such blemishes in our works, all of them may justly be condemned, were it not that our God has pity upon us and bears with us. As he says by his prophet, he accepts our services as a father does when his child brings him something to please him. Though it may not be perfect, nor indeed of any value, yet the father is content with it — not because the work is worth anything, but because he loves his child. God shows us that it is out of his mere goodness that he accepts our works; it is not because he regards any merit or worthiness in us, but because he loves us he accepts them and even regards them as righteous works, as though there were no fault to be found with them — although they are very imperfect.

Salvation is by faith alone, not by works

This text is, therefore, so far from helping the papists in the slightest to show that their works deserve anything in God's sight, and that faith alone does not save us, that it actually serves to confound them. For if we note well St Paul's words, this text necessarily implies that we must be saved by faith alone, because, as I said earlier, God can crown no works in us, except those which we have done through his mere grace.

And, therefore, when the papists speak of their meritorious works, they put themselves on a par with God, thinking that they work together with him (for that is the language they use). They say that they make some good gesture, that their will is good, and so God helps them when they are well-disposed, and joins hands with them to a certain extent. And being thus puffed up with pride, they persuade themselves that it is in man to do well. And this is what makes them drunk with negligence, because they think they are able to do well when they want to, and in this way they give themselves over to all manner of wickedness, so that they are full of uncleanness within and carried away with evil inclinations; indeed, they are bewitched and blinded — they cover their eyes so that they can see nothing at all.

Again, they are puffed up with their free will, and with their virtues and merits. And then, because they cannot deny that we are sinners and liable to God's punishment, they add their acts of penance, saying, 'If I have not done my duty in some respect, this will supply what I lack.' This is the situation of these miserable wretches. But when they have done all they can, what rest do they have in their consciences? They surely must always be greatly troubled and disquieted, because they have no certainty of their salvation. Indeed, it is one of the principal articles of their faith to say that it is presumptuous for people to be assured of their salvation. And God's judgement of them is just, because, like wild beasts, they have lifted themselves up against him. Thus these poor wretches stand wavering, which is to say that they are unbelievers, having no hope of salvation.

But as for us, because we are assured that it is of his own free goodness that God calls us and takes us to be his children in the name of our Lord Jesus Christ, and not because we have deserved it, we can also be confident that our works are acceptable to him. And why are they acceptable? Is it because of their worthiness? No, no, it is because he does not hold us accountable for their imperfections — though they may justly be found fault with — but he accepts us as if we had served him perfectly.

At the same time, we flee to God for forgiveness of sins and call upon him: 'O Lord, because you are pleased to bear with us and to be so merciful to us, we are so much the more bound and indebted to you; and since you are pleased to accept our works, which are faulty and imperfect, we acknowledge that it is of your gracious goodness alone.'

This consideration, I say, makes us hang our heads and humble ourselves. But as for the papists, though they are loud in speaking highly of their works and merits, yet they cannot avoid having their mouths stopped; for God confounds them in their pride, because they make war against him. And therefore if there were no other texts in all Holy Scripture apart from this one, it would still be enough to show that there is no way for us to be saved but by faith alone. We put our trust solely in the free goodness of our God, who not only receives us and shows mercy to us, but also accepts our works, even though they are unworthy and are like an offensive smell to him on account of the imperfections that are in them. Nevertheless he accepts them because he is pleased to regard them as though they were perfect and pure, and to receive them in the name of our Lord Jesus Christ.

Grace and its fruits

Selections from John Calvin on the Pastoral Epistles

Chapter 13

A lesson on prayer

'If we have faith, we must show it by calling upon God. If prayer is of no account to us, that is a sure sign that we are unbelievers, however much we may claim to believe the gospel.'

13.
A lesson on prayer

'I desire therefore that the men pray everywhere, lifting up holy hands, without wrath and doubting' (1 Tim. 2:8).

The link between faith and prayer

After St Paul has told us that our Lord Jesus Christ came into the world and gave himself as a ransom for all, and that the message of salvation is carried in his name to all peoples, both great and small [see chapters 2 and 4], he then exhorts everyone to call upon God. For this is one of the true fruits of faith: to know that God is our Father, and to be moved by his love. The way is open for us to run to him, and we have ready access to approach him in prayer once we are convinced that his eyes are upon us and that he is ready to help us in all our needs.

Until God has called us, we cannot come to him without being guilty of too much impudence and daring. Is it not folly and rashness for mortals to presume to address God? Therefore, we must wait until God calls us, which he does by his Word. For when he promises to be our Saviour he shows that he will always be ready to receive us. He does not wait till we come seeking him; rather, he offers himself and exhorts us to pray to him — and, in doing so, tests our faith.

This is why St Paul says elsewhere that we cannot pray to God until the gospel has been preached to us (Rom. 10:14). We understand from that passage that God is ready to receive us, although we are not worthy. Once we know his will, we may come to him boldly, because he reveals himself to us. So the apostle goes on to say, later in Romans, 'Praise the Lord, all you Gentiles! Laud him, all you peoples!' (Rom. 15:11). By this he gives us to understand that, since the gospel applies to the Gentiles as well as to the Jews, every mouth ought to be open to call upon God for help.

We see, therefore, how Paul links this doctrine, that we must call upon God in all places, with what he has said in the preceding verses. In other words, he says, 'My friends, you see that God has received you into his flock, although previously you were excluded from his church and he had no acquaintance with you.' For, indeed, the Gentiles were strangers to all the promises which God had made to his people Israel. 'But now,' the apostle says, 'God has gathered you into his flock. He has sent you his only begotten Son, because of the fatherly love which he had for you. Now, therefore, you may boldly call upon him, for it is to this end and for this purpose that he has given you this witness of his good will.'

Whenever the goodness of God is witnessed to us and his grace promised to us — wretched sinners though we are — whenever we hear that our sins were forgiven us by the death and suffering of our Lord Jesus Christ; and that he has paid our debt and torn in pieces the writing of requirements that was against us (Col. 2:14); and that atonement has been made to God for us — then the way is opened for us to pray to him and implore his blessings. As it is said in Hosea, 'I will say to those who were not my people, "You are my people!" and they shall say, "You are my God"' (Hosea 2:23).

Therefore, as soon as our Lord God makes us taste his goodness and promises that, having sent his only begotten Son for us, he will accept us in his name, let us not hesitate to come to him, for it is almost as if he commanded us to pray, and the one follows on from the other. If we have faith, we must show it by calling upon God. If prayer is of no account to us, that is a sure sign that we are unbelievers, however much we may claim to believe the gospel. Thus we see what a great blessing God bestows on us when we have the privilege of being able to pray to him.

Our Lord God assures us that if we call upon him it will not be in vain; we shall not be deceived in our expectations if we come to him, nor shall we be rejected if we keep to the way that St Paul has set out for us — that is, if we have Jesus Christ as our mediator and we come on the grounds of the merits of [Christ's] death and passion, knowing that it is his responsibility to keep us. We know also that having once made reconciliation to God the Father on our behalf, he will now be merciful to us if we come to him in this name and in this way.

Once we have come to know what a great and inestimable privilege God has bestowed on us in giving us freedom to call upon him by prayer, we must be diligent in the exercise of it. We must be careful to call upon God both morning and evening, for we need his assistance every minute of every hour. Besides, every day we hear his promises declared to us and he stirs us up, either by word or deed, to come to him.

We also need to note that we cannot pray to God unless we have the spirit of adoption — that is, unless we are assured that he takes us as his children and testifies this to us by the gospel. So much for this point.

As often, therefore, as we read in Holy Writ, 'Pray to God,' or 'Praise him,' we must know that the fruit of our faith is expressed by these words, and because God has revealed himself to us and drawn near to us, he has also given us ready access to his presence. We may, therefore, come and seek him, with the assurance that it will not be difficult to find him, because he comes to meet us.

Old Testament restrictions no longer apply

We see next what St Paul meant by the word 'everywhere'. We see that in the First Epistle to the Corinthians he greets the faithful 'who in every place call on the name of Jesus Christ our Lord, both theirs and ours' (1 Cor. 1:2). In that passage he joins the Gentiles with the Jews — as if to say that he would not confine the church of God to one particular people. It was indeed so under the law, but after the wall of separation was broken down and the enmity between Jews and Gentiles was abolished, its scope was made much wider, so that now those of all nations and peoples may call upon God, because his grace is common to us all.

Moreover, St Paul also meant to show that the ceremonies of the law were abolished after Jesus Christ was manifested to the world. For in the time of the law, men were constrained to come to the temple and to gather together there, in order to call upon God. It is true that the Jews prayed, each man at home in his own house, but it was not lawful to offer a solemn sacrifice except in the temple at Jerusalem, for that was the place which God had chosen. Why was that? Because the people were slow to learn, it was necessary to have sacrifices, until the time when the truth should be declared more plainly. The temple, therefore, was a sign representing that we must have one object on which to fix our eyes when we come to God. And on what are we to fix our eyes? On our Lord Jesus Christ. We cannot come near to God unless we have someone to lead us; he is too highly exalted in the glory and infinity which transcends the heavens. Therefore, we need another to whom we can look to bring us near to God — that is, to our Lord Jesus Christ. The Jews had this in a figure; we have it in reality and in truth.

Again, God thought it proper to keep them, as little children, in the unity of faith by means appropriate for their unenlightened state; but now that the gospel has been made so clear to us, we no longer need those old shadows. Seeing, therefore, that the order which God had established under the law is now abolished — I mean, the order of the temple of Jerusalem and all the rest of the ceremonies — we must move on from there.

This is why our Lord Jesus Christ said to the woman of Samaria, 'The hour is coming when you will neither on this mountain, nor in Jerusalem, worship the Father... But the hour is coming, and now is, when the true worshippers will worship the Father in spirit and truth' (John 4:21,23). In those days there was a great controversy between the Jews and the Samaritans, for the temple in Samaria had been built in spite of the Jews, and those who worshipped there claimed to follow the example of Abraham, Isaac and Jacob. Because the Jews had the Word of God, Jesus Christ said that in [Old Testament] times they knew what they worshipped, for they were governed by a teaching that was beyond doubt. 'You Samaritans,' he said, 'were idolaters. But now you must contend no more, either for the temple of Jerusalem, or for the temple of Samaria.' Why not? Because God is to be called upon in spirit and in truth throughout the whole world.

The shadows have given way to the substance

Now that Jesus Christ has come, we are no longer to have the old shadows of the law. Let us instead content ourselves with the knowledge that we have a temple which is not material or visible. Indeed, because all the fulness of the Godhead dwells in our Lord Jesus Christ and because he is our Brother, it is sufficient for us that he should reach out his hand to us, and be ready to present us before the presence of God. It is enough that by him we have an entrance into the true, spiritual sanctuary. It is sufficient that God receives us, that the veil of the temple is torn down and that we no longer need to worship afar off in the court of the temple, but may come and cry with open mouths, in every language, '*Abba,* Father.'

St Paul deliberately uses the word '*Abba*', which was a word commonly in use at the time in the Hebrew, or rather Aramaic, language. He puts the two words, '*Abba*' and 'Father', in Hebrew and Greek to show us that everyone is now free to call upon God in his own language. Nor is there any longer a fixed place to which we must come in order to worship, but since the gospel has been preached throughout all the world, we must show that today everyone may call upon God and 'pray everywhere', throughout the world.

It is true, we may now have church buildings, but not in the same way as the Jews had; that is, it is not necessary for us to come to a particular place in order to be heard by God, but we only have such buildings for our convenience. Let us, therefore, learn that all ceremonies came to an end at the coming of Christ. This is a point which is important for us to understand in order to draw us away from all the trivia and nonsense practised by the papists, and from the superstitious notions which only obscure the true meaning of prayer.

The Jews had their lights, perfumes, incense, and so forth in order to pray to God; and they had the priest in all his special garments, in order to teach us that we need a mediator between God and ourselves, and that this mediator must not be a man of the common order. The papists still keep all those things, and what is the result of their doing so? In practice it is as if they renounced Jesus Christ. It is not their intention to do so, but that is what it amounts to.

It pleased God to be served by means of shadows (as St Paul shows in Colossians 2) before the coming of Jesus Christ, who is the true embodiment, or substance, of what these things represented. Are not, then, those who seek to introduce such ceremonies today guilty of estranging themselves from Christ? Do they not reveal their ignorance of the fact that when he took our flesh upon himself, lived in the world, suffered and died, that it was for this purpose — that we might look to him and have no more to do with these childish figures, which served only for a time? Thus the papists, with all the foolish things which they use, not only obscure the glory of our Lord Jesus Christ, but utterly deface it, as far as it is possible to do so.

Let us, therefore, learn to worship God and simply call upon him, without all this confusion, without things devised by our own brains and without borrowing from the Old Testament law things that are no longer proper for us. We now have a full revelation in the gospel; let us not therefore do God the injury of extinguishing the glorious light which he has caused to shine before our eyes. Seeing that the Son of righteousness, our Lord Jesus Christ, is now made manifest to us, why should we talk any longer of walking in dark shadows, which were only of use when we were far from that great brightness which afterwards appeared? For if we once begin to turn aside from the Word of God we shall never come to an end of doing so.

The papists make pilgrimages and seek to find God by running backwards and forwards, this way and that, but, when they have done all that, are they any better for having done so? If we are to pray to him as the gospel commands us to do, and in the way God everywhere reveals himself, as he calls us to him, we must do what he tells us. Those, therefore, who run back and forth to perform their devotions show plainly that they are making false gods for themselves and that, in so doing, they are forsaking the living God and withdrawing themselves wholly from him.

But since God has bestowed such grace upon us in revealing himself to us in the gospel as a Father, and since he exhorts us daily to pray to him, let us make use of this privilege which he has conferred upon us. In other words, seeing that [our faith is] grounded upon the promise of the gospel, and since we have access to God through Jesus Christ, let us have no doubt that God will take pity on us and listen to all our requests.

The attitude with which we are to come to God

St Paul also says that we are to do this 'without wrath and doubting', or rather 'disputing', for the second word that he uses really means 'disputing'. Why should he use such a word? When we come to offer our prayers to God, we must not come in a despondent frame of mind, or fretting and fuming, as though we would adopt an attitude of defiance towards him, like someone who comes to pray to God when he is angry, or complaining, or distressed because of afflictions that God has sent, for we do not honour God when we pray to him in a reproachful manner, as it were.

There are many who make a show of praying to God, but they do so by protesting against him, by chafing, fretting and fuming because they are not dealt with according to their own fancy. They will come to God, but it is to be defiant towards him. It is like when there is a disagreement between a husband and wife and he says, 'You should do this; you are not behaving as you should,' or as if a woman should ask her husband for something with the accusation: 'Oh, you don't care for me!' This is the way many people approach prayer, but it would be better for them not to pray at all than to come with a heart that is so full of bitterness and anger against God. We are, therefore, to pray to God with peaceable hearts. This is also why St Paul shows us that, besides the need for diligence in our prayers we must also see that they include thanksgiving. In other words, however much we may be seething with emotion, we must always content ourselves with the good will and pleasure of God, and if we do not immediately receive what we ask for, we must be content to await his pleasure.

We must first be at peace with one another

So then, we must pray to God without complaining, without fretting or fuming and, indeed, without answering back or asking him why he leaves our prayers unanswered. But it appears that St Paul had another meaning in this text; he had in mind the circumstance which we have mentioned before — namely, that the Jews would gladly have shut out the Gentiles. For they thought, 'We are the children of God; he has chosen us. And shall not the stock of Abraham have more privileges than the uncircumcised nations?' The Gentiles, on the other hand, mocked the Jews saying, 'They are behaving like children. They are still learning their ABC, not knowing that the ceremonies of the law have been abolished. We, on the other hand, have reached the age of maturity, so we do not need extra things to help us, such as those given under the law.'

Thus the Jews despised the Gentiles and looked down on them and would not receive them into their company. The Gentiles, on the other hand, mocked the Jews as being primitive, because they continued to hold fast the rudiments of the law. And so arose many schisms, one party setting themselves against the other; and the church was, as it were, torn in pieces, and yet we know that, above all things, God commends to us [the importance of] unity and brotherly love.

Indeed, how does the model of prayer given us by our Lord Jesus Christ begin? 'Our Father in heaven…' He does not say that each one of us is to call on God individually as Father.

When I say 'our', I speak in the name of all; and everyone must say the same. Therefore, we shall not have access to God by prayer, unless we are joined together, for those who separate themselves from their neighbours shut their own mouths, so that they cannot pray to God as our Lord Jesus Christ has commanded. In short, we must agree together and be bound in a bond of peace before we can come near and present ourselves to God.

Because these discords and debates of which we have been speaking existed between the Jews and Gentiles, St Paul shows that they cannot call upon God without being refused and turned away, until they are at peace with one another. This is the reason why he says here that they are to pray without contention and debate. In other words, they were not to enter into arguments and contention with one another. The Jews must not elevate themselves above the Gentiles because they were called first; nor must the Gentiles condemn the Jews for the slowness of their understanding. All these contentions must cease, and a perfect reconciliation must be made, to show that they all have the Spirit of adoption; that is to say, that they are governed by the Spirit of God, even that Spirit who brings peace and unity.

And from this we must make this more general point: that before we can come to prayer with the right attitude, we must have this brotherly love which God commands, and this unity and closeness. For God would not have each one of us to remain by himself, but would have a full harmony and concord in the words we utter. Although each of us speaks, though each one individually and privately prays to God in secret, yet we must present a united front to heaven and all say, with the same affection, and in truth, 'Our Father'. This word 'our' must bind us together and make us in such fellowship one with another that there will be, as it were, but one voice, one heart and one spirit between us. This is something we are to take away from this passage.

Moreover, when we pray, let us also join together with other churches. If we wish to pray aright, we must not act like those who seek only to divide that which God has joined together. Let us not, under colour of some trifling little ceremony which is of no importance, separate ourselves from one another so as to, as it were, dismember the body of Christ and tear it to pieces; for those who conduct themselves in this manner show plainly that they are possessed with the spirit of Satan, and are carried away in a frenzied attempt to sever and tear apart the knot and the bond which God has established between his children.

Therefore, let all such controversies be rooted out and trodden under foot, and let us in liberty and with freedom pray to God, in the confident assurance that our Lord Jesus Christ, who has revealed and manifested himself to all of us, will draw us to himself in order to present us to God the Father. It is true that we cannot join with those who separate themselves from us. The papists, for example, call themselves Christians; can we not have fellowship with them in prayer? No, because they have forsaken Christ Jesus. We know that if we turn aside from him in even the least little thing, we have gone right off the path and find ourselves wandering aimlessly about in the fields. Therefore, since the papists have separated themselves from Jesus Christ, the distance between them and us is too great. But we must reach out our hands to all who are willing to submit themselves to Jesus Christ, so that we may all come with mutual accord to present ourselves before God as our Father.

In the same way that this applies to the church in general, so each of us individually must take steps to live, as far as possible, in harmony with our neighbours, if we desire to be heard by God as we pray together. This is why our Lord Jesus Christ says that if a man comes to offer his gift at the altar, he must leave his offering there and go and be reconciled to the brother whom he has offended, rather than think that God will receive him if he is so troubled in his mind with bitterness towards his brother (Matt. 5:23-24). Do we want God to be merciful to us? If we do, we must lay aside all enmity one against another, for if we are divided among ourselves, God will reject us. He will receive none but those who are members of his Son, and we cannot be members of Jesus Christ unless we are governed by his Spirit, who is the Spirit of peace and unity, as we have already shown. Let us, therefore, learn from this text to live with one another in friendship and brotherly love, if we wish God to receive us and open his heart to us in welcome when we come to him.

When we see anything that might hinder our prayers, we must remember that the devil goes about to put stumbling-blocks in our way. Let us, therefore, avoid such things as the most deadly plagues. There are many who seek only to get involved in disputes, as though the Word of God was meant to separate us one from another. We have already seen that the true intent of the gospel is to call us to God so that we may be joined together and made one in our prayers and requests to him. Those who indulge in contentious debates and seek their own advantage over that of others are doing all they can to bring to naught the glory of God. They pervert all good doctrine; they turn God's purposes upside down and fight against them, endeavouring to bring them to naught. Therefore, they must not think that God will hear them when they pray to him, seeing they lack this unity and concord [which are necessary] to go to him in the name of, and through the means of, the Lord Jesus Christ.

We must be cleansed before coming into God's presence

St Paul adds that we are to pray, 'lifting up holy hands'. By this he would have us understand that we must not abuse God's name by coming to him in all our defilement, but that we must be purged and made clean. For prayer is called a sacrifice, and there is a good reason for this. We know that in the time of the law, when they offered sacrifices, they first washed themselves. And why was this? By that requirement of the law our Lord meant to show us that we are full of defilement; we are unclean, and are not worthy to come to him until we have been cleansed and made bright and clean. It is true that the figures of the law have been abolished and brought to an end, and that we must come to Christ, for he is, indeed, the one who truly cleanses us. Yet it is still true that none of us is to entertain any defilement in ourselves, for Christ Jesus was given to us in order that he might renew us by his Holy Spirit, and that we might not be given over to our wicked desires.

God does not command us to bring our defilement and corruption into his presence, but will have us prepare ourselves before we pray to him. How shall we do this? We must have recourse to the forgiveness of sins, and when we would pray to God we must remember to speak in this way: 'O Lord, I am utterly confounded and ashamed, for I am full of uncleanness and defilement, so that I must be rejected unless I am cleansed by another — that is, by our Lord Jesus Christ.' Thus, we must acknowledge our spots and blemishes and run to this fountain where we may be washed; that is, since Jesus Christ has shed his blood to wash away our sins, we shall be accounted pure in the sight of God, and completely clean. We also need to note that, although there is nothing in us but corruption, when Jesus Christ gave us the spirit of sanctification, he cleansed us from our faults and gave us free access to God. Therefore the apostle says that he wants men to pray to God, 'lifting up holy hands'.

In the time of the law and the Old Testament, God instructed the people by means of this ceremony of requiring them to be purified before they offered sacrifice, and even before they made a solemn profession of faith in the temple. It is true that these practices no longer apply to Christians, but we must keep the substance that they represented. And what is this substance? It is this: although we have no visible water in which to wash ourselves, yet we must come to the blood of our Lord Jesus Christ, which is our spiritual washing.

Sometimes when the Holy Spirit is mentioned he is represented by the image of clean water. 'Then I will sprinkle clean water on you, and you shall be clean; I will cleanse you from all your filthiness…,' says the Lord speaking by the prophet Ezekiel (Ezek. 36:25). This promise refers specifically to the coming of Jesus Christ. So then, God shows us that instead of the old figures which he gave to the Jews, and instead of literal water, he gives us that which it truly represents, and assures us that we shall be made clean by the Holy Spirit.

St Paul is, therefore, seeking to show us that, instead of the outward rites of washing which were practised in the past, we must have this spiritual purity of being washed by the Spirit of God in order to come and present ourselves before him. It is true that he speaks in particular of 'hands', but we know that in Scripture the word 'hands' is used to mean all actions.

When David says, 'I will wash my hands in innocence; so I will go about your altar, O LORD' (Ps. 26:6), he is indeed thinking of the figures of the law, but he shows us how we are to apply this to our own time. We shall understand this more easily by looking at the opposite and seeing how God reproaches the Jews by means of his prophet Isaiah because they came into his temple with filthy hands. 'Do you come here to pollute my holy place [he asks], when you come to make a show of calling upon me in my temple, and yet you have your hands full of blood, you are full of malice and deceit, you are murderers, thieves and perjurers? And what do you mean by coming in this way with your filthy hands to make requests of me, unless it is to make war against me and provoke me to anger as much as you can?' (see Isa. 1:12-16). In the same way that our

Lord God accused the Jews of coming before him with 'hands full of blood', so, on the contrary, here he commands us by the mouth of St Paul to 'lift up holy hands' — that is, not to be caught up in our evil desires, and to testify the same thing by our whole lives.

Thus we see what St Paul meant. Seeing we have this privilege of easy access to God in prayer and of drawing near to him as our Father, we must not think that he will hear us if we come to him in our natural state of defilement, if we bring with us all the refuse and corruption of our nature, for he cannot abide such abuse of his name. On the contrary, seeing that Jesus Christ has come to cleanse us and since this is the responsibility of his Holy Spirit, of whom he has made us partakers, each of us is to devote himself to purity; and since we cannot do it ourselves, we must have recourse to our Lord Jesus Christ, who is the fountain of all purity — as, indeed, it is to him that we must look for all goodness.

The significance of the gesture

We must also note, in closing, that when St Paul speaks of 'lifting up hands', he is referring to the custom that was used, whenever people prayed to God, of putting their hands together and lifting them up. Of itself, this is of no importance, but the practice can be a good and proper one if it is used for the purpose for which it was intended. In our ignorance, we always imagine that we are too far from God and that he is not near to us. When we have this outward sign, it confirms to us that God is near to us when we seek him. And on the other hand, we see our own slothfulness: we are so idle that we need to be stirred up to prayer, and lifting up our hands in such a manner can act as a means of stirring us up to seek God. And, again, we must not pray to God as though he were an idol that required to be served in a sensual manner. Instead, we must be lifted to a higher plane than that of our senses, and must rid ourselves of all earthly affections and all things that keep us back and tie us down to this earth. And because we do not have wings to fly up to heaven, if we lift up our hands, this is a symbol of the fact that we lift our hearts on high by faith.

So whenever we put our hands together and lift them up to heaven, this should lead us to God and to a consideration of our weakness and should remind us that it is to him alone that we are to have recourse, and that we cannot have access to him unless we lift ourselves above the world — that is, unless we withdraw ourselves from all earthly passions, thoughts and foolish ideas that we might have, and put all these things away from us. In the same way, when we say, 'Our Father in heaven', we are reminded that we must seek him there and must climb up there by faith; though we still live on earth, our affections must be lifted up on high.

And in regard to this [custom of lifting up our hands], let us learn to renounce every practice that God does not allow, and to know that our salvation is in him alone. Our trust must be in him alone, and it should be enough for us to know that he is the one who comes to our aid and helps us. For if we do not believe this, the gesture, good though it may be in itself, will be vain and superfluous. We should also note that those who lift up their hands to heaven but at the same time remain earth-bound condemn themselves just as much as though they had written down their own condemnation and ratified it by their own hand and seal, condemning themselves as hypocrites, liars and perjurers. For if I come to affirm in the sight of God that I am seeking him who is above, and yet I remain attached to the things of this life, I am making a show of putting my trust in him, but in fact I am putting it in myself, or in created things. I am claiming to be lifted up to heaven by faith, when in fact I am drowning in the things of earth.

Let us, therefore, learn, whenever we pray to God, that we must free ourselves from all earthly cares and wicked inclinations, knowing that there are many things that hinder us from coming directly to God. When we lift up our hands to heaven, it must be for the purpose of seeking God there by faith — which we cannot do unless we withdraw from earthly cares and from all wicked inclinations of the flesh.

Grace and its fruits

Selections from John Calvin on the Pastoral Epistles

Chapter 14

Abundant grace

'Unbelievers are like a covered pot; God showers his gifts upon them, but they do not receive them, for they are so tightly covered that there is no getting into them... But if we have our mouths open by faith, we shall be filled.'

14.
Abundant grace

'But when the kindness and the love of God our Saviour toward man appeared, not by works of righteousness which we have done, but according to his mercy he saved us, through the washing of regeneration and renewing of the Holy Spirit, whom he poured out on us abundantly through Jesus Christ our Saviour, that having been justified by his grace we should become heirs according to the hope of eternal life' (Titus 3:4-7).

In this passage St Paul bases the whole cause of our salvation upon God's goodness. He intends that we should learn to acknowledge with all humility that it is to God that we are beholden for all things, and that none of us has any reason to glory in ourselves. Accordingly, St Paul has excluded all that people can imagine in themselves by way of merits, saying that we have not done any work at all that would place God under any obligation to us. Rather, we become righteous when it pleases God to accept us through his free mercy.

St Paul goes on to add the means by which [this is accomplished]. God has poured out on us a spiritual cleansing, and this has been carried out by our Lord Jesus Christ, so that we are purified from all that defiled us, with the result that God now takes us into his favour and is pleased with us.

The source of our salvation

Let us notice, then, that St Paul first shows us the source of our salvation, namely, the love that God had for us. We must always come back to this point of knowing how it came about that God has drawn us out of the accursed state in which we were by nature. Since there is a great distance between God and us, however, it is necessary that we should have explained to us the means by which we may most easily come to him. That means is our Lord Jesus Christ, with all the grace of his Holy Spirit.

This is the subject we are now about to consider. However, we must always bear in mind the connection between the principal cause of our salvation and what is added here, which is that God has not only loved us, but also expressed his love and showed us how we may come to him and enjoy the salvation which he offers us. And it is said expressly that he has 'poured out' on us 'the washing of regeneration and renewing of the Holy Spirit'; and that this is carried out by our Lord Jesus Christ.

The means by which our salvation was accomplished

It is certain that whenever we want to find the means by which our salvation was accomplished we must begin with the Son of God. For it is he who has reconciled us to God the Father; it is he who has washed us with his blood; it is he who has purchased righteousness for us by his obedience; it is he who is our advocate and the one by whom we find grace at the present time; it is he who brings us the Holy Spirit; it is he who has obtained for us the adoption by which we are made the children and heirs of God. So we need to take note that we must look to Jesus Christ for every aspect of our salvation, for we shall not find even the tiniest part of it anywhere else.

St Paul does not imply any particular significance by the order [in which he mentions various aspects of salvation], or mean that the washing of which he speaks is the most important of them. Rather, his intent in this passage is to show us, using an example from everyday life, by what means we may be joined to God and made partakers of the salvation that springs from the fatherly love to which he has referred. For we are so lacking in understanding that God has to stoop down in order to reveal to us things that otherwise would be hidden from us, including those that relate to the health of our souls, which transcend our ability [to understand] and are beyond the reach of our comprehension. Therefore, when there is any mention of God's spiritual kingdom, this is one of the secrets that are incomprehensible to us; it fact, it is like an unknown language as far as we are concerned. That is why St Paul, as it were, presents it to us piecemeal in easily digestible portions so that we may more easily grasp the effects of the things he has taught us.

Our need for cleansing

What St Paul is saying, then, is that God, for our own benefit, has poured out cleansing upon us. In other words, by nature, we are defiled and unclean, and have in us nothing but refuse and corruption; we are cursed in the sight of God, who must reject and disdain us, and even drive us so far away that we would be banished without any hope of returning.

The first point, then, which St Paul has shown us here is that the uncleanness that defiles us is such that God must loathe us.

Now let us go about boasting about ourselves [if we dare]! And when anyone speaks to us about our salvation, dare we seek it in our own merits, seeing that everything that is polluted and defiled displeases God, who is the fountain of all purity and cleanness? Surely not! Since there is nothing in us but outright filthiness, God must of necessity be our enemy. How, then, can we purchase any favour from him with our own worthiness? We must conclude, therefore, that men are out of their wits and insane, or worse, when they dare attribute to themselves any aspect of their salvation, and when they do not acknowledge the infinite and unmixed grace of which St Paul is speaking here.

Baptism as a sign of the Spirit's work

After the word 'washing' he adds that it consists of 'regeneration and renewing of the Holy Spirit'. In saying this, St Paul no doubt had an eye to baptism and meant to set forth to us this doctrine as clearly as if it were seen in a mirror. For because we are untaught, God is not content merely to witness to us by his gospel that we have been washed and made clean in the blood of our Lord Jesus Christ, but he has also given us a visible sign of this. When we are baptized it is almost as if God had demonstrated visibly that of ourselves we bring to him nothing but utter filthiness, and that it is for him to make us clean. That is what baptism shows us.

And so, instead of saying that our sins are forgiven us and that life is offered to us, St Paul says that God has poured out cleansing upon us. Thus we see how he brings us back to our baptism, in which the grace that is spoken of here may more easily be seen. However, he also shows us that the washing to which he refers does not reside in the visible water, for how strange it would be if our souls were to be cleansed by an earthly element that will pass away! The water has no such power. Still, because of our lack of understanding it is for our benefit to begin at the water, so that we may go on to higher things. We must, I say, begin at the water, but we must not stop there. For the outward sign that is presented to our vision serves to lead us to the Holy Spirit, so that we may know that it is from him that the efficacy of baptism proceeds. And so, although he uses the illustration that I have spoken of, he shows us that our trust must not be tied to that; instead we must attribute the effect of baptism and the substance which it represents to the Holy Spirit.

We must become new creatures

St Paul also shows what manner of grace is obtained for us from the Holy Spirit in being baptized — namely, the grace of regeneration and renewal. Now this word 'regeneration' [or 'new birth'] signifies that we are born again — not that we come anew out of our mothers' wombs, but that God makes us new creatures by condescending to imprint his image on us. For what do we bring with us, as children of Adam, but all that is accursed? Therefore, it must be for God to change us. And to the end that we may know that there is nothing in us but wickedness, that we are utterly without favour [in God's eyes], that what we call reason is mere folly, and that what is termed free will is merely a cursed slavery to sin — to the end that we may know all this and condemn it in ourselves, it is said that we must be recast, in a new mould, and be totally changed.

So you see what the word 'regeneration' signifies. St Paul has expounded it by saying that we are made new, and this is how other scriptures speak of it — and, indeed, it is common enough for us to talk about being made 'a new person'. By this it is meant that, until we have renounced all that we have from our father Adam, there is nothing in us but rebelliousness against

God, malice, hypocrisy and wicked lusts. In short, human nature in its present corrupt state is an abyss of all kinds of evil, until God reaches out his hand to remedy it. And St Paul adds that all this is done by our Lord Jesus Christ. For how should we possess God's Spirit if he were not given to us by the one who has in himself the fulness of the Spirit?

So then, let us understand that in order to be cleansed we must become new creatures, having nothing that contributes to our salvation, except as a gift, and by means of the person of our Lord Jesus Christ. The conclusion is that whenever a question arises about our salvation, we must always be fully persuaded of this: that we would have perished without all hope of recovery, if God had not had pity on us. Therefore let his mercy be esteemed as the principal cause and source of our salvation.

The sole foundation for assurance

But even that would not serve to confirm us in a proper trust. It is indeed true that showing men that they were lost and ruined if it were not for God's receiving them to his mercy is enough to make them glorify God and abase themselves. For must they not be utterly cast down, on the one hand, and yet at the same time overjoyed, when they consider how greatly they are indebted to so merciful a Father? So even that one article of truth by itself is enough to humble men and to make them acknowledge God's goodness.

Even so, we could not rest upon God with firm and settled trust unless he revealed himself to us still further and expressed his love to us in a more intimate way. Let us learn, therefore, to resort to our Lord Jesus Christ, who is clothed with our nature in order that we might enjoy fellowship with him. Since he is man, we should not need to seek far. So then, our salvation is proclaimed when the certainty we ought to have of it is affirmed. It is true that God must always keep it in his hand; for if we were responsible for keeping it ourselves, alas, what would become of it? However, although it is God who reserves our salvation in heaven for us (as St Peter says), so that it is exempt from all dangers in this world, we have such a sure guarantee of it that it is as certain as though God had given it to us here and now. How can that be? Because Jesus Christ joins himself to us and calls us his brethren.

So we must resort to him. If we mean to have a solid foundation for our assurance, if we mean to call upon God without any doubting, if we want to be sure of our adoption and of our heavenly inheritance, we must make Jesus Christ the anchor and ground of our faith.

The work of the Spirit in applying Christ's work to us

Let us note, thirdly, that it is not enough for us merely to own the name of Jesus Christ; we must also know his office and power. I mean, we must understand why the Father has sent him and what he brings us. That is why St Paul treats here of the washing by means of which we are renewed and made new creatures.

We need, therefore, to note that Jesus Christ came provided with all the good things that were necessary for the spiritual welfare of our souls. The Holy Spirit was given to him in all his fulness, so that he should confer on each of us an appropriate measure and portion of the Spirit. It is said that the Spirit of God rested upon him, even the Spirit of wisdom, the Spirit of purity, the Spirit of discretion and the Spirit of strength.

In a word, when it comes to having all the elements of eternal life, there is not one thing which we shall not find in Jesus

Christ. Nor can we come to God, as I said before, except through our Lord Jesus Christ. Finally, seeing we have such a mediator, we may be sure that God loves us and owns us as his children. And if we wish to know how this is done, let us come to this doctrine of St Paul's, which is this: our Lord Jesus Christ, having washed us by his death and passion, having shed his blood to rid us completely of all our spots, that they might appear no more in the sight of God the Father; having been crucified to put away sin and set us free from the tyranny in which we were held — now communicates all those things to us by the grace and power of his Holy Spirit. And it is fitting that his death and resurrection should profit us, for if we did not have the Holy Spirit, Christ's sufferings would have been in vain.

It is true that his death and passion would still have had sufficient power to save us, but in the meantime we should have been deprived of it and shut out from it. So in order that Jesus Christ might make the fruit of his death and resurrection effectual in us, it was necessary for him to make us partakers of his Holy Spirit. This is the essential point which we need to remember on this subject. These things would merit being discussed more at length, but sometimes prolonged discussion of such matters only tends to obscure them still further. That is why I have attempted to summarize these things briefly, that even the most untaught among us might grasp in a few words where they should seek salvation and the steps by which they are to approach the subject.

We must understand, first of all, then, that God the Father has been full of pity towards us. Secondly, we must be led to Jesus Christ. And, thirdly, we must know how it is that we come to have salvation in Jesus Christ — namely, by the fact that he has accomplished all things necessary for our salvation, and that he now bestows them upon us by the power and grace of his Holy Spirit.

God's abundant grace

Now St Paul adds further that this cleansing was poured out upon us 'abundantly'; in other words, God did not pour it out a drop at a time, so to speak, as if he had been stingy with us, but he showed himself to be so generous that we have good reason to be content with it. And this serves a double purpose.

The first is to stir us up all the more to magnify the riches of our God as they deserve. For although our God showers ever so many blessings upon us, to our way of thinking it is nothing. We are, as it were, locked up, so that instead of opening our hearts, affections and thoughts to receive God's grace that is offered to us, we are so entangled in unbelief and unthankfulness that God can find no such way of gaining access or entrance to us as would be required for his gracious gifts to be received as they deserve. For this reason he speaks here of the abundance which we have in our Lord Jesus Christ. So abundant is this grace that if we rightly understand God's mercy as it is expressed in him, we shall have both length and breadth enough to fill and satisfy us thoroughly.

And secondly, he intends also to draw us away from every tendency to put our trust in vain objects — something into which we stray too easily. How many are there who rest themselves wholly upon Jesus Christ? It is true indeed that we will confess him as our Saviour, and say that he is the one by whom we are reconciled to God, yet at the same time we also seek other, additional sources of help. We never come to an end of this, because we are so prone to ranging far and wide and cannot rest wholly upon Jesus Christ and assure ourselves that all the perfection of our welfare is to be found in him.

St Paul shows us here that we must indeed be guilty of gross ingratitude, since we are not satisfied with the goodness that God shows us in his only Son. And why is this? Because in him such riches are to be found that it must be said that we are never capable of being satisfied when we cannot confine ourselves to him. Those are the two reasons why St Paul used the word 'abundantly'.

The present and future aspects of our salvation

Now he first says that God 'saved us', and then he adds that this is so that 'we should become heirs according to the hope of eternal life'. We must see how these two matters agree — namely, that God has saved us, and that he will make us 'heirs according to the hope of eternal life'. Now, first of all, he has shown us here that, as far as God and our Lord Jesus Christ are concerned, our salvation is already perfect and there is nothing lacking in it; and yet, in spite of that, we do not yet possess it, except by hope. We do not as yet experience the full accomplishment of it in practice.

These, therefore, are the two points we have to note. The first is that as soon as we believe in Jesus Christ we have passed from death to life, as it is said in the fifth chapter of St John's Gospel. And we must not imagine, as the papists do, that Jesus Christ has merely opened to us the gate of salvation and that it is then in our power to enter if we wish; in other words, that he has only begun [the work], and it is up to us to finish it. Those are wicked and accursed blasphemies. But let us assure ourselves that our salvation is complete and perfect, at least as far as God is concerned. Nevertheless, we do not enjoy it as yet, for it is incumbent on us to fight, here in this mortal life; we must experience trouble and disquiet, so much so that it may seem as if we are surrounded by death a thousand times over and plunged into the depths of hell.

Our salvation is thus hidden, as we are told in the eighth chapter of Romans. Yet for all that, there is a sense in which we are already heirs by hope; that is to say, we are sure that although God tries us and we feel our own infirmities, which might cast us into anguish of mind and doubting, yet we steadfastly believe that God does not change. And since he has chosen us and given us assurance of his adoption, our hope which we have in him feeds and maintains the certainty of our faith. And even though we must wait, the inheritance is now ready for us, and it remains only for us to take possession of it when the day comes.

The practical application of this doctrine

Now that we see what the teaching of this text is, it remains for us to put it to use. And whenever anyone speaks to us of God's mercy, let us be sure that all trust in our own merits is demolished, and consequently any glory we might have is utterly defaced, so that we have no grounds for boasting, because we bring nothing to God but receive all things from him.

We also need to know that we could not even conceive of the goodness and love of our God if we did not have a pledge of it in our Lord Jesus Christ. Therefore let us not enter into lofty or profound speculations when we want to be assured of our salvation, as we know many do, their heads being full of fantasies. They are never content till [their ideas] have encompassed both heaven and earth. But let us go at once to Jesus Christ, for God bears with our weakness in that he will have us to be grounded upon his only Son. And we need not travel by any long or circuitous route to come to our Lord Jesus Christ, for he has come down here to us — so much so that he was abased lower than all men, according to the psalm which says that he was the laughing-stock of the world and made as naked as an earthworm (Ps. 22:6).

Again, it is said by the prophet Isaiah that he was disfigured like one afflicted with a loathsome disease (Isa. 52:14). And why was this? So that we might receive the grace that he offers us. And how was he so abased? St Paul uses the same word also in his epistle to the Philippians (Phil. 2:7-8). He does not cease to draw us daily to himself and he does this so graciously and with the greatest gentleness and kindness imaginable. For he wills us by his gospel to come; yet he does so by encouraging and beseeching us, as St Paul says in his Second Epistle to the Corinthians (5:20).

Seeing, then, that our Lord Jesus Christ is so loving, that this message is daily brought to us, that he desires only to count us as members of his body; and that our Lord's invitation ought to sound continually in our ears: 'Come to me, all you who labour and are heavy laden, and I give you rest … and you will find rest for your souls' — seeing that all this is so, I say, let us not wilfully run astray, but let us be firmly anchored on Jesus Christ, for we cannot go wrong in resorting to him. And when we know that we are reconciled to God the Father by his means and are given a full righteousness, let us likewise understand that he distributes all these things to us by his Holy Spirit.

The principal thing is that we should remain content with Jesus Christ, not seeking to add anything to the grace that he brings us, and that we should not deal as the papists do, who when they have confessed that Jesus Christ is the mediator, look to various saints to be their patrons and advocates and attempt to lay hold on the merits of the apostles and martyrs. It seems to them that the satisfaction [of God's justice] made by our Lord Jesus Christ is nothing unless they add bits and pieces to it. They are also under the impression that they can serve up a more appetizing mixture by the addition of their own merits. Not content with the perfect sustenance that is given for their souls in the Son of God, they add to it their own sauces which they have concocted out of their own heads and brains. But let us, for our part, take care that we are completely satisfied with the riches of God's goodness, which he has made available to us in the person of our Lord Jesus Christ.

And along with that, let us understand (as I said earlier) that Jesus Christ does not communicate his grace to us, unless he has made us partakers of his Holy Spirit. For what shall it avail us that our Lord Jesus Christ has shed his blood, if we are not washed with it by the Holy Spirit? What shall it avail us that Jesus Christ has taken away sin and the tyranny of the devil by being crucified, if we are not brought and united to him by the grace of his Holy Spirit? So then, let us pray to our good God to put us in possession of the thing which he has purchased for us by the death and resurrection of his Son our Lord Jesus Christ by pouring out the gifts of the Holy Spirit upon us.

How do we receive these gifts? First, by being enlightened and given faith, that we may know that God is our Father and may be assured in our own experience of his goodness. Secondly, by having a spirit of godly fear, so that we may renounce our own wicked lusts and desires and devote ourselves to serving the one who rightly rules over us. Thirdly, by having a spirit of strength and constancy, which will enable us to fight against all the assaults that Satan makes upon us, and to withstand all his temptations. And finally, by having a spirit of wisdom to keep us from all the crafty schemes of our enemy. To that position we must come, so that the death and passion of our Lord Jesus Christ may profit us, and that his resurrection may have its full power and effect in us. And let us understand that all these things are witnessed to us in baptism.

Therefore, if we are conscious that we lack the gifts of the Holy Spirit, let us not doubt that we shall have them if we need them. Why? Because God did not deceive us when he ordained the figure of baptism, for in it we have a sure sign that he is not stingy towards us but pours out generously (at least in so far as he sees it to be appropriate for us) all the gifts that we lack and that we stand in need of.

Do we, then, perceive a lack of strength in ourselves? Do we perceive that there is the darkness of ignorance in us? Do we perceive that we are so entangled in [the things of] this world that we cannot attain to the spiritual things? Then let us run to God, and let our baptism act as a sign pointing us to him. For, as I have already said, in baptism our Lord shows us that he will not fail us in any way, if only we flee to him for refuge. But, on the other hand, we need to take note that the mere fact of being baptized is nothing. When we have received the visible sign, to what end will it serve us, except to our greater condemnation, if we do not also have that which it represents? And the responsibility for that will be laid at our door. If we find that there is any shortcoming in this respect, we must lay the blame on our own unbelief more than we do.

But again, St Paul attributes the power of our renewal and regeneration to this washing that he speaks of. However, he is addressing the faithful, who do not reject God's grace, but open their mouths that he may fill them, according as we are exhorted to do in the psalm (Ps. 81:10). Let us take good note of the fact that unbelievers are like a covered pot; God showers his gifts upon them, but they do not receive them, for they are so tightly covered that there is no getting into them. Or else they are as hard as rocks. It may rain for a whole day on a rock, yet the rock will not have absorbed any of the moisture, because it is too hard. That is how it is with all who refuse God's grace. But if we have our mouths open by faith, we shall be filled. And therefore it is not without good reason that St Paul addresses himself to the faithful, saying that God has poured out this spiritual cleansing upon them and has made them partakers of it. Oh, how we ought to put into practice the doctrine which is contained in this passage!

The hope of eternal life

And now let us come to the last part of the text, where he says that we are saved because we are 'heirs according to the hope of eternal life'. St Paul shows us what our faith is grounded upon and in what it consists, namely, in our being heirs of God. For properly speaking, our salvation is ours only by rights of inheritance. We are not heirs by nature, but by adoption, because it pleases God to take us as his children. We are born as children of wrath — that is to say, we are under a curse — and, far from our being able to call God our Father, he utterly rejects us. Yet for all that, he does not refrain from adopting us. How is this possible? St Paul sends us back to our Lord Jesus Christ, who with good reason is called the only Son of God. For he is God's only Son by nature, and that title belongs to him by right. Nevertheless, inasmuch as we are grafted into his body and have become his members, we too are adopted as God's children. This is how we come to inherit the kingdom of heaven. Are we heirs? Then we are saved. But let us note that it is as yet only by hope.

It is helpful to us to be reminded of this, for God will not have us to be idle in this world. Even though he has perfected our salvation in the person of his Son, he will lead us to it by the order he has laid down, which is, that when we have once received assurance of his goodness and received the thing that he offers us by his gospel — that is, justification by his grace alone — he will also keep us occupied in fighting against Satan, and that not for one day only, but throughout our whole lifetime we must go through with all the battles that God is pleased to send our way. And moreover, we must strive to forsake all our own affections, lusts and desires — yes, and even our own wisdom. For the area in which God chiefly intends to test our obedience is that of bringing our own personal desires into submission, so that we may not be too wise in our own opinion, but instead may seek to submit ourselves wholly unto him, so that when our own desires would drive us hither and thither, we may have a bridle to hold us back; and that, even in the teeth of our own desires, our own passions may not reign over us, but that God may have the mastery.

So then, seeing it is God's will to keep us occupied in this manner all the days of our life, let us learn to turn for encouragement to what is said here concerning hope. Why do we need to do this? Because, if [on the one hand] someone tells us that we are saved, we also see how the devil does not cease trying to bring about our ruin, and that he has the means to bring it about, were we not preserved by the wonderful power of our God. Then again, on the other hand, we see what mysteries surround us, and that our life is so wretched that even unbelievers are in a better situation than we are, and seem to enjoy a happier state than that of God's children. We see all these things, and they would be enough to dismay us, if we were not assured of that which St Paul tells us in this text, namely, that we are heirs through hope. That, I say, is the thing which maintains us in the certainty of our faith, so that even if we are mocked in this world by unbelievers and they work against us in a thousand spiteful and outrageous ways, yet we must never cease to assure ourselves that we enjoy God's favour.

And again, although our true life is hidden and we seem to be on the point of being overthrown, and although we may be like sheep led to the slaughter (as it is said in Romans 8:36) and though we may be trampled under foot, rejected by the world and scorned by all men — yet we must not let that prevent us from taking hold by faith of the inheritance that is prepared for us in heaven, and from concluding from this that, although we may seem to face utter ruin, yet, even so, we shall not fail to be saved. And why is that? Because our salvation is in good and safe hands; God is the one who keeps it safe.

'Yes, that is all very well' [someone may say], 'but still we are assailed on all sides.' Well, even if that is so, we shall not be a prey to Satan, since God the Father will exert his strength to defend us, and our Lord Jesus Christ will carry out the functions of his office, because he has taken responsibility for us. We know how he has said that he will not allow any of those who have been given to him to perish (John 6:39). And we know that inasmuch as God is almighty, our salvation is exempt from all danger. See how we may take comfort from this, and how we may defy both Satan and the world, and, indeed, all the temptations that may assail us!

In short, we may already speak confidently of everlasting life, even though we are not merely on the very edge of the abyss, but even on the point of being made to tumble in, and though we may be threatened with death every minute of the hour. But let us also take note that when St Paul speaks of eternal life, he intends to draw us away from this world, to which we are too closely wedded. There is no one who does not naturally desire to live, and to live well, but we lack the wisdom to choose the true life. Instead we take hold of a mere shadow, as though a man were to try to catch the moon between his teeth, as they say.

The word 'life' is enough to make us madly in love with it, but at the present time we only catch a shadow of the real thing. Everyone clings to this fleeting life, and the world keeps us entangled in its web, and at the same time we despise the everlasting life to which God calls us, and which has been purchased for us by the death of our Lord Jesus Christ. So let us bear in mind that we are only passing through this world, and that in this passage St Paul spurs us on in order to rouse us to aspire to the heavenly life and to make us run at a fast pace through this world and not be halted in it for anything. And because we are so weak and our reason is unable to climb so high, let us always fix our eyes on our Lord Jesus Christ. And since we know that God's Son came down here and will hereafter receive us into his glory — and, indeed, that God has made him head over the angels as well as over us — let us be assured that, although we are in this world, we are here only as pilgrims and do not cease to be citizens of heaven, to which we are being led by hope. This is why [the apostle] says in another place that we are seated already in the heavenly places (Eph. 2:6). How is that? By hope.

So then, let us note well that hope is not a dead thing, nor a light fancy of our own devising. It is rather the Holy Spirit working in us in such a way that, although we are trapped in these bodies which are subject to decay; although we feel such a heavy burden [weighing us down] that it seems to us that we are about to be dragged down into hell; although our sight is so pitifully short and dim, and even though all our strength should fail us — yet God, notwithstanding all these things, works by the power of his Holy Spirit in such a way that we are still lifted up and enabled to keep on our way and press on to reach the inheritance that has been prepared for us, not doubting that we shall arrive, because our Lord Jesus Christ will then appear, and that life which at the present time is hidden from us will finally be revealed.

Chapter 15

Grace, godliness and glory

'We are always skilful enough at putting forward clever arguments when it comes to our own rights — we do not need to ask anyone's advice on that... But why are we not clear-sighted when it comes to maintaining the rights of everyone else?'

15.
Grace, godliness and glory

'For the grace of God that brings salvation has appeared to all men, teaching us that, denying ungodliness and worldly lusts, we should live soberly, righteously, and godly in the present age, looking for the blessed hope and glorious appearing of our great God and Saviour Jesus Christ, who gave himself for us, that he might redeem us from every lawless deed' (Titus 2:11-14).

We see from the verses which precede this passage that when we hear of the goodness of God which has been shown to us in the person of our Lord Jesus Christ, we ought to be stirred up to holiness of life. For it is only reasonable that God, who bought us at so great a cost, should possess us; especially since he shows us that the object of our redemption is that, having been set free, we should serve our God all the days of our life (as Zechariah tells us briefly in his song in Luke 1:74-75).

For (as St Paul says in Romans 6), we were in chains and in bondage to sin, but we have now been set free, to the end that sin should no longer reign over us. How can that come to pass? By our being subject to the righteousness of God. And yet, in this case there is neither coercion nor constraint; it is a subjection which is better and more to be desired than all the kingdoms of the world. If a man insists on having his free will to serve his own desires, he might as well plunge himself into the depths of hell, allowing the devil to coerce him and drive him as he wishes. Why do I say that? Because our desires are enemies of God, and sin overpowers us and takes over our lives when we give free rein to our flesh. So there is no other way to have true freedom than to be in reverent subjection to God and his justice.

The things we must forsake

But we must proceed with the matter which is before us, which is that in order rightly to consecrate ourselves to God we must forsake all unrighteousness and all worldly desires. Now we know that in us there is nothing but all manner of wickedness and that it is not possible for God to wring any goodness out of us until he himself has formed us anew; until then, we do not even know what it is to serve God. For although we may claim to practise some form of devotion, yet we are dull and heedless, and not so much as one vein in our bodies is inclined to true religion, until God has utterly changed us and fashioned us anew.

It is true that if we look at unbelievers, they may seem to devote themselves to God and to have some zeal to do good. But the Scripture does not lie when it tells us that men are rebellious against God. They go completely contrary to his will and would gladly be exempt from his control, if it were possible. Why do such people practise ceremonies in an attempt to discharge their duty towards God if not because they [know that they] cannot escape God's hand or avoid having him as their Judge? If they were once able to do that, it is certain that they would then despise all majesty and throw everything into disorder.

Until God has changed us and brought us back to himself, there is nothing in us but such ungodliness that would cause every one of us to live in a manner no better than the beasts of the field; we would never think of the kingdom of heaven, no, nor even consider what it means to have been created — for every one of us would become like brute beasts.

And because ungodliness tends to be concealed, and mischief lurks within and is not revealed to the public gaze, St Paul goes on to speak of 'worldly lusts'. This bears witness to what is within us — namely, that we are weighed down with wickedness and, whereas nature should point us to God, or at least to know and see evidence of his existence, we are worse than the brute beasts. For although the beasts do not have the ability to discern the difference between good and evil, they at least keep themselves within bounds and limits; and although they are led by their appetites, at least when they have eaten their food they lie down to rest; when they have rested, they get up and go; when they are hungry, they feed, or at least look for food. But as for man, it is pitiful to watch him. It seems that he sets out to contort himself out of all recognition. We see how headstrong he is about satisfying his lusts, leaving us in no doubt that he loves his own comfort and convenience. It seems that no one can be happy unless he has put everything in disorder, and thrown all heaven and earth into confusion. In a word, since we are so entangled in the things here below that we do not give a thought to the kingdom of heaven, it appears that we are utterly perverted, that there is not one drop of good in us, and that we are blind in all our desires. Why is that? Because they tend altogether in the direction of this world — and we are created for heavenly goals.

We would indeed be in a sorry state if we looked no further than to things on earth, since we are subject to so many miseries, so many cares, so many vexations and so much anguish. The brute beasts have a better life. Their fears are only for the present moment; they are not anxious about anything; they are not led by ambition; they do not anticipate the inconveniences that may befall them; they do not envy one another as men do; they do not foretell the future a hundred years after their death, but are content with such fodder as they have before them. But look at men: they are in continual torment. And yet, what would become of us if God should let us alone? The world holds us fast, the world possesses us, and we are so tied to it, or rather buried in it, that we are obsessed with it and think of nothing but this fleeting life.

Seeing this is so, let us understand that to come to God we must abandon our nature which we have from Adam and become new creatures. That is why St Paul begins at this point, that we must forsake all ungodliness and worldly desires. And he adds immediately that the grace of God is given to the end that 'we should live soberly, righteously, and godly in the present age'.

The three aspects of the righteousness God requires

Here he describes the life of a Christian in three things: that there is to be holiness, or reverence, towards God, so that God will be obeyed; that we are to show justice or uprightness towards our neighbours; and that we are to be characterized by honesty and steadfastness, so that we are not wild or wanton [in our conduct], but that our lives may be modest and chaste. That is the true perfection which God requires, and towards which we are required to advance, in order that we may profit from it all the days of our life.

It is true that throughout Scripture, whenever it sets out to show us what perfect righteousness consists of, normally only two aspects of this are mentioned, as, for example, when the law was divided into two tables. [These teach us that] it is incumbent on us to serve God in all purity, and also to live soundly and roundly in all respects with our neighbours. This might well suffice; however, steadfastness, or sobriety, is laid down here as a third requirement and is joined inseparably with the other two. For how can we keep the spiritual sabbath rest that is commanded if steadfastness does not reign in us? Or how can we be patient in our afflictions?

St Paul previously linked together the service of God and love for neighbours as a principle. Yet there is no contradiction in what he is saying now. For steadfastness means that a person should control himself and not be ruled by his own desires, but be in subjection under the hand of God, and be governed not by his own preferences, but by what is pleasing to God. When we have brought ourselves to such a state of mind, then we have the sobriety of which St Paul speaks.

And now we may easily conclude that by using those three words ['soberly', 'justly' and 'godly'] St Paul meant to show that God does not, as it were, haul us about mechanically, but laid down for us a certain infallible way, out of which we are not to stray of our own accord, as they do who invent devotional practices of their own in an attempt to please God. They take pains to please him, but it is all just so much beating about the bush. Let us, therefore, make sure that we keep to the right way, for St Paul tells us that it is a waste of time when people gad about in this way following their own imaginations. Why must we stay in the right way? Because it is only when our lives are ruled according to God's law that we can rest assured that they are pleasing to him.

Righteous living: our conduct towards others

As far as the word 'justly' [NKJV, 'righteously'] is concerned, that one word is intended to include all the rights which we ought to yield to our neighbours, treating them with spontaneous kindness and uprightness, as our Lord Jesus Christ taught us, when he told us to do nothing to anyone else which we would not want to have done to ourselves.

Therefore, when we have to conduct business with our neighbours, let us avoid all underhand dealings, spitefulness or cruelty. Let us not be in the habit of exploiting people. Let none of us seek our own gain, nor let ambition or vainglory lead us to take others for a ride, or squeeze out of them everything we can. Rather, may we seek only to live together on such good terms with our neighbours that no one may have any reason to complain about us. And especially let no one be wedded to his own profit, but let us endeavour to profit everyone, for that is justice, which may be briefly defined as yielding to everyone that which is his by right. However, our Lord Jesus Christ expresses it even more simply when he puts it in terms of doing to others as we would be done by.

We are always skilful enough at putting forward clever arguments when it comes to our own rights — we do not need to ask anyone's advice on that. It is true that if a man has a case at law, he will go to a lawyer to help him present his case in such a light that his rights will be stated more clearly. But, for all that, you will never find anyone who is such an idiot that he does not have the wit to say, 'This belongs to me!' It is true that he may not be able to present his case so well that he can prove his rights in all points of law, but he has skill enough in general to say, 'This is mine; I have been wronged in this matter.' But why are we not clear-sighted when it comes to maintaining the rights of everyone else? Is it not because we are corrupt? So then, it is certain that the only thing that that prevents us from being characterized by such integrity is our own sinful nature. For if we are asked to give a general ruling on a matter where our emotions are not involved, we are well able to say, 'This is what you should do; this is right.' We need no great learning, nor a university education, in order to judge such a case justly. If the question were put to us as a matter of general principle, we would have no doubt or hesitation about the right decision. But if there is any factor liable to bias our judgement, we no longer know the meaning of the word 'integrity'. Let us, therefore, learn that to please God we must live with our neighbours in such a way that no one can complain about us. Note that for a principle.

Many men labour in vain to please God with religious ceremonies, as we see among the papists, where many such ceremonies are performed. And for what purpose? To please God. But at the same time one person is given to fleecing others, and another to deceit and spite; and payment has to be made for all this by having a great many masses sung. Is that not downright mockery of God? Yes, for we know what we are called to do: not to engage in petty trifles of this sort but to learn to occupy ourselves in practising righteousness. God will have our minds to be set on that. The true fruit that he requires, and which is acceptable to him, is integrity of life, coming to the aid of those who need our help and avoiding all kinds of wrong and injury to others.

Holy living: giving God his rightful place

But here holiness [or 'godliness] is paired with righteousness, and with good reason. For it is not enough that others should be satisfied with us and that we should not be responsible for causing anyone's hurt or hindrance in any way. We must give God the first place [in our lives], as he deserves. If wives ought to be subject to their husbands, how much more ought we to be subject to God! Women are their husbands' companions; nevertheless, they owe respect to their husbands as to their heads and must submit to them. Now, our Lord Jesus Christ has entered into a spiritual marriage with us, which is much holier than all the marriages in the world. If we do not keep faith with him — either by practising superstition and idolatry, as some do, or by wallowing and becoming steeped in the mire and dirt of papistry — I ask you, what will become of it? It is true that they may say they have not offended anyone. No, not here below. But is it right that God's majesty should be wronged in this way? Someone will say, 'I steal no man's goods.' No, but at the same time you are a traitor towards God, as St Paul also says. Therefore, when this doctrine is preached to us (that we must deal incorruptibly with everyone, without hurting or hindering anyone, but rather procuring their benefit), let us apply it to ourselves. And at the same time let us condemn these wretched fools who fill their heads with all manner of worthless baggage, supposing that they honour God with their ridiculous playthings — for all these contrivances are just so much abuse. Why? Because God will have mercy and not sacrifice. He requires uprightness, faithfulness and justice, as he says by his prophets and as our Lord Jesus also declares (Hosea 6:6; Isa. 56:1; Matt. 9:13;12:7; 23:23).

The thing which God uses to test us, to show whether we fear him or not, is the matter of our walking uprightly and our living one with another in such a way that we harm no one. That is required of us. But at the same time we must not forget God, nor neglect to resort to him, nor to put our whole trust in Jesus Christ, nor to exercise ourselves continually in calling upon the name of God the Father, all the more so since necessity moves and drives us to call on him every minute of every hour.

We must glorify God, acknowledging that we are dependent on him for all good things; and we must be careful to succeed in doing the things he commands in the first table of the law — to observe those things above all else, and then to proceed to keeping the rest [of the commandments]. For God's law cannot be divided, nor ought it to be. Indeed, there are two tables, and it is proper to distinguish between them, so that we may be aware that the service of God comes first, and that love for others is added in second place. But even so, God has not given one part of his law to the Jews, and another to the Gentiles. Rather, he wants both of them to receive the whole law.

God has knit the two [tables of the law] together in such a way that it is not lawful for men to separate them. It is said that the one who does not perform all things contained in the law will be cursed (Deut. 27:26). It is true that none of us can fulfil all that God commands; we shall all come short of that. And although God guides us by his Holy Spirit, yet we shall always be hindered by our own feebleness. But however much we may fall short, the mark we must aim at must be to submit ourselves to God thoroughly and in all respects. For as St James says, he who forbids fornication also forbids theft, so that we offend God's majesty and violate the whole law when we commit any sin at all. Therefore, let us learn to combine righteousness with holiness — which is to say, let us so live among our fellow men, without doing any wrong, outrage, or violence to them, that God is not deprived of his rights; that is to say, so that we do not fail to worship him in purity, nor think that we have done all that is required of us when others cannot condemn us in that respect. For it is said that if we play the hypocrite before others and are ashamed to follow Jesus Christ, he will also deny us in the presence of the angels of heaven. Let us assure ourselves of that, and let us learn that both our bodies and our souls must be dedicated to God.

If a woman casts lascivious glances in the direction of a man known for sexual immorality, she will be considered a lewd woman even though she does nothing more. If a servant not only allows his master to be slandered, or a child his father, but also joins hands with the slanderers, showing that he is one of them, what must such betrayal indicate? If we keep company with the wicked and dissemble in such a way that we appear to give assent to their ungodliness, we are certainly betraying God. So let us not flatter ourselves when men clap their hands at us, or rather by their applause cover our defilement. We must come before the one who will condemn us twice over for disguising his truth in this way by hypocrisy and concealment. That is what we need to remember on the subject of 'godly' living.

Sober living: the stability of character needed to live in this way

Now, there is also the matter of steadiness [or 'sobriety'] which, as I said, adds nothing to God's law, but only shows what St Paul meant by holiness and righteousness. If we are unstable, it is not possible for us to be submissive to God when he sends afflictions to tame us. If we do nothing but pine here on earth, being burdened with numerous miseries and encumbrances, shall we be able to worship our God and praise his name without having the steadiness and sobriety of which St Paul speaks? Or if we behave like young bulls let loose, and great licentiousness is offered — in dancing and wanton songs and other enticements that lead to disorderly conduct — how will each of us be content to live quietly with his own wife, without attempting infidelity by our relations with other married folk? For if such stumbling-blocks are allowed to exist, if loose behaviour and inconstancy are tolerated and such gaps, so to speak, are left unplugged, fornication and adultery will surely have free play and there will no longer be such things as faithfulness and upright conduct to be found among men, but everyone will throw off restraint and permit himself all kinds of misconduct. One will devote himself to cruelty and extortion, and another will take to looting and robbing everywhere in a way that is totally out of hand.

So then, let us observe that when St Paul speaks here of sobriety he adds nothing to God's law, any more than when he spoke previously of patience he intended to add anything to what is contained in the two tables of the law. He means simply to show how we may obey God by cutting out worldly excess, so that God may control us quietly and reign over us without hindrance.

The hope which sustains us

St Paul says expressly that we must live such a life of sobriety and purity, 'looking for the blessed hope and glorious appearing of our great God and Saviour Jesus Christ'. In this way St Paul shows us that God keeps us here below to put us through our paces, as it were, to see what sort of persons we will be, and therefore this life of ours is a continual battle. God does not permit us to be idle, but keeps us occupied, in order that he might have a sure proof of the awe and honour that we owe him. And that is of great benefit to us. For we see how every one of us complains because God does not grant us our desires, but is utterly opposed to them, whereas we would gladly have him guide and govern us according to our own inclinations and, in a word, to permit each of us to be his own master.

Here St Paul declares that there are good reasons why we should occupy ourselves in God's service throughout our lives, and why he should test us regarding our service to him. Nevertheless, since we are grieved by the length of time [we must continue to endure trials], he also teaches us that our service must be marked by waiting and hoping for the coming of our Lord Jesus Christ. He shows us that we must not muse upon the present state of the world if we intend to be steadfast and constant in serving God. On the contrary, we must give close attention to the hope we have been given, that the Son of God will come to judge the world.

Let us bear in mind accordingly that God intends to test his faithful ones. He permits and ordains their grief and vexation during this earthly life. They pass through many troubles, and things do not fall out as they would like them to. God seems to have forsaken them, and even to be their enemy. But we must understand that he has a good reason for doing all this and that we need to be exercised in this way. If a man were to deliver silver or gold to us, we would want to know whether it was good or not; and if we doubted its genuineness, we would test it by fire. Is not our faith more precious (as St Peter says) than all the corruptible metals that are tested so carefully? (1 Peter 1:7). There is good reason, then, that our faith, being of great value, should be put to the test, which occurs when God sends us affliction and will not have us always seeking our own profit rather than serving others — even those who are unkind and churlish and who repay us with evil when we endeavour to do them good. God has appointed it so, and not without cause.

But let us also consider the shortness of life, so that we do not become weary. We are so prone to pick and choose that even those who have shown some inclination to dedicate themselves to God keep a check on themselves and [think that] it is lawful, when they have made some progress, to stop midway. So they are grieved and ask, 'Will this last for ever?'

At the same time we forget the frailty of life. If a man has only a short way to go, he manages to persevere; even though his legs are as weary as can be, he drags them after him to his lodging. And especially if a man has travelled ten or twelve days' journey already, the nearer he comes to his journey's end, the gladder he is, and he takes heart and goes through with it. Now, since we see that we are not far from the end that we aspire to come to, why do we not take heart in view of that and persevere, being encouraged to do so by the Holy Spirit?

Nevertheless, we should not only keep in mind the shortness and swiftness of life, and the fact that we shall soon have finished our race and therefore we ought not to faint. We must also have an eye to the hope to which we are called. Why? Because the reason why we are slack in devoting ourselves to God is that we see no profit before our eyes, nor can we touch it with our hands. We want God to reward us. Now it is certain that God does not turn his back on us when we have done well by devoting ourselves to him. Yet, however well we may fare, he will not maintain us so comfortably in this world that we take occasion to fall asleep here. We know how he has said that those who devote themselves to the things of the present world have received their reward already. So our Lord encourages us to look up to heaven. This is because our life here is full of disquiet and a great many troubles that hem us in on all sides. Look how many afflictions we endure. These are so many jabs of the spur sent by God to urge us forward, so that we might be drawn closer to him and that we might devote ourselves to the consideration of heavenly things and as a result be totally withdrawn from the things of this world. This is the reason why St Paul here purposely speaks of hope. In other words, it is not surprising that people grow weary when they should be serving God. And why is that? Because they have their eyes fixed on earthly things, and then they come to a complete stop.

Now, we should think about the coming of our Lord Jesus Christ, whereas every one of us turns away from it. That is why the world has such a hold on us and dazzles our eyes with its enticements, and why we are utterly infatuated with it. Let us learn what it means to serve God, knowing that life passes quickly here below, and that God has placed us here on the sole condition that we are to walk as strangers, for we may not settle down comfortably here. Although God gives us some rest, yet we must continue to go forward, keeping on our way to him until the coming of our Lord Jesus Christ. Until we have come to see this, it is certain that, however fair a show we may put on, our life will be nothing but vanity. And therefore the principal point we need to grasp in order to govern our lives aright is that God has not placed us here to dwell here for ever, but that we should constantly press on towards him, while always having the assurance of the blessed coming of our Lord Jesus Christ.

The promise of Christ's appearing as the grounds of our confidence

That is why after the word 'hope', St Paul goes on to speak of the coming, or 'glorious appearing of our great God and Saviour Jesus Christ'. When he speaks of the blessed hope it is as if he is saying, 'My friends, we must not go towards the kingdom of heaven as if we were risking all, uncertain whether we shall arrive there or not, for we know that God has promised us the kingdom.' Now, God is faithful, and therefore let us be content to rely on him, as the one who is trustworthy. Besides, we have good assurance and warrant for doing so. Otherwise, what would be the outcome? For we see that our Lord Jesus Christ has come into the world. Is it a small thing that the eternal God should be abased to such an extent, in the human nature which he took upon himself, that he not only suffered a death that was shameful in the eyes of men, but that he was also cursed by God and banished from his presence? Behold, the Son of God, the head of the angels, the one who is the source of life, the living image of God, to whom all glory and majesty belong, has come down so low as to become like us, and has received all our infirmities, except only for sin. It is true that there was no spot in him, but he made himself subject to cold and heat and other sufferings; in short, he endured all human infirmities, and in the end he had to endure being cursed by God — not for his own sake, but because he bore the burden of all our sins, and the curse of God came down upon his head because he was made the principal debtor, in order that he might discharge us of our debts.

And now, do we think that the Son of God, having done such a deed, will suffer his death and passion to be of no effect, if we believe in him, or that after having been crucified he will abandon us, who are the members of his body, now that he is in his heavenly kingdom? That would make his death and passion ineffectual. And then, whenever we were shaken by any distrust, so that we exclaimed in surprise [at what was happening to us], what would come of it? We do not [now] see the Son of God; he is hidden from us, yet we know him to be our Saviour. And yet, that would do us no good if he were not to appear again in his glory. His death and passion would be no more than an interlude between the acts of a stage play, and there would have been no point in God's changing the whole order of nature as he did by coming down here and taking on him the likeness of sinners — though he himself was no sinner — and revealing himself in the flesh if, notwithstanding all this, he no longer acknowledged us, for then all would slip away and vanish, and we would receive no benefit from it.

Therefore let us embrace the salvation that was purchased for us, and so be assured that our Lord Jesus Christ will come again, though for the present we do not see him. It is incumbent on us to note well what St Paul says to the Colossians, when he tells them that we must not lose heart, though we may be sadly discouraged in this world and it may seem that we prosper no better by serving God.

It grieves the faithful when they see the wicked in control, while they themselves are oppressed. 'Where is God?' they say. 'He is not concerned about us.' But St Paul tells us that we must bear all things patiently. Where is our life? he asks. It is not in ourselves, but in our Lord Jesus Christ (Col. 3:3-4). And we see that Jesus Christ is [concealed from our view] in the Father's glory until he is revealed to us again at the last day. No marvel, then, he says, if our life is hidden with him and we are like trees in the winter. When the leaves have fallen from the trees, the trunks may look dry and dead, but they still have life within them. Therefore let us receive our Lord Jesus Christ and refer everything to him, assuring ourselves that our life is enclosed in him. And since he has not yet been manifested, let us wait for him patiently, and let it not grieve us that we have to languish here in the midst of so many miseries and afflictions.

Now we see why St Paul, having spoken of this present world and shown that it is like a passing shadow (1 Cor. 7:31), brings us to our Lord Jesus Christ, saying that we must persevere in hope. Now, we need to learn that the true constancy of the faithful is to be found in hope, for hope is that which nourishes our faith. What is the difference between faith and hope? By faith we embrace God's promises, not doubting that he will perform them. But it is not enough that we believe after that fashion, once for all time. We must continue steadfastly in that state of mind throughout our lives — and that is done by hoping. And so hope is nothing else but that which gives rise to, or directs, faith so that it does not vanish away, or prove to be a temporal or transitory thing, but so that it holds out and continues to the end.

It is true that in the meantime we shall have to face many encounters. We must fight, I say, if we intend to hope and not faint, or fall away from our hope. But we would sometimes be greatly disheartened by this doctrine, if we were not firmly resolved at all times that, inasmuch as Jesus Christ, who is our life, has not yet come again, we must accept that our welfare is bound up in him. Although we do not see him, we must not for that reason cease to keep the eyes of our faith open, so that we may have as a secure anchor the knowledge of who it is into whose hands we have entrusted our goods.

If a man were in danger in his own house — whether of fire, or of enemies, or of robbery — and if he had some other secure place, or some trustworthy friend, and had put all his treasures into that person's keeping, he would be content and would not run every minute to look at it and check that all was well. A man could be content to leave all his possessions in the hand of some friend of his; he could find it in his heart to trust him and leave his goods with him all year long. Now, it is God who undertakes the keeping of our salvation. If it were left in *our* hands, it would be quick pickings [for any thief], and the devil would soon snatch it away from us; but God takes care of it and keeps it, calling it a pledge. Seeing this is so, what honour do we render him if we do not trust him to keep it well and safely? If a man takes a thing to keep for someone, or accepts a pledge from someone, and then misuses it, that would be theft of the foulest and worst kind, because he betrayed a trust. Do we think that God will be guilty of such a breach of trust, especially when we consider that we have so many promises of his to the effect that, having once taken charge of our salvation, he will surely bring it to accomplishment? Therefore, whenever we are tempted to be discouraged, or when we are conscious of becoming careless and slothful, let us learn to look to the coming again of our Lord Jesus Christ and to place our confidence firmly in the promises of the salvation that will be ready for us at that time. Thus we see how we should put into practice the doctrine contained in this passage.

God's greatness revealed in Christ

Now, although St Paul speaks of 'our great God' and of 'our … Saviour Jesus Christ', we must not separate God the Father from his Son. St Paul means that God will appear in the person of our Lord Jesus Christ, according to his statement that God will be all in all things. This is well worth noting [as an argument] against those who want to deny the deity of Christ and have imagined him to be, as it were, a newly made God — as did that detestable creature who was punished in this city [Servetus]. He indeed admitted that Jesus Christ was God, but said that Christ had not existed [as God] from eternity, but that his divine nature dated only from the creation of the world, and that the Father had, so to speak, subjected him to a process of distilling as a result of which he appeared to be God when he was born into the world. Lo and behold, we have here a God forged in haste!

Now, those who were of the same opinion (as, for example, the heretics of old) armed themselves with this text which we are considering. 'Look here!' they said. 'St Paul names a great God, and afterwards Jesus Christ. And therefore it follows that Jesus Christ is an inferior God — an underling.' But those who say such things only mock Holy Scripture. For St Paul says that we must not imagine any majesty of God, except in Jesus Christ (Col. 1:15-19). For in him, as he says in another place, dwells all the fulness of the Godhead bodily (Col. 2:9). Paul speaks of them in rather physical terms, so that we might more easily comprehend the infinite nature of God, and that our unthankfulness might be all the more reprehensible if we were to imagine anything about God other than what we see revealed in our Lord Jesus Christ. That is the reason why he says that we shall see God in all his greatness at the coming again of our Lord Jesus Christ.

But why does he speak of God's greatness? Because at the present time it is diminished by our ignorance and unbelief and because our lack of understanding, while we are in this world, is so pitiful. It is true that we are ready enough to confess with our mouths that God is great, that he is incomprehensible, and that he is so exalted that our minds cannot grasp him. Everyone will readily acknowledge this. But at the same time we see in what contempt people hold him. We see that they cannot find it in their hearts to trust him, and that we cannot persuade them to be in subjection to God and to show reverence towards his majesty. We see how his heavenly kingdom is forgotten, to such an extent that if only the smallest opportunity of worldly gain is set before us, we run after it, we despise God openly and we give no thought to the promises of the gospel. In a word, men are so spiteful that they seek only to bring dishonour on God, and if each of us were really honest with himself we should have to admit that our whole lives tend in that direction.

Thus you see that until God draws us to him, our nature serves no purpose but to detract from his glory, and in the end to get rid of it completely, if we had the power to do so. But St Paul, showing us that we must not busy ourselves with these temporal things, nor spend our time gazing at this world, says that in due time we shall see the great God. Not that God will be made greater than he is (for we know that in himself he neither grows nor diminishes), but that we shall have another kind of eyes with which to look upon him.

Let us take good care that when we see him it will not be to our utter confusion. For the wicked will have to see him against their will — and the one they will see is none other than the same one who is our Redeemer, Jesus Christ. For he is so closely joined with God the Father that the whole fulness of the Godhead dwells in him. Yes, the wicked and the reprobates will see him in the teeth of their own wishes and it will be to their utter confusion. But as for us, let us seek to see by faith, here and now, the greatness of God. Although our vision is dimmed by the world; and although we see that the worldlings who proudly defy God and mock at his gospel appear to be triumphant, while those who live circumspectly seem to be nothing in comparison to them; and although we see a great number of hypocrites, who put on a good face here below, while all the time they seek only to deface God's glory — although we see all these things, let us not cease to look upon the greatness of God with the spiritual eyes of faith, waiting in anticipation of the day when we shall be able to see him face to face. This will take place at the time when we too shall be transformed into that same glory; and indeed, we bear a little trace of it even now, because God reigns in us by his Holy Spirit.

A wide range of excellent books on spiritual subjects is available from Evangelical Press. Please write to us for your free catalogue or contact us by e-mail.

Evangelical Press
Faverdale North Industrial Estate, Darlington, DL3 0PH, England

Evangelical Press USA
P. O. Box 84, Auburn, MA 01501, USA

e-mail: sales@evangelical-press.org

web: http://www.evangelicalpress.org